P9-DIJ-383

PRAISE FOR PREVIOUS EDITIONS OF

Idaho Off the Beaten Path®

"Rushing around Idaho is inherently pointless . . . you can miss
the spirit and the majesty in an unplanned moment, the
unexpected person, the odd place, off the beaten path."
—*USA Today*

"[This book] makes traveling across the state exciting, whether
you're taking the kids up to college at Moscow or heading over
to Idaho Falls to visit Grandma."
—*Idaho Statesman*

Help Us Keep This Guide Up to Date

Every effort has been made by the author and editors to make this guide as accurate and useful as possible. However, many changes can occur after a guide is published—establishments close, phone numbers change, facilities come under new management, etc.

We would love to hear from you concerning your experiences with this guide and how you feel it could be improved and be kept up to date. While we may not be able to respond to all comments and suggestions, we'll take them to heart, and we'll make certain to share them with the author. Please send your comments and suggestions to the following address:

The Globe Pequot Press
Reader Response/Editorial Department
P.O. Box 480
Guilford, CT 06437

Or you may e-mail us at: editorial@GlobePequot.com

Thanks for your input, and happy travels!

OFF THE BEATEN PATH® SERIES

Off the Beaten Path®

SEVENTH EDITION

idaho

A GUIDE TO UNIQUE PLACES

JULIE FANSELOW

travel

Guilford, Connecticut

The prices, rates, and hours listed in this guidebook
were confirmed at press time. We recommend,
however, that you call establishments to obtain
current information before traveling.

To buy books in quantity for corporate use
or incentives, call **(800) 962–0973**
or e-mail **premiums@GlobePequot.com.**

Text design by Linda R. Loiewski
Maps by Equator Graphics © Morris Book Publishing, LLC
Illustrations by Carole Drong
Illustration on page 36 of the River Dance Lodge drawn from photos used with
permission from Peter Grubb
Illustration on page 69 of Idaho Anne Frank Human Rights Memorial drawn from
photos by Julie Fanselow
Spot photography throughout © FoqStock/Index Open

ISSN 1535-4431
ISBN 978-0-7627-4781-8

Printed in the United States of America
10 9 8 7 6 5 4 3 2 1

For Natalie, who was born to travel

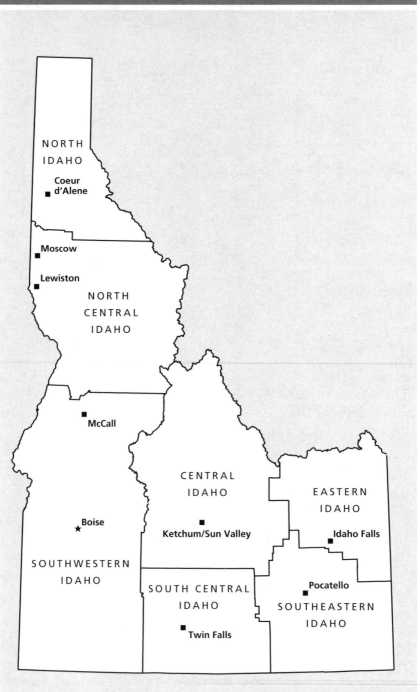

NORTH
IDAHO

Coeur
d'Alene

Moscow

Lewiston

NORTH
CENTRAL
IDAHO

McCall

CENTRAL
IDAHO

EASTERN
IDAHO

Boise

Ketchum/Sun Valley

Idaho Falls

SOUTHWESTERN
IDAHO

SOUTH CENTRAL
IDAHO

Pocatello

SOUTHEASTERN
IDAHO

Twin Falls

Contents

Acknowledgments

Many Idahoans too numerous to name recommended special spots throughout the Gem State for this book. My thanks to all, especially to Tom Ashenbrener, Darryl Davidson, Linda Langness, John McGimpsey, Steve Medellin, and Tara Rowe, who provided new suggestions for this edition. I'd also like to acknowledge the staff of the Idaho Department of Commerce and everyone at the local chambers of commerce and visitors bureaus who keep me up-to-date on what's happening around Idaho. Thanks, too, to the people at The Globe Pequot Press and the editors at *Journey, Sunset, Hemispheres,* and *VIA* magazines, for whom I've written about Idaho.

As always, my deepest gratitude goes to my family. My husband, Bruce Whiting; our daughter, Natalie Fanselow Whiting; and my father, Byron Fanselow, have accompanied me to many of the places described in this book. Our trips are usually whirlwinds of activity, covering hundreds of miles each day with a stay each night in a different motel. Natalie, born in 1994, has already visited all of Idaho's forty-four counties, many of them several times. When you figure many people spend their lives in one place, without even seeing the next state, I believe that's quite an achievement. But at the same time, I sometimes feel our knowledge of Idaho runs a mile wide and an inch deep. So it's my hope that we'll someday be able to spend an entire week together rafting the Salmon River, a long weekend in a cabin at Warren, or just an entire afternoon on the beach at Pend Oreille.

Introduction

When I first moved to Idaho, I had about two weeks before I was scheduled to start my job at the newspaper in Twin Falls. What better way to spend the time, I figured, than on a quick orientation trip around my new home state? Two weeks would be plenty of time to take a drive through Idaho's mountainous midsection, followed by a beeline for the Canadian border, a detour through Montana to Salmon, and a swing through Eastern Idaho.

Or so I thought. A week or so later, I'd meandered across maybe a quarter of my intended route. As someone who had grown up on the fringes of Pennsylvania suburbia and come of age in rural Ohio, I knew more than a little bit about back roads and small towns. But I knew next to nothing about a landscape that would force me, by virtue of geography and scenery, to really slow down and savor the journey, not to mention a piece of huckleberry pie here and a buffalo burger there. Two decades later, I still haven't seen all Idaho has to offer—especially not now, when international cuisines are joining mountain fare on the state's menus and an increasingly urban Idaho has as many cultural delights as recreational destinations. I expect it will take a lifetime, and that's fine.

In a sense, all of Idaho could be considered off the beaten path. It's true that here—like elsewhere—interstates now cross the state from east to west. But Highway 12, the only route across North Central Idaho, didn't link Lewiston to Missoula, Montana, until 1961. The White Bird Grade on the state's only major north-south road, Highway 95, wasn't completed until 1975. When it's closed by bad weather or rock slides, travelers must make a five-hour detour through Oregon and Washington. And until the early 1990s, it was nonstop cross-country from Boston to Seattle on Interstate 90, except for one stoplight in the town of Wallace, Idaho.

Idaho was the last of the continental United States to be settled by whites pushing westward (although Native Americans were here 10,000 to 15,000 years ago). When pioneers pressed west on the Oregon and California Trails, most kept right on going through what would become Idaho. When British fur traders staked their claims in the Northwest, they did so hundreds of miles west near the mouth of the great Columbia River. Idaho's first permanent town, Franklin, wasn't settled until 1860, and many of today's communities didn't exist at all until early in the twentieth century.

The state's tourism slogans of recent years tell the story, too: "Idaho: The Undiscovered America" and "Idaho Is What America Was." The state's population is swelling, most notably in the southwestern corner, where Boise—

frequently touted as one of America's most desirable places to live—has given way to a creeping urban sprawl that is home to more than a third of the state's population. But no matter where you are in Idaho, you don't have to travel far to escape: Owyhee County, south of Boise, and the Central Idaho Rockies, northeast of the capital city, remain so sparsely settled they could qualify as frontier. All across Idaho, residents and visitors have plenty of opportunities to get happily lost for a day, a weekend, or longer, on a seldom-traveled forest road, in an abandoned mountaintop fire tower, in a country antiques store, or in a tucked-away cafe.

A few notes on how to use this book: There are seven chapters, each covering one of the tourism regions designated by the Idaho Travel Council. Each chapter leads off with a general overview of the region. With roads few and far between in many areas of Idaho, it is impossible to avoid retracing a route once in a while, but I've tried to keep backtracking to a minimum. Although each chapter leads off with a general map of the region and its attractions, you will want to use a more detailed map in planning your travels. You can get a free highway map by calling (800) VISIT-ID (847-4843). Maps are also available via the state's travel Web site at www.visitidaho.org, or by writing the Idaho Travel Council at 700 West State Street, Boise 83720. The *Idaho Atlas & Gazetteer,* published by DeLorme Mapping, P.O. Box 298, Yarmouth, ME 04096, is another excellent reference, as are the maps published by the various units of the U.S. Forest Service in Idaho.

It's still possible to travel 50 miles or more in Idaho without passing a gas station. And just because a town is listed on a map or road sign, that's no guarantee you'll find a filling station or other services there. So before you set out off the beaten path, make sure your vehicle is in good shape and the fuel tank is full. Carry a good full-size spare tire and jack, a gasoline can, and a basic emergency kit, including flashers. A shovel and ax also can come in handy on unpaved back roads, the former in case you encounter a snowdrift, the latter in the event a tree has fallen in your path. (Both these things happen not infrequently on Forest Service roads in Idaho's high country, even in the dead of summer.) Most of the places mentioned in this book are accessible using any two-wheel drive vehicle in good condition, but a few are unsuitable for large RVs or vehicles towing trailers. When in doubt, inquire locally before setting off on an unfamiliar back road.

I've tried to list prices for most attractions, but bear in mind these are subject to change. Use the prices as a guideline, and call ahead for updates or more information. In the listings at the end of each regional chapter, restaurant cost categories refer to the price of a single entree without beverage, dessert, taxes, or tip. Room rates are per double per night.

More Idaho Travel Tips

The Idaho Transportation Department has a Web site that features the state's many designated scenic byways. Explore online, or order a free glove box–size guide at www.idahobyways.gov.

Idaho's tourism division offers an e-mail newsletter, *Idaho Journeys,* for people who like to travel in the Gem State. It includes inside travel tips, destination information, and even the occasional recipe. To sign up, go to www.visitidaho.org and click on "about," then "newsletters."

InIdaho is another highly useful tool for planning the perfect Idaho vacation or week-end getaway. Travel counselors with this free service have up-to-date information and expertise to help you match activities and accommodations throughout the state with your budget and tastes. Visit www.inIdaho.com, or call (208) 634-4787 or (800) 844-3246, and they'll help you out.

If, like many Idahoans and visitors, you're here mainly for Idaho's riotously abundant recreational opportunities, you'll want to check out the Yahoo groups that focus on these pursuits. The Boise-based *idahooutdoors* group has this as its description: "We do hiking, backpacking, climbing, hot springing, rafting, skiing, snowshoeing, telemarking . . . most anything outdoors. This group is open to anyone who is inter-ested in the Outdoors in Idaho and wishes to know about and participate in group outings." Other Yahoo groups focus on river running and bird-watching in the Gem State. To find them, simply search "Idaho outdoors" at http://groups.yahoo.com/.

Restaurants

$10 or less	Inexpensive
$11 to $20	Moderate
$21 and over	Expensive

Places to Stay

Up to $75 per couple per night	Inexpensive
$75 to $150 per night	Moderate
$151 and over per night	Expensive

Also remember that Idaho, unique among states, is divided north-south into two time zones. The northern part of the state is on Pacific time, while the south runs on Mountain time. (The Salmon River between North Fork in the east and Riggins in the west is the rough dividing point.)

It should be noted that Idaho has more federally designated wilderness lands—nearly four million acres—than any other state in the lower forty-eight, with an additional nine million acres of roadless public land. Much of Idaho is, therefore, accessible only by boat, on horseback, on foot, or by chartered plane flown into a backcountry airstrip. For more information about exploring Idaho's wilderness areas, contact the Idaho Outfitters and Guides Association, P.O. Box 95, Boise 83701. The phone number is (208) 342-1919; the Web site is at www.ioga.org/.

It is my hope that *Idaho Off the Beaten Path* will inspire you to hit the open road and discover this great state. Whether you seek an unusual family vacation destination, a romantic weekend rendezvous, or a fun one-day getaway; whether you desire mountain peaks, high desert stillness, or crystalline lakes, Idaho awaits your exploration. If, in your own travels, you come across changes in the information listed here or a great place that might be mentioned in a future edition of this book, drop me a line at julie@juliefanselow. com, or write me in care of The Globe Pequot Press, P.O. Box 480, Guilford, Connecticut 06437. Thanks—and happy travels!

Idaho Facts

POPULATION (2007 ESTIMATE):

- 1,499,402

STATEWIDE TOURISM INFORMATION:

- (800) VISIT-ID or www.visitidaho.org/

MAJOR NEWSPAPERS:

- *The Idaho Statesman* (Boise)
- *Boise Weekly* (alternative news and views)
- *Idaho Press-Tribune* (Nampa)
- *The Times-News* (Twin Falls)
- *The Idaho State Journal* (Pocatello)
- *The Post Register* (Idaho Falls)
- *The Coeur d'Alene Press*
- *Lewiston Morning Tribune*
- *The Idaho Spokesman-Review* (North Idaho)

HELPFUL STATEWIDE PHONE NUMBERS AND WEB SITES:

- State of Idaho Home Page—www.accessidaho.org
- Idaho weather—www.wrh.noaa.gov/boise/
- Road conditions report—Dial 511 or
  (888) 432-7623 or visit http://511.idaho.gov/.

- Idaho Department of Parks and Recreation—
  (208) 334-4199 or www.idahoparks.org
- Idaho Department of Fish and Game—(208) 334-3700
  or http://fishandgame.idaho.gov/.
- United States Forest Service—(208) 373-4100 or
  www.fs.fed.us
- Idaho RV Campgrounds Association—(208) 345-6009
  or www.rvidaho.org

TRANSPORTATION:

Air:

Idaho's major airport is in Boise, which is served by Alaska Air, Big Sky, Delta, ExpressJet, Frontier, Horizon, Northwest, Salmon Air, Sky West, Southwest, United Airlines, and USAirways. Other airports with scheduled service—sometimes via commuter carriers—include Hailey (Sun Valley), Idaho Falls, Lewiston, Twin Falls, and Pocatello. Many people traveling to North Idaho choose to fly into Spokane, Washington (just 33 miles from Coeur d'Alene). And the airport in Salt Lake City (161 miles from Pocatello) is reasonably convenient to destinations in the Southeastern, Eastern, and South Central regions of Idaho.

Bus:

Greyhound provides service to more than twenty Idaho cities, including Boise, Cascade, Coeur d'Alene, Idaho Falls, Lewiston, McCall, Moscow, Pocatello, Riggins, and Twin Falls. For more information call (800) 231-2222 or visit www.greyhound.com. Regional bus service also is available from Northwestern Trailways (on the U.S. Highway 95 corridor in North Central and Southwestern Idaho; call 800-366-3830 or visit www.northwesterntrailways.com/) and Rimrock Stages Trailways (along Interstate 15 in Eastern and Southeastern Idaho; call 800-255-7655 or see www.rimrocktrailways.com).

Train:

Amtrak's Empire Builder route passes through Sandpoint in North Idaho.

CLIMATE:

Because Idaho is so big, its climate cannot be easily summed up in a paragraph. But generally Idaho is drier than the Pacific Northwest and milder than the rest of the Rocky Mountain region. In Boise, daytime highs range from about 90°F in July to the mid-30s in January, with nighttime lows in the 50s in summertime and the 20s December through February. In the panhandle region, summer daytime temperatures are typically in the 80s, dipping to about 50°F at night.

In the winter expect North Idaho daytime highs at just about the freezing mark and lows about 20°F. Humidity is low around most of the state.

Precipitation varies widely, from only 9 inches of rain and 17 inches of snow falling annually at Twin Falls in South Central Idaho to 30 inches of rain and 75 inches of snow at Sandpoint. The best time to visit depends on your interests, but generally spring and fall are especially pleasant in the southern regions, while mid-July through mid-September are the best times to visit North Idaho and the Central Idaho mountains. The high country often has snow until after the Fourth of July.

FAMOUS IDAHOANS:

Famous Idahoans past and present include former Mormon church president Ezra Taft Benson, Edgar Rice Burroughs (author of *Tarzan*), Philo Farnsworth (inventor of television), baseball great Harmon Killebrew, NFL quarterback Jake Plummer, writer Ezra Pound, businessman J. R. Simplot, musicians Josh Ritter and Curtis Stigers, skier Picabo Street, and actress Lana Turner. Other celebrities who have made homes in the state include Jamie Lee Curtis, Patty Duke, Ernest Hemingway, Patrick McManus, Tom Hanks, Steve Miller, Demi Moore, Arnold Schwarzenegger, and Bruce Willis.

RECOMMENDED READING:

Guidebooks and Travel

Hiking Idaho by Jackie and Ralph Maughan (2nd edition; The Globe Pequot Press, 2001). A classic statewide guide that describes more than 100 trails,

Idaho for the Curious by Cort Conley (Backeddy Books, 1982). This fascinating, weighty book concentrates on history along the state's highways.

Moon Handbook: Idaho by Don Root (5th edition; Avalon Travel Publishing, 2004). If you buy only one other travel guidebook, this should be your choice. It is exhaustive and witty.

Traveling the Lewis and Clark Trail and *Traveling the Oregon Trail* by Julie Fanselow (The Globe Pequot Press, 2007 and 2001, respectively). These books are comprehensive modern travel guides to the famous trails, both of which run through Idaho.

History

Big Trouble: A Murder in a Small Western Town Sets Off a Struggle for the Soul of America by J. Anthony Lukas (Simon & Schuster, 1997). A long but worthwhile examination of early Idaho labor strife.

Building Idaho: An Architectural History by Jennifer Eastman Attebery (University of Idaho Press, 1991).

Camera Eye on Idaho by Arthur A. Hart (Caxton Press, 1990). A fascinating survey of pioneer photography in the state from 1863 through 1913.

History of Idaho by Leonard J. Arrington (University of Idaho Press/Idaho State Historical Society, 1994). This two-volume set was completed as part of the state's centennial celebration in 1990.

Roadside History of Idaho by Betty Derig (Mountain Press Publishing, 1996).

Natural History

Idaho Wildlife Viewing Guide by Aimee Pope (2nd edition; The Globe Pequot Press, 2001). Describes ninety-four viewing sites statewide.

Roadside Geology of Idaho by David Alt and Donald W. Hyndman (Mountain Press, 1989).

Rocks, Rails and Trails by Paul Karl Link and E. Chilton Phoenix (Idaho Museum of Natural History, 1996). A photo-packed look at the geology, geography, and history of Eastern and Southern Idaho. It's also available online at http://imnh.isu.edu/digitalatlas/.

Literature and Miscellaneous

Idaho 24/7 edited by Rick Smolan and David Elliot Cohen (Dorling Kindersley, 2004). Many of Idaho's top photographers contributed to this day-in-the-life document of life statewide.

Idaho Loners: Hermits, Solitaries, and Individualists by Cort Conley (Backeddy Books, 1994). Idaho is a state of individualists, and veteran writer Conley interviewed some of the most singular for these profiles.

Idaho's Poetry: A Centennial Anthology edited by Ronald E. McFarland and William Studebaker (University of Idaho Press, 1989).

So Incredibly Idaho! by Carlos A. Schwantes (University of Idaho Press, 1996). A photographic and literary tour of Idaho's varied landscapes.

Where the Morning Light's Still Blue: Personal Essays about Idaho edited by William Studebaker and Richard Ardinger (University of Idaho Press, 1994).

Written on Water: Essays on Idaho Rivers edited by Mary Clearman Blew (University of Idaho Press, 2001).

For Children

Idaho (Hello USA series) by Kathy Pelta (First Avenue Editions, 2002).

Idaho (Portrait of America) by Kathleen Thompson (Steck-Vaughn, 1996).

A Rendezvous with Idaho History by Dorothy Duttan and Caryl Humphries (Sterling Ties, 2000). This textbook is frequently used in the state's schools.

OTHER FAST FACTS:

- Idaho is among the nation's fastest-growing states. The population has risen about 50 percent since 1990.
- Idaho has more white water than any other state, with about 3,100 miles of river rapids.
- Idaho is the only state with an official seal designed by a woman.
- Idaho elected the nation's first Jewish governor.
- Yes, Idaho is the nation's leading potato producer. But you knew that.

North Idaho

For decades the lakes of North Idaho were a private playground for the people of the Northwest. If you grew up in eastern Washington, Idaho, or Montana, chances are your family vacationed on the shores of Lake Coeur d'Alene at least once. If you didn't, your neighbors probably did. But outside this corner of the country, few people had North Idaho on their radar screens.

Today, however, North Idaho has been discovered. Coeur d'Alene and Sandpoint are hot spots. Even scruffy old Wallace and Kellogg, long the victims of declining mining fortunes, are enjoying a tourism-centered renaissance. Consequently, you may need to work a bit harder to get off the beaten path in this region. But it can be done.

Interstate 90 runs through Coeur d'Alene and the Silver Valley surrounding Wallace, and it's the only high-speed road in the region. Elsewhere, even on U.S. Highways 2 and 95, two-lane stretches, stunning scenery, and occasionally heavy traffic are apt to slow you down. If you'd really like to leave the crowds behind, try the road up the east side of Priest Lake, the Coeur d'Alene Scenic Byway (Highways 97 and especially 3), or Highway 200 east of Sandpoint (the Pend Oreille Scenic Byway). These routes are part of the *International*

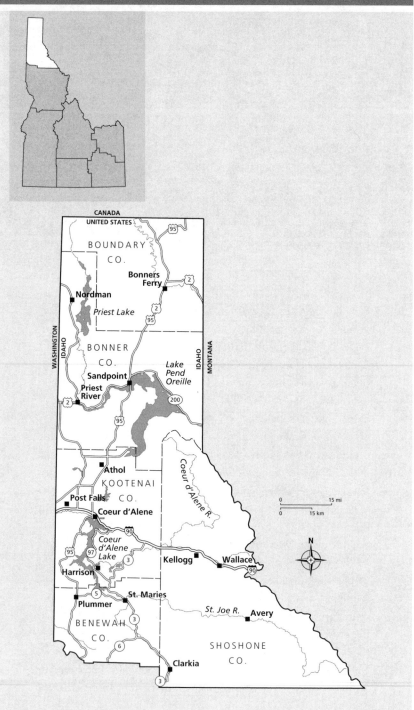

Selkirk Loop, a 280-mile scenic byway that connects Idaho and Washington with British Columbia. A few years ago, *Sunset* magazine called the loop the Northwest's most scenic drive, and it's hard to argue. The route is remote, yet there are enough towns and services along the way to fill a long weekend or even a week's road trip. For more information and a travel planner, write the International Selkirk Loop, P.O. Box 920, Bonners Ferry 83805; call (888) 823-2626; or visit www.selkirkloop.org.

For more North Idaho travel information, call (888) 333-3737, write the North Idaho Tourism Alliance, P.O. Box 850, Coeur d'Alene 83816, or log on to www.visitnorthidaho.com.

Lakes and Forests

Everywhere you look in North Idaho, you see either dense forests, expansive lakes, or both. This part of the state is most noted for its three large lakes—Coeur d'Alene, Pend Oreille, and Priest Lake (which actually is two lakes)—and the recreation-oriented resort towns on their shores. But rivers also run through this country, their Indian names music to the ears, their wild rapids and placid pools pure tonic for the soul. Two of these rivers—the Kootenai and the Moyie—meet at Bonners Ferry, the seat of Boundary County. East of town under a bridge spanning US 2, the Moyie flows through one of Idaho's most impressive canyons. The 1,223-foot-long steel truss *Moyie River Bridge,* built in 1964, is the second highest in the state, just 12 feet shy of the Perrine Bridge over the Snake River Canyon at Twin Falls. Stop at the rest area just east of the bridge for a good view of the span, or take the road to Upper and Lower Moyie Falls, two cascades that drop 100 feet and 40 feet, respectively.

Also along the Moyie River is Snyder Guard Station, a cabin first used as a forest ranger headquarters in 1908. Today the cabin is one of several available for rent from the Idaho Panhandle National Forests. The guard station, available from

---

JULIE'S FAVORITES IN NORTH IDAHO

Under the Sun Bonners Ferry	**Coeur d'Alene's Old Mission State Park** Cataldo
Lake Pend Oreille Sandpoint	**Sierra Silver Mine Tour** Wallace
Clark House Hayden Lake	**Trail of the Coeur d'Alenes** Mullan to Plummer

May 15 through September 30, was placed on the National Register of Historic Places in 1982. Sleeping arrangements include one double bed, two cots, and a set of bunk beds; plus you'll get electric heat, running water for hot showers, and a kitchen—all for $35 a night or $175 a week. A horse corral outside makes this a fine equestrian retreat, too.

Snyder Guard Station is 22 miles northwest of Bonners Ferry via Meadow Creek Road (County Road 34). To reserve the cabin call (208) 267-5561 or write the Bonners Ferry Ranger District, 6286 Main Street, Bonners Ferry 83805. For a directory of lookouts and cabins available for rent throughout Northern Idaho and surrounding states, write the U.S. Forest Service's Northern Region Headquarters, P.O. Box 7669, Missoula, MT 59807.

West of Bonners Ferry, the 2,774-acre **Kootenai National Wildlife Refuge** serves as an oasis to migrating waterfowl and a bird-watcher's paradise. In spring look for mallards, pintail, American widgeon, and tundra swans. Canada geese come through in August and September, while the mallards fly through later in the fall. All summer you may see cinnamon and blue-winged teal, common goldeneyes, and wood ducks. Wildlife spotted at the preserve include moose, muskrats, deer, beaver, and more.

The refuge is open to visitors during daylight hours year-round. In addition to excellent wildlife watching, you'll find some nice short trails. To find the refuge, drive 5 miles west of Bonners Ferry on Riverside Road. Stop at the refuge entrance for a self-guiding map to the refuge's foot trails and a 4½-mile driving tour. For more information call (208) 267-3888 or visit kootenai.fws.gov.

Idaho is a remote state, and its people are self-sufficient. Because Bonners Ferry is 535 miles from Boise, the state capital, and a good two-hour drive from the nearest metro area, people know how to make do for themselves. So it's no surprise that there are some real finds in Bonners Ferry's tiny downtown. **Under the Sun** at 7178 Main Street is a wonderful twenty-first-century general store with housewares, gifts, clothing, and more. A small cafe in the back serves lunch from 10:00 a.m. to 3:00 p.m. Monday through Saturday, with mostly organic soup, salad, and sandwich fare. **Groove Studio** at 7169 Main Street features a good selection of works by local artists. These two businesses are relatively new, but down the street, **Bonners Books,** at 7195 Main Street, has been supplying Idaho's far north with eclectic new and used reading material for decades as one of the state's best independent bookshops. If you're feeling lucky, you can play some slots at the casino in the **Best Western Kootenai River Inn** at 7169 Plaza Street, owned in part by the Kootenai Indians.

Although much smaller than Coeur d'Alene, Sandpoint rivals its neighbor as the most interesting town in Northern Idaho. Sandpoint's abundant natural attractions include Lake Pend Oreille, Idaho's largest, and **Schweitzer**

Mountain Resort. Schweitzer is one of the West's biggest ski areas, with nearly 3,000 skiable acres; that and its fairly remote location help make it one of the least crowded. From the top, skiers are treated to unbeatable views of Lake Pend Oreille. At the bottom, guests can relax in a slopeside room or condo or party in Sandpoint. Schweitzer has a full range of offerings in the warmer months, too. Summertime visitors can picnic atop the mountain, take a half-day or overnight guided llama trek, go mountain biking, or play golf. For more information on Schweitzer, call (208) 263-9555 or visit www .schweitzer.com.

Sandpoint is a shopping paradise, with a bevy of unique stores. Even people who don't like to shop will find this town hard to resist. Sandpoint is home base for *Coldwater Creek,* the upscale women's clothier, which has a store on First Street. But there are dozens of other interesting retailers here, too, with strengths in outdoor gear and fine art. The only downside to visiting Sandpoint is the traffic, which frequently backs up for blocks in the downtown area. A long-awaited bypass route has been talked about for years, but it was still in the planning stages as of late 2007. When you visit, park your car on the fringe of downtown and enjoy the walk!

Sandpoint's pride and joy is the *Panida Theater,* originally opened in 1927 and dedicated to "the people of the Panhandle of Idaho," thus the name. For years the Panida was considered one of the premier movie palaces of the Northwest, but like many theaters, it fell on hard times in the late 1970s and early 1980s. The community rallied to buy and restore the Panida, and it is now home to a full calendar of films and performing arts.

The Panida is at 300 North First Street. Call (208) 263-9191 or visit www .panida.org for upcoming events. The *Festival at Sandpoint* is another staple

TOP ANNUAL EVENTS IN NORTH IDAHO

Sandpoint Winter Carnival
(mid-January)

Depot Days Wallace
(early May)

Independence Day Celebration, Kellogg
(July 4)

Festival at Sandpoint
(August)

Art on the Green, Coeur d'Alene
(first weekend in August)

Coeur d'Alene Tribal Pilgrimage to Cataldo
(August 15)

North Idaho Fair, Coeur d'Alene
(late August)

of the local arts scene. Held midsummer on Lake Pend Oreille, the concert series features an inspired menu of music ranging from roots rock to the Spokane Symphony Orchestra. See www.festivalatsandpoint.com for upcoming shows. For tickets call (888) 265-4554.

Lake Pend Oreille is the center of sea kayaking activity in Idaho, and *Full Spectrum Tours* was the state's first licensed outfitter for the sport. The company offers rentals, lessons, and a wide menu of trips. If you have only a few hours, consider a Full Moon Paddle or Bird 'n' Boat trip, on which paddlers scope out wildlife on the Clark Fork Delta. Travelers with more time may want to arrange a "Gilligan's Special" combination paddling-camping trip. For more information call (208) 263-5975, visit Full Spectrum's Web site at www.kayaking.net, or stop in the store at 321 North Second Avenue in Sandpoint.

Highway 200 runs east from Sandpoint through the communities of Hope and East Hope, both recreational gateways to the northeastern reaches of Lake Pend Oreille. Near here, in 1809, Canadian explorer David Thompson established Kullyspell House, the earliest fur trade post in the American Pacific Northwest. Nothing remains of the post, but a monument to Thompson's efforts

Echoes of Ruby Ridge

Randy Weaver and his family moved to remote North Idaho in 1983 to live off the land, practice a radical brand of Christian fundamentalism, and turn up at the occasional gathering of the state's fringe neo-Nazi movement. Because most Idahoans have a live-and-let-live philosophy, the Weavers didn't attract much attention—until 1990, when Randy was caught selling illegal arms to an undercover Bureau of Alcohol, Tobacco, and Firearms agent. Released after a court appearance, he decided to hole up on his property and make the law come to him. After a year and a half of surveillance, federal marshals moved in. It's never been proven who shot first, but by the time the gunfire ended, three people were dead: decorated U.S. Marshal William Degan; Weaver's fourteen-year-old son, Samuel; and Weaver's wife, Vicki, who was holding her baby when she fell. Following an eleven-day standoff, Weaver surrendered. He subsequently went to trial on murder and conspiracy charges, beating all but a failure-to-appear rap with the aid of flamboyant defense attorney Gerry Spence, and he left Idaho. He eventually relocated to Montana with his daughters, after receiving an out-of-court settlement from the federal government to conclude a wrongful death lawsuit he filed.

The story of Ruby Ridge still echoes loudly in North Idaho. Local businesspeople and residents are still asked about the incident and the location of the Weavers' cabin. (The property was long a site for curiosity seekers, but it is now under new ownership and is off-limits.) For an insightful look into the Weaver incident and its aftermath, read *Every Knee Shall Bow: The Truth and Tragedy of Ruby Ridge and the Randy Weaver Family* by Jess Walter.

sits along the highway at Hope. The **Old Ice House Pizzeria & Bakery** at 140 West Main Street in Hope serves up thin-crust New York-style pies, plus sweets including baklava, muffins, and cookies. The phone number is (208) 264-5555.

Wolves are highly controversial critters in Idaho. In Cocolalla, 11 miles south of Sandpoint, a roadside business called **Wolf People** offers travelers an easy chance to stop and meet these misunderstood creatures. Between three and five wolves can be viewed most days, part of a pack of about twenty wolves that live nearby on a fifty-acre preserve. (Born and raised in captivity, these Timber, Arctic, and Tundra wolves don't have the wilderness skills needed to survive on their own.) Wolf People offers a gift shop, educational programs, and wolf sponsorships. All in all, it's a lot more commercial than the nonprofit Wolf Education and Research Visitor Center down in Winchester (see the North Central Idaho chapter for information), but founder Nancy Taylor seems to have her heart in the right place. Hours are 9:00 a.m. to 6:00 p.m. daily except Saturday in summer, and 9:00 a.m. to 5:00 p.m. daily except Saturday from Labor Day through Memorial Day. Visit the Web site at www .wolfpeople.com, or call (800) 404-9653 for more information.

Southwest of Sandpoint, Lake Pend Oreille flows into Priest River, toward a town of the same name. Head north from the town of Priest River to **Priest Lake,** Northern Idaho's least-used big lake. Named for the Jesuit priests who came to Northern Idaho to spread their gospel among the Native Americans, Priest Lake is bordered to the east by the Selkirk Mountain Range, whose more than 7,000-foot peaks stand majestic against the lake's altitude of some 2,400 feet above sea level. Priest Lake is actually two lakes—the main body of water and Upper Priest Lake, which is connected to the much larger lower lake by a 2-mile-long water thoroughfare. Area marinas rent boats and other watercraft that can be used to ply the lakes and thoroughfare as well as explore island campsites dotting the water. The eastern shore is almost entirely undeveloped save for **Priest Lake State Park** and a few marinas. Nevertheless, this was where Nell Shipman—an early silent film star—had a studio during the 1920s, way up at Lionhead on the lake's northeastern tip.

At the south end of Priest Lake, the **Old Northern Inn** welcomes vacationers to a gracious, antiques-filled bed-and-breakfast. Amenities include a small private marina, a swimming and sunning beach, and a deck overlooking the lake. The inn is open Memorial Day through mid-October, with four rooms and two suites, all with private baths. Rates range from $95 to $150 double occupancy, including a home-cooked breakfast for two. Children over age twelve are welcome. For more information or reservations, call (208) 443-2426, write The Old Northern Inn, P.O. Box 177, Coolin 83821, or see www .oldnortherninn.com.

The west side of Priest Lake has more commercial development than the east side, but still nothing compared to the shores of Coeur d'Alene and Pend Oreille. **Hill's Resort** has been welcoming guests to Luby Bay since 1946 and has won wide acclaim for catering to families. Aside from water-based activities, Hill's is accessible to good hiking, mountain biking, volleyball, golf, tennis, hunting, cross-country skiing, and about 400 miles of groomed snowmobile trails. And then there's the food. Baby back ribs, Margarita shrimp, and huckleberry pie are among the specialties, and the view of Priest Lake is a welcome side dish. Hill's has lakefront housekeeping units in four buildings, along with cabins that sleep between four and twelve people. Call (208) 443-2551 for reservations or more information.

Huckleberries are plentiful in Northern Idaho, and some of the best berry patches are located along Priest Lake. Because huckleberries need sunlight to ripen, the best picking is often along abandoned logging roads and areas opened to sunshine by forest fires. Look for shrubs about 1 to 5 feet tall, with tiny pink or white urn-shaped flowers that blossom in June or July. The berries themselves are purplish black to wine red in color, and they generally ripen in July or August, although some berries on slopes facing north may linger as late as October.

Humans like huckleberries a lot, but so do black bears and grizzly bears. The Selkirk Mountains are one of a handful of places where the legendary grizzlies still range in the United States, so caution must always be used. (Wear bells, keep a clean camp, and retreat from the area should a bear turn up.) For a pamphlet showing prime berry picking areas and a few recipes, contact the Idaho Panhandle National Forests' Priest Lake Ranger District, 32203 Highway 57, Priest River 83856.

State Highway 57 ends at Nordman, but a 13-mile trip up Forest Road 302—past the locally famous shoe tree, where travelers discard worn-out foot gear—leads to the **Roosevelt Grove of Ancient Cedars,** where you can see a virgin forest of trees ranging up to 2,000 years old. Short hiking trails from the grove lead to views of Upper and Lower Granite Falls.

The Coeur d'Alenes

Idaho has its share of gourmet restaurants in unlikely locations, and **Chef in the Forest** certainly fits that description. Set on Hauser Lake north of the town of Post Falls, this chalet-style destination restaurant draws many patrons from eastern Washington and Montana's Flathead Valley as well as from all over Northern Idaho.

Chef in the Forest changes its menu regularly, but diners are likely to find such entrees as house specialty roast duckling with fresh brandied raspberry sauce; rack of lamb; and German sauerbraten, a Bavarian marinated pot roast complete with gingersnap sauce, potato pancakes, and braised red cabbage. You'll also find such fare as Cioppino, an award-winning dish featuring lobster, crab, scallops, and shrimp baked in an earthenware crock and served with rice pilaf and garlic bread.

Entrees at Chef in the Forest range in price from $21 to $38. A tempting variety of appetizers and desserts complements each main course, and the wine list has about fifty-five selections. To get to Chef in the Forest, watch for the sign on Highway 53 west of Rathdrum; the restaurant is located at 12008 Woodland Beach Drive. Chef in the Forest is open for dinner only from 5:00 p.m. Wednesday through Sunday. For reservations, which are suggested, call (208) 773-3654.

Post Falls is one of Idaho's fastest-growing towns, a chock-a-block with strip malls and subdivisions that stretch from the Washington state line to Coeur d'Alene. But Post Falls has its share of character, too. In the downtown area, amiable chef Raci Erdem presides over two popular and lively restaurants. YOU LOVE GARLIC. WE LOVE YOU, promises the streetside mural outside *The White House Grill* at 712 North Spokane Street. Greek, Turkish, and Italian fare is on the menu here, all heavy on the garlic (and feta, too). Hours are 11:00 a.m. to 10:00 p.m. Monday through Thursday, 11:00 a.m. to 11:00 p.m. Friday and Saturday. *The Oval Office,* Erdem's other eatery, has a wider bistro-style menu and a martini bar. It's at 612 North Spokane Street, and hours are 3:00 p.m. to 11:00 p.m. Tuesday through Sunday.

Chef in the Forest

On a hot day many Post Falls residents can be found at *Q'Emilin Park,* with its grassy lawn and beach. (Q'Emilin, pronounced "ka-MEE-lin," is an Indian term that means "throat of the river.") Few, however, know that a magnificent canyon nearby awaits exploration. The gorge is also home to an outcropping of rocks popular with local rock climbers. To find the canyon, just stroll back beyond the boat dock and parking area.

One of Idaho's most storied state parks can be found near the town of Athol at the south end of big Lake Pend Oreille. In 1941 the U.S. Navy built the second-largest naval training center in the world on this site at the foot of the Coeur d'Alene Mountains. Over fifteen months during World War II, 293,381 sailors received basic training at Farragut Naval Training Station. Following the war the site served for a time as a college before being transformed into *Farragut State Park* in 1965. Since then the park—one of Idaho's largest— also has hosted several national Boy Scout and Girl Scout gatherings.

The park visitor center displays exhibits detailing the Navy presence at Farragut, which hasn't disappeared entirely: The military still uses 1,200-foot-deep Lake Pend Oreille as a submarine testing site. But recreation reigns at Farragut these days, with good opportunities for camping, hiking, cross-country skiing, boating, and wildlife viewing. Mountain goats patrol the steep peaks along Pend Oreille's south shore, and deer, moose, elk, and bear are also in residence. Farragut State Park is open year-round, with a $4-per-vehicle state park admission charge. For information call (208) 683-2425; write Farragut State Park, 13400 East Ranger Road, Athol 83801; or visit www.idahoparks.org/parks/farragut.aspx.

It might be a stretch to call the Northwest's largest amusement park a truly off-the-beaten-path attraction, especially when it sits along Highway 95 about 20 miles north of Coeur d'Alene. But *Silverwood Theme Park* truly is out of the way for the thousands of urbanites from Spokane, Boise, Seattle, and beyond who nonetheless flock here for summer fun. Silverwood offers plenty to make even a long drive worthwhile, including several top-notch roller coasters and the Boulder Beach water park. But the park's most charming attraction may be its live performances. The magic and ice shows are must-sees. Silverwood admission, which includes both the amusement park and Boulder Beach, runs about $36 for visitors age eight and up and about $20 for children ages three to seven and senior citizens. See the park's Web site at www.silverwoodthemepark.com or call (208) 683-3400 to plan a visit. The park is located at 27843 North Highway 95, Athol 83801.

The Coeur d'Alene area takes the title as Idaho's bed-and-breakfast capital, with about twenty establishments providing homey hospitality and new ones opening all the time. One reason for this may be Idaho's relaxed marriage laws.

Comfy Camping

Not everyone likes to sleep on the ground, and not everyone has camping equipment. If you fit either category, you can still enjoy Idaho's state parks by reserving any of the new-in-2003 camping cabins available throughout the state.

The year-round cabins, which measure 12 feet square, can sleep up to five people for $45 a night. They're furnished with log-style beds, a table and chairs, lamps, power outlets, heat (and even air-conditioning in some locations), lockable windows and doors, and a porch complete with swing. A fire ring and picnic table are situated outside each cabin, and restrooms, water, and showers are located nearby. Campers bring their own sleeping bags, cookware, and eating utensils. The wheelchair-accessible cabins are perfect for people with disabilities, too.

Cabins are available at these state parks: Bruneau Dunes, Dworshak, Farragut, Hells Gate, Henrys Lake, Lake Walcott, Massacre Rocks, Ponderosa, Priest Lake, and Three Island Crossing. Older cabins and yurts are available in several parks, too. For complete information or reservations, see www.idahoparks.org/lodging/cabins.aspx. Idaho also has several dozen cabins and lookouts available for rent on U.S. Forest Service land. To find them, visit www.recreation.gov, click on "camping," and search for cabins and lookouts. Some are extremely rustic; others have complete kitchens and even indoor plumbing.

No waiting period is required either before or after the license is obtained, so couples from Washington, Canada, Montana, and other spots often steal away to the Gem State to seal their vows, and Coeur d'Alene is a favorite destination. There's even a local bed-and-breakfast association available to offer information on all the local establishments, whether you are newlyweds, nearly weds, or traveling on business. The association's Web site is at www.bb-cda.com.

For one of Coeur d'Alene's most unusual bed-and-breakfast experiences, the ***Roosevelt Inn*** gets high marks. This handsome former schoolhouse, listed on the National Register of Historic Places, turned one hundred in 2005; it's been a bed-and-breakfast since 1994. Guests here have access to a twenty-four-hour hot tub and spa, a CD library, snacks and beverages, and lots of books, plus it's only a short walk to downtown or Lake Coeur d'Alene.

Room rates at the Roosevelt run from $89 to $229 in the off-season and from $119 to $319 during the summer, certain holidays, and for some special events. The top price gets you the Bell Tower Suite, suitable for honeymoon or anniversary stays with a fireplace and a view of the lake. Prices include a gourmet breakfast. For more information call (800) 290-3358; write to 105 East Wallace Avenue, Coeur d'Alene 83814; or learn more online at www.therooseveltinn.com.

Along Hayden Lake just north of Coeur d'Alene, the ***Clark House*** is among the most elegant inns in the Northwest. In the late 1980s the F. Lewis

Clark Mansion on the shores of Hayden Lake was scheduled to be burned down after years of neglect and rampant vandalism. The mansion was completed in 1910 as a summer home for Spokane flour mill magnate F. Lewis Clark and his wife, Winifred. Clark was an unusually astute businessman who, fresh out of Harvard, built the C & C Mill in Spokane, later selling it for $200,000 more than he had invested. Clark knew Spokane would grow to the east, so he turned his attention to buying land in the Idaho panhandle. Here, too, his investments proved shrewd, turning Clark into a millionaire.

The 15,000-square-foot Hayden Lake villa was considered the most grand and expensive in Idaho when it was completed in 1912. Everything about the home was opulent, from the French hand-painted wallpaper to the Czechoslovakian crystal chandeliers. Unfortunately tragedy struck the Clarks not long after the mansion's completion. In 1914, while wintering in California, Clark disappeared while walking on the beach in Santa Barbara. His hat was found on the beach, but a body was never recovered, and authorities never determined whether the death was an accident or a suicide. Just a few years later, Winifred Clark was forced to leave the mansion in foreclosure proceedings.

The mansion played many roles over the next decades, serving as a children's home, church retreat center, military convalescence center, and a restaurant. But the grand building had stood vacant for many years when Monty Danner purchased it in 1989. Eighteen months later, after he replaced more than 1,000 window panes, installed new heating and electrical systems, and attended to countless other details, Danner rechristened the mansion the Clark House.

The inn has ten guest rooms—some the size of midsize apartments—ranging in price from $125 to $250 per night, double occupancy, including breakfast. All have private baths, some with Roman tubs for two; four have their own fireplaces; and the larger rooms are stocked liberally with books. The F. Lewis Clark Suite, the inn's showplace, features such sumptuous furnishings as a king-size canopied bed and billowing gold draperies hung on walnut rods. But even the more modest rooms are memorable and welcoming.

The guest quarters are hard to leave, but the rest of the house is worth a long look, too. Especially noteworthy are the murals by acclaimed artist Jack McCullagh, a frequent Academy Awards nominee for film set design (and winner of the scenic design prize at the Cannes film festival in France). Guests also are free to wander the twelve acres of grounds, play croquet, take in the lake views from the verandah, or soak in an enclosed hot tub.

In recent years Clark House has become as well-known for its food as for its lodging. Multicourse gourmet dinners are served seven nights a week by reservation, and the inn frequently hosts weddings, corporate retreats and business meetings, private dinner parties, and other events for up to fifty people. The Clark House is geared to adults and is considered "inappropriate for children under twelve." A two-day minimum stay is required weekends from Memorial Day through Labor Day. For reservations call (800) 765-4593; write the Clark House, 5250 East Hayden Lake Road, Hayden Lake 83835; or visit www.clarkhouse.com.

Coeur d'Alene has plenty of good restaurants. One of the best (and least pretentious) is **Moon Time,** a neighborhood-style pub about a mile from the lakefront at 1602 Sherman Avenue. Menu favorites include spicy gumbo, baby back ribs, and a great array of sandwiches. Try the handmade Anasazi Bean Burger with a side of roasted corn pasta salad and a Moon Unit brownie for dessert. Moon Time has live music and $1 pints of beer every Thursday after 9:00 p.m. For more information call (208) 667-2331 or see www.wedonthaveone.com.

North Idahoans don't just like good food when they dine out, but when they eat in, too. For great picnic fare, Northwest beer and wine, organic produce and meats, and lots more good stuff, Coeur d'Alene-area chefs and amateur foodies turn to **Pilgrim's Market** at 1316 North Fourth Street. Fresh and local are the mantras here. The market is open from 9:00 a.m. to 8:00 p.m. Monday through Saturday, and from 10:00 a.m. to 6:00 p.m. Sunday. Call (208) 676-9730.

In 1990 readers of *Condé Nast Traveler* magazine voted the Coeur d'Alene Resort the best resort in the continental United States. The Coeur d'Alene isn't exactly off the beaten path—its copper-topped presence dominates the city's lakefront—but it does have one amenity no other resort in the world can claim: the **Floating Green** on the resort golf course. The brainchild of resort co-owner Duane Hagadone, the green is a par three on the fourteenth hole. It's also a moving target, floating between 100 and 175 yards from the blue (longest) tees. The movement is controlled by a computer, with the hole's length displayed each day at the tee. More than 30,000 golfers play the course each year, and during one memorable season, 22,000 golf balls, 50 golf clubs, and 2 golfers landed in the lake. The golf balls are removed from the lake weekly by salvage divers, but there's no word on what happens to errant golf clubs or golfers!

The Coeur d'Alene Resort Golf Course is notable for other elements of its design, too. The links were constructed on the site of a former sawmill, and planners strove to incorporate as much of the natural environment into the course as possible. An osprey nest perches on a piling beside the thirteenth tee, and Fernan Creek and its trout spawning beds parallel the eleventh fairway. For these efforts the course was given a special award for environmental sensitivity from the Urban Land Institute. Alas, the Coeur d'Alene golf experience doesn't come cheap. Greens fees run from $200 to $270, with stay-and-play packages available. The fee includes eighteen holes, caddy service, a custom-designed golf cart for each twosome, range balls, tees, and a personalized bag tag. For more information or reservations, call (800) 935-6283.

If the Coeur d'Alene beachfront is too bustling for your taste, head instead to *Tubbs Hill,* a 120-acre wooded city park on the peninsula just southeast of downtown. The main trail on Tubbs Hill begins on the west side at the south end of Third Street; from there, spur trails provide access for great hiking. Dogs are allowed on a leash. For more information on Tubbs Hill, call the city parks department at (208) 769-2252. Another quiet spot amid Coeur d'Alene's growth is The Nature Conservancy's *Cougar Bay Preserve,* featuring eighty-eight acres of wetlands along the northwest shore of Lake Coeur d'Alene. Visitors will find more than 5 miles of hiking trails and a canoe-kayak launch. Many critters make homes here, including waterfowl, shorebirds, songbirds, moose, beaver, otter, and deer. The preserve entrance is about 2 miles south of Coeur d'Alene on US 95; look for the sign on the left (east) side of the road. The boat access area is about three-quarters of a mile north of the entrance. More information is available from The Nature Conservancy at (208) 676-8176.

The oldest standing building in Idaho is preserved handsomely at *Coeur d'Alene's Old Mission State Park,* accessible via exit 39 off I-90. The Sacred

Norman, Is That You?

Sun Valley aside, Coeur d'Alene is about as fancy as Idaho gets. But never let it be forgotten that this town, famous for its pricey bed-and-breakfasts and posh resort, is also home to—scary movie music, please—the **Bates Motel.**

OK, so this vintage-style motor court at 2018 Sherman Avenue wasn't the setting for Alfred Hitchcock's immortal 1960 film *Psycho.* That hasn't stopped the Bates Motel from putting a shower curtain on its business cards, nor from doing a brisk business in souvenir towels, key chains, and T-shirts.

The clean and comfy lodge has had its name since former owner Randy Bates bought the old Highway 10 Motel years ago and decided to have some fun by renaming it. Dusty Van Iderstine runs the place these days, and he's added some new twists, including an annual Halloween celebration—although, as Van Iderstine says, "Of course, it's Halloween year-round here."

The Bates Motel is one of Coeur d'Alene's best lodging bargains. The rooms, origi-nally used as cabins up at Farragut Naval Station, rent for $30 to $45 in the off-sea-son and $42 to $56 in summer, and each has a refrigerator, microwave, and TV. Call (208) 667-1411 for more information or reservations.

Heart Mission was primarily built between 1848 and 1853, the work of Coeur d'Alene Indians laboring under the supervision of Father Antonio Ravalli, a Jesuit missionary. The tribe called the mission "The House of the Great Spirit." Begin your tour by asking to see a slide presentation of the same name at the park visitor center.

The Coeur d'Alene Indians welcomed the Jesuits, for they believed the "Big Prayer" brought by the priests would give them an advantage over their enemies. There proved to be many parallels between the Native Americans and the Catholics: Each had a sense of the miraculous, the crucifix and rosaries were akin to the Indians' sacred charms, the chants of the Jesuit priests weren't unlike the natives' tribal songs, and the Catholics' incense, like the Indians' sage, was said to help carry prayers skyward.

Ravalli designed the mission in classical Roman Doric style. In addition to serving as architect, he helped adorn the inside with devotional paintings and European-style chandeliers fashioned from tin cans. Wooden ceiling panels were stained blue with huckleberry juice to resemble the sky. Incredibly, when the Coeur d'Alenes were sent to a reservation, the boundaries drawn did not include their beloved mission. A new mission was built at DeSmet, 60 miles away. But the Sacred Heart Mission (also called the Cataldo Mission) remains an important site for history buffs, as well as for Catholics and the Coeur d'Alenes who make a pilgrimage to the site each year for the Feast of the Assumption. This event, held every August 15, includes a Mass, barbecue, and Indian dancing. Other annual happenings include a Historic Skills Fair with living history demonstrations the second Sunday each July and a Mountain Man Rendezvous the third weekend of August. Old Mission State Park is open year-round 9:00 a.m. to 5:00 p.m. Admission is $4 per vehicle. Phone (208) 682-3814 or visit at the park Web site at www.idahoparks.org/parks/oldmission .aspx for more information.

Coeur d'Alene's Old Mission State Park is also the headquarters for the **Trail of the Coeur d'Alenes,** a 72-mile paved path among the longest of its kind in the United States. In an innovative solution to an environmental problem, the asphalt trail seals what was once the heavy metals-contaminated Union Pacific railroad bed between Mullan and Plummer. The mostly flat trail is open for cycling, skating, and pedestrian use. The state and the Coeur d'Alene Tribe both manage it.

The nicest stretch of trail is the 40 or so miles between Enaville and the old Chatcolet Bridge south of Harrison. Here, the trail runs far from I-90, winding along the Coeur d'Alene River and numerous lakes. Bike rentals and lodging are available in Kellogg and Harrison, among other towns, and picnic waysides dot the route. Be sure to carry drinking water and snacks. Many cycling enthusiasts combine the Trail of the Coeur d'Alenes and the Route of the Hiawatha near Wallace (see the next section) for a great bike-based vacation in North Idaho. You can get a map at any of the twenty trailheads; from Coeur d'Alene's Old Mission State Park; or by writing the Coeur d'Alene Tribe, P.O. Box 408, Plummer 83851. You can also get more information at these Web sites: http://friendsofcdatrails.org and www.idahoparks.org/parks/trailofthecoeurdalenes.aspx.

The small town of Harrison has become a hub of activity and tourism for the Trail of the Coeur d'Alenes. Vacationing cyclists and bird-watchers rule the roost at the *Osprey Inn,* which was built as a rooming house for lumberjacks in 1915. Its five guest rooms each have a private bathroom, and three of the rooms include lake views. Rates run from $75 to $120 in summer, less in the off-season, including breakfast. For information or reservations call (208) 689-9502, see www.ospreyinn.com, or write The Osprey Inn, 134 Frederick Avenue, Harrison 83833.

Silver and Garnets

For more than a century, Idaho's Silver Valley—also known as the Coeur d'Alene Mining District—was the undisputed world leader in silver, lead, and zinc production. By 1985, a hundred years after mining began, the region had produced one billion ounces of silver, and the total value of wealth coaxed from the mines had topped $5 billion. But as mining fortunes fluctuate, the Silver Valley —like many Western communities formerly dependent on natural resources—is looking to recreation and tourism to rebuild its economy. The region's location along I-90 has proven a blessing, with many attractions visible from the freeway, but a few places require a detour from the four lane.

The *Enaville Resort* is one such spot. Dining in this restaurant is kind of like eating at a flea market. The walls are covered with collectors' plates, NASA memorabilia, and black velvet paintings, and patrons sit at extra-rustic furniture amid bulbous tree burls. The decor leaves a bit to be desired, frankly, but the food keeps people coming back. The special here is Rocky Mountain Oysters. ("Make sure we have them. Sometimes the bulls don't cooperate," the menu cautions.) A full portion served with bread, soup or salad bar, and choice of potatoes costs $12.95, and a side order goes for $6.95. Other options include steaks priced from $9.95 to $16.95; a good selection of seafood; chicken-fried steak; and buffalo burgers. A smorgasbord of salmon, cod, oysters, shrimp, barbecued chicken and ribs, and sautéed mushrooms is available Friday from 5:00 to 9:00 p.m.

For much of its history, which stretches back more than a century, Enaville Resort also has been known as "the Snake Pit." Ask five people why, and you'll likely get five different answers. One popular tale recalls when water snakes used to inhabit the area around the outdoor privies used before indoor plumbing came along. Patrons occasionally caught the snakes, put them in a container, and brought them inside. The business also served as a way station for railroaders, miners, and loggers. In addition to food, they sometimes sought female companionship, and the women available at the roadhouse were supposedly called "snakes." The Enaville Resort is open daily for lunch and dinner, with breakfast, lunch, and dinner served Saturday and Sunday. It's located 1.5 miles from exit 43 off I-90, up the Coeur d'Alene River Road. For more information call (208) 682-3453.

Sitting atop the old, mostly dormant Bunker Hill Mine in Kellogg, **Silver Mountain** resort has made a name for itself with the world's longest single-stage, people-carrying gondola. Each car transports eight people on a nineteen-minute, 3-mile ride that covers 3,400 vertical feet. The gondola runs in the summer as well as in the winter. After reaching the top, many warm-weather riders like to either hike or bike down the mountain on trails that range from 2 to 22 miles long. Skiers have their choice of sixty-seven runs covering 1,500 acres. The resort opened a year-round indoor water park, Silver Rapids, in the Spring of 2008. Its signature attraction, the FlowRider, unleashes 10,000 gallons into a "wave box" that simulates the thrills of surfing, skateboarding, and snowboarding. Visitors looking for tamer pleasures will find a lazy river and kids' activity lagoon. For more information on Silver Mountain, call (877) 230-2193 or visit www.silvermt.com.

Kellogg is doing its best to augment Silver Mountain with other attractions. Its small downtown features some interesting locally owned shops such as **Bitterroot Mercantile,** which stocks everything from Idaho-made goods to birdhouses and many beautiful antiques. It's at 117 McKinley Avenue; the phone number is (208) 783-5491. Around the corner, **Josie's Full of Beans** is a wonderful little coffee shop in the old McConnell Hotel at 210 South Main Street. Good vibes abound here, from the high-ceilinged brick and wood decor to the free wireless Internet.

Leave the interstate at exit 54 east of Kellogg to see the **Sunshine Mine Memorial,** which recalls the worst United States hard-rock mining disaster since 1917. On May 2, 1972, a fire broke out in the mine and, although eighty-five made it out safely and two were later found alive, ninety-one people died in the blaze. The monument features a miner hoisting a jack leg and a poem penned by then-state senator Phil Batt (later Idaho's governor). Small memorials placed by the miners' families are scattered beneath the trees on each side.

Wallace, Kellogg's neighbor to the east, seems to be having more success than Kellogg in mining its glory days. The entire town is listed on the National

Register of Historic Places, and it's well worth a day or two of exploration. The *Sierra Silver Mine Tour* is billed as the only one of its kind in the Northwest. Visitors ride a trolley-style bus to the mine portal, where hard hats are issued for the trip underground. Once in the mine the tour guides—themselves experienced miners—talk about and demonstrate the equipment and techniques used to mine silver ore. Interestingly this mine was once used as a working classroom for Wallace High School students who wanted to pursue a career underground.

Along with the mine visit, tour patrons are treated to a drive-around orientation of Wallace. The seventy-five-minute tours leave every thirty minutes from 420 Fifth Street in Wallace. Tours are given from 10:00 a.m. to 4:00 p.m. June through August and from 10:00 A,M. to 2:00 p.m. in May and September. Cost is $10.00 for adults, $9.50 for senior citizens age sixty and up, and $8.00 for children ages four to sixteen. Bring a jacket because mine temperatures average about 50°F. For more information call (208) 752-5151; write Sierra Silver Mine Tour Inc., P.O. Box 712, Wallace 83873; or see www.silverminetour.org.

Idaho on Film

Lights . . . camera . . . disaster! With its wide range of unspoiled scenery, Idaho has landed some major roles in Hollywood, although it sometimes seems the state's involvement in movies has calamitous connections of one sort or another.

For example, the town of Wallace served as the setting for *Dante's Peak,* the 1997, exploding volcano film starring Pierce Brosnan and Linda Hamilton. Despite lukewarm reviews, Wallace is proud of *Peak,* and you can still buy souvenirs of the film at some businesses around town. The same can't be said for *Heaven's Gate,* which was partially made in Wallace in 1979. The film is often cited among Hollywood's all-time biggest flops. But disaster movies, whether intentional or not, are nothing new in North Idaho: A silent film, *Tornado,* was filmed in the 1920s on the St. Joe River.

On the opposite end of the state, Preston, Idaho, recently found fame as the setting for the offbeat 2004 hit *Napoleon Dynamite.* Preston native Jared Hess made the independent film for $400,000; it earned $45 million in its first six months of theatrical release, and more than double that in its first year on DVD. (See the Southeastern Idaho chapter for more information on *Napoleon's* sweet success story.) Other films made entirely or partially in Idaho include Clint Eastwood's *Bronco Billy* and *Pale Rider; Northwest Passage* with Spencer Tracy; *Continental Divide* (with John Belushi in a tender-hearted role); *Smoke Signals,* written by Sherman Alexie; Nell Shipman's *Told in the Hills; River of No Return* with Marilyn Monroe; *Breakheart Pass; Sun Valley Serenade;* and *Dark Horse,* a family film about a troubled teenager's redemption. For information on filmmaking in Idaho, visit the Idaho Film Bureau's Web site at www.filmidaho.org or call (208) 334-2470.

Just down the street from the mine tour office, the **Wallace District Mining Museum** at 509 Bank Street is a good spot to learn more about the mining industry and other area history. A short film, *North Idaho's Silver Legacy,* is packed with interesting tales from Wallace's past. Exhibits include several mine models, a beautiful local history quilt, and the world's largest silver dollar (3 feet in diameter, with a weight of 150 pounds). It's also the final resting place of "Old Blinky," which until September 1991 was the last stoplight on I-90 between Seattle and Boston.

The mining museum has a gift shop and ample parking and is open daily from 9:00 a.m. to 5:00 p.m. May through September and daily from noon to 5:00 p.m, October through April. The cost is $2.00 for visitors age sixteen to fifty-five, $1.50 for senior citizens, 50 cents for kids ages six to fifteen, or $5.00 for a family. For more information call (208) 556-1592 or write Wallace District Mining Museum, P.O. Box 469, Wallace 83873.

On the same block at 524 Bank Street, **Silver Capital Arts** displays and sells collectible minerals and fossils, antiques, Idaho-made silver and gold jewelry, mining souvenirs, and more. The **Wallace Wine Cellar** is here, too. **Indelible Tidbits** at 604 Bank Street doubles as a one-hour photo processing lab and a fly-tying shop. Owner Shauna Hillman offers a Fly of the Month Club, featuring a different angling aid sent to your favorite fly-fisher. For more information call her at (208) 753-0591.

Train fans will enjoy a stop at the **Northern Pacific Depot Railroad Museum** at 219 Sixth Street in Wallace. The last train ran out of the Wallace depot in 1980; since then, the facility has been moved to accommodate the freeway and renovated to tell all about the Northern Pacific, which at one time boasted "2,000 miles of startling beauty." There is an extensive collection of Northern Pacific memorabilia, a model railroad display, and even a quilt bearing the railway's famous red and black, yin and yang symbol.

The chateau-style Wallace depot has a fascinating history all its own. Built in 1901 with 15,000 bricks salvaged from what was to be a grand hotel in Tacoma, Washington, the station was visited two years later by then-president Theodore Roosevelt. It also has survived a string of near disasters: a 1906 flood, a 1910 fire that burned half of Wallace, and a 1914 runaway train that crashed only a few feet from the depot. The Northern Pacific Depot Railroad Museum is open daily from 9:00 a.m. to 7:00 p.m. June through August. In May and September, hours are 9:00 a.m. to 5:00 p.m. In April and October, the museum is open Monday through Friday from 10:00 a.m. to 3:00 p.m. Admission is $2.00 for adults, $1.50 for seniors age sixty and up, and $1.00 for children ages six through sixteen. Children age five and under get in free. The museum is closed November through March. Call (208) 752-0111 for more information.

Northern Pacific Depot Railroad Museum

Last but certainly not least, the ***Oasis Rooms Bordello Museum*** at 605 Cedar Street documents another formerly important Wallace industry, one that thrived until 1988. The Oasis Rooms were hardly unique; at one time five brothels stood along Wallace's main street, and prostitution was an acceptable misdemeanor in the eyes of local law enforcement. After all, Wallace had three times as many men as it did women, "so women had an opportunity and the townspeople didn't seem to object if the women stayed to themselves," explains Michelle Mayfield, who runs the museum with her husband, Jack.

But in 1973, according to the *New York Times,* Democratic governor Cecil Andrus ordered that Wallace's brothels be shut down, possibly in response to an *Idaho Statesman* article in which Republican attorney Stanley Crow charged that Andrus had agreed to go easy on gambling and prostitution in North Idaho in return for a $25,000 campaign contribution. (Andrus denied the charge.) After the fuss subsided, the brothels quietly went back into business. But by the late 1980s, beset by the AIDS crisis and the faltering mining economy, only one house was left. The Oasis Rooms' employees would often make themselves scarce for a few days if FBI agents were rumored to be in town—and in January 1988, they left and never came back.

For that reason, the Oasis Rooms tour is a fascinating look at how these women worked and lived. The rooms are pretty much as the "girls" left them, with clothing, jewelry, and makeup strewn about. Mayfield opens a drawer in the office to reveal a pile of timers, each with a different woman's name affixed. A box of Mr. Bubble sits on the bathtub ledge, "Heather" written on it.

Mayfield explains that in the brothel's heyday, an employee might make $1,000 to $2,500 a week, and some women put themselves through college with their earnings. (The Oasis Rooms would not hire anyone from Wallace or the surrounding area.) But it's clear they worked hard for their money. A menu left on the wall when the Oasis Rooms closed revealed different services priced from $15 (for eight minutes of "straight, no frills") to $80 (for a bubble bath and an hour-long encounter). The madam kept 40 percent of all fees.

The Oasis Rooms Bordello Museum is open May through October from 10:00 a.m. to 5:00 p.m. Monday through Saturday, and from 11:00 a.m. to 4:00 p.m. Sunday. The tour costs $5 per person. For more information call (208) 753-0801. To schedule a group tour or make an off-season appointment, phone (208) 752-3721.

Photos from the past are displayed at the **Beale House Bed and Breakfast,** located 4 blocks from downtown in one of Wallace's most prominent old homes, a 1904 Colonial Revival. Hosts Jim and Linda See have collected pictures from their home's past owners, as well as from the University of Idaho's Barnard-Stockbridge Photographic Collection. Beale House has five guest rooms, one with a fireplace, another with a balcony, another with two full walls of windows. Room rates start at $150, including breakfast. There's also a spacious, fully furnished cottage available on the grounds, ideal for families or two couples traveling together. For more information call (888) 752-7151, or write The Beale House, 107 Cedar Street, Wallace 83873.

East of Wallace, the **Route of the Hiawatha** mountain bike trail has stirred big excitement among cyclists. The 13-mile trail was built atop what was once the Milwaukee Road rail bed. Riders cross trestles (all with good guardrails) and pass through tunnels, including the 1.7-mile-long Taft Tunnel, which is why cyclists need to have a headlamp on their helmets. The mountain vistas are spectacular, and there's a fair chance you'll see wildlife. But the ride's biggest plus is that, with the help of a shuttle service, it's all downhill—actually a gentle grade of about 2 percent—making the Route of the Hiawatha a good choice for families. To get to the East Portal trailhead, where most people start, take I-90 over the Montana state line to exit 5 (Taft) and follow the signs. Trail day passes cost $9 per person, $5 for kids ages three to thirteen. The shuttle costs $9 for adults, $6 for children. The trail is open for riding or hiking late May through early October, and you can rent bikes, helmets, and lights at Lookout Pass Ski and Recreation Area, located at I-90 exit 0 on the Idaho-Montana border. For more information see www.ridethehiawatha.com or call (208) 744-1301.

From Wallace backtrack along I-90 to Highway 3, the **White Pine Scenic Byway.** This route leads through country crisscrossed by the St. Joe and St. Maries Rivers. The St. Joe in particular is interesting; at about 2,200 feet above sea level, it is reportedly the highest navigable river in the world. These days it's also gaining renown for its fly-fishing and challenging rapids.

For a stay near the town of St. Maries (pronounced Saint Mary's), consider the *St. Joe Riverfront Bed & Breakfast.* Cary and Val Day, who owned a travel agency in Spokane for many years, built the 3,700-square-foot home specifically as a bed-and-breakfast, and it shows. Lovely landscaped grounds and gardens meet 135 feet of riverfront, where guests have access to a beach and fire pit. Four guest rooms, each with private bath, reflect the family's wide travels; one, the Tuscan Room, has bright blues and yellows evocative of Italy, while the Vineyard Room decor features shades of plum, burgundy, and green. Room rates run $99 to $249, including gourmet breakfast. Ask about special interactive cooking weekends—in which guests enjoy dinners prepared around a culinary theme—and the ever-rollicking murder mystery parties. For more information or to make reservations, write P.O. Box 488, 816 Shepherd Road, St. Maries 83861; call (208) 245-8687; or visit www.stjoeriverbb.com.

Southeast of St. Maries on Highway 3, look for two great places to have fun and maybe pick up some unique Idaho souvenirs (if you don't mind getting your hands dirty). The star garnet is found in only two places in the world, Idaho and India. And in Idaho the best place to find these dark beauties is the *Emerald Creek Garnet Area* 6 miles west of Clarkia on Forest Road 447. Star garnets are so named because they have rays that seem to dance across the gem's purple- or plum-colored surface. There are usually four rays, but some gems—the most valuable kind—have six. In ancient times people believed garnets conferred a sense of calm and protection from wounds.

Garnets are typically found in alluvial deposits of gravel or sand just above bedrock, anywhere from 1 to 10 feet underground. The deposits along the East Fork of Emerald Creek are particularly rich. The Forest Service formerly allowed people to dig in the beds, but due to concerns for water quality, wildlife habitat, and public safety, the gravel beds are now off-limits. However, visitors can still wash stockpiled gravel in sluice boxes to find garnets. You can get a permit at the sluice area, which is a half-mile hike from the parking lot. Permits are good for one day, and the cost is $10 for adults and $5 for children age six to twelve. Buckets, shovels, and special screen boxes are provided.

The garnet area is open from 9:00 a.m. to 5:00 p.m. Friday through Tuesday, Memorial Day weekend through Labor Day. Bring drinking water and snacks, sunscreen, a change of clothes, and a container for holding your garnets. Veteran garnet hunters say that lined rubber gloves, a small hammer and brush, and a collapsible stool are handy to have, too. Motorized equipment and pets are not allowed at the site. There is no shade in the parking lot, so it's best to leave pets at home.

The Idaho Panhandle National Forest offers the Emerald Creek Campground nearby, as well as year-round indoor accommodations for up to fifteen people at the Clarkia Guest Bunkhouse, where rooms go for $30 to $45 a night ($200 for the whole facility). For more information call the Forest Service in St. Maries at (208) 245-2531.

Also near Clarkia is the locally famous ***Fossil Bowl,*** just south of town. The Fossil Bowl is first and foremost a motorcycle racing track, but when owner Francis Kienbaum was bulldozing a new turn on the track in 1971, he unearthed a prime fossil area with a world-class stash of fifteen-million-year-old leaves, as well as a few fossilized insects, fish, and flowers. For $8 per person (no charge for young children), anyone can dig at the site. The fossils are found by chopping blocks from the soft clay hillside, then prying apart the layers with a knife. Some undisturbed layers that have yet to be exposed to the elements can yield magnificent leaves in their original dark green or red—until the air turns them black, usually within a minute.

The Fossil Bowl still hosts motorcycle races on Sunday mid-April through October, and anyone visiting on that day will get double for their entertainment dollar. The original fossil site is right by the racetrack, making for some dusty digging on race days, but another site farther from the commotion is now available as well. Digging is permitted daily except in winter, but the Kienbaums suggest you call first to check on hours.

Visitors also may be interested in the Fossil Bowl's antiques collection, which includes century-old woodworking machinery. Although it's situated on Highway 3, the Fossil Bowl's legal address is Eighty-fifth and Plum—"85 miles out in the sticks and Plum the hell away from everything," Francis's son, Kenneth, explains. For more information call (208) 245-3608.

Places to Stay in North Idaho

BONNERS FERRY

Best Western Kootenai River Inn
Highway 95
(800) 346-5668
fax: (208) 267-3744
Moderate

Bonners Ferry Log Inn
Highway 95 North
(208) 267-3986
Inexpensive-Moderate

Northside School Bed & Breakfast
6497 Comanche Street
(208) 267-1826
Moderate

SANDPOINT

Best Western Edgewater Resort
56 Bridge Street
(800) 635-2534
fax: (208) 263-3194
Moderate-Expensive

K2 Inn
501 North Fourth Avenue
(208) 263-3441
fax: (208) 263-5718
Inexpensive-Moderate

LaQuinta Inn
415 Cedar Street
(800) 282-0660
fax: (208) 263-3395
Moderate

Selkirk Lodge at Schweitzer Mountain
(800) 831-8810
fax: (208) 263-7961
Expensive

PRIEST LAKE (NORDMAN)

Elkins
404 Elkins Road
(208) 443-2432
Moderate-Expensive

Hill's Resort
4777 West Lakeshore Road
(208) 443-2551
(see text)
Moderate-Expensive

The Old Northern Inn
(208) 443-2426
(see text)
Moderate

POST FALLS

Red Lion Templin's Hotel
414 East First Avenue
(800) RED-LION
fax: (208) 773-4192
Moderate

Riverbend Inn
4105 West Riverbend Avenue
(208) 773-3583
fax: (208) 773-1306
Inexpensive-Moderate

Sleep Inn
157 South Pleasantview Road
(208) 777-9394
fax: (208) 777-8994
Inexpensive-Moderate

HAYDEN LAKE

Clark House
5250 East Hayden Lake Road
(800) 765-4593
(see text)
Moderate-Expensive

COEUR D'ALENE

Bates Motel
2018 Sherman Avenue
(208) 667-1411
(see text)
Inexpensive

Best Western Coeur d'Alene Inn & Conference Center
414 West Appleway Avenue
(800) 251-7829
fax: (208) 664-1962
Moderate-Expensive

Coeur d'Alene Resort
115 South Second Avenue
(800) 688-5253
fax: (208) 664-7276
Moderate-Expensive

Flamingo Motel
718 Sherman Avenue
(208) 664-2159
fax: (208) 664-2150
Moderate

LaQuinta Inn & Suites
2209 East Sherman Avenue
(800) 531-5900
fax: (208) 769-7332
Inexpensive-Moderate

Roosevelt Inn
105 East Wallace Avenue
(800) 290-3358
fax: (208) 664-4142
Moderate-Expensive

Shilo Inn
702 West Appleway Avenue
(800) 222-2244
fax: (208) 667-2863
Moderate

HARRISON

Osprey Inn
134 Frederick Avenue
(208) 689-9502
fax: (208) 689-3363
(see text)
Moderate

KELLOGG

Baymont Inn & Suites
601 Bunker Avenue
(208) 783-1234
Moderate

Morning Star Lodge at Silver Mountain
610 Bunker Avenue
(866) 344-2675
Moderate-Expensive

Silverhorn Motor Inn
699 West Cameron Avenue
(208) 783-1151
fax: (208) 784-5081
Inexpensive-Moderate

WALLACE

Beale House Bed and Breakfast
107 Cedar Street
(208) 752-7151
(see text)
Moderate-Expensive

Wallace Inn
100 Front Street
(800) 643-2386
fax: (208) 753-0981
Moderate

ST. MARIES

The Pines Motel
1117 Main
(208) 245-2545
Inexpensive

St. Joe Riverfront Bed and Breakfast
816 Shepherd Road
(208) 245-8687
(see text)
Moderate-Expensive

Places to Eat in North Idaho

BONNERS FERRY

**The Creamery
(deli/coffeehouse)**
6428 Kootenai Street
(208) 267-2690
Inexpensive

**Springs Restaurant
(American)**
in the Kootenai River Inn
(208) 267-8511
Moderate

**Under the Sun
(organic specialties)**
7178 Main Street
(208) 267-6467
(see text)
Inexpensive

SANDPOINT

Bangkok Cuisine (Thai)
202 North Second Avenue
(208) 265-4149
Moderate

**Eichardt's Pub Grill
(American)**
212 Cedar Street
(208) 263-4005
Inexpensive-Moderate

**Fifth Avenue Restaurant
(family)**
807 North Fifth Avenue
(208) 263-0596
Inexpensive-Moderate

**Hydra Restaurant
(steak/seafood)**
115 Lake
(208) 263-7123
Moderate

The Landing (Northwest)
Highway 95 (south end of
the Long Bridge)
(208) 265-2000
Moderate-Expensive

**Trinity Café
(Southern-inspired fare)**
116 North First Avenue
(208) 255-7558
Moderate

HOPE

**Old Ice House Pizzeria &
Bakery**
140 West Main Street
(208) 264-5555
(see text)
Inexpensive-Moderate

PRIEST LAKE

Elkins (American)
40 Elkins Road
(208) 443-2432
Moderate-Expensive

Hill's Resort (American)
4777 West Lakeshore Road
(208) 443-2551
(see text)
Moderate-Expensive

HAUSER LAKE

**Chef in the Forest
(fine dining)**
12008 Woodland Beach
Drive
(208) 773-3654
(see text)
Expensive

POST FALLS

**Mallard's Restaurant
(American)**
at Red Lion Hotel
(208) 773-1611
Moderate

Milltown Grill (American)
306 Spokane Street
(208) 457-1724
Inexpensive

HELPFUL WEB SITES FOR NORTH IDAHO

North Idaho Visitor Information
www.visitnorthidaho.com

Sandpoint Chamber of Commerce
www.sandpointchamber.com

**Coeur d'Alene Visitor and Convention
Services**
www.coeurdalene.org

Idaho Spokesman-Review
www.spokesmanreview.com

Coeur d'Alene Press
www.cdapress.com

HAYDEN LAKE

Clark House (fine dining)
5250 East Hayden Lake
Road
(800) 765-4593
(see text, reservations
necessary)
Expensive

COEUR D'ALENE

Beverly's (fine dining)
in the Coeur d'Alene Resort
(208) 765-4000
Expensive

**Brix Restaurant
(fine dining)**
317 Sherman Avenue
(208) 665-7407
Moderate-Expensive

**Cedars Floating
Restaurant (seafood)**
off Highway 95 south of
town
(208) 664-2922
Expensive

**Coeur d'Alene Brewing
Co. (brewpub)**
209 Lakeside Avenue
(208) 664-BREW
Inexpensive-Moderate

**Hudson's Hamburgers
(American)**
207 East Sherman Avenue
(208) 664-5444
Inexpensive

**Java on Sherman
(coffeehouse)**
324 Sherman Avenue
(208) 667-0010
Inexpensive

Moon Time (casual pub)
1602 Sherman Avenue
(208) 667-2331
(see text)
Inexpensive-Moderate

Mulligan's (American)
in the Coeur d'Alene Inn &
Convention Center
414 West Appleway Avenue
(208) 765-3200
Moderate

Takara (Japanese)
309 Lakeside
(208) 765-8014
Inexpensive-Moderate

**The Wine Cellar
(Mediterranean)**
313 Sherman
(208) 664-WINE
Moderate

KINGSTON

Enaville Resort (family)
I-90 exit 43
(208) 682-3453
(see text)
Moderate

KELLOGG

**Silver Spoon Restaurant
(American)**
699 West Cameron Avenue
(208) 783-1151
Moderate

**Veranda Restaurant (fine
dining)**
12 Emerson Lane
(208) 783-2625
Moderate-Expensive

WALLACE

**Albi's Steakhouse
(American)**
Sixth and Pine Streets
(208) 753-3071
Moderate

**The Jameson Restaurant
& Saloon (American)**
304 Sixth Street
(208) 556-6000
(closed winters)
Inexpensive-Moderate

1313 Club (American)
608 Bank Street
(208) 752-9391
Inexpensive-Moderate

ST. MARIES

Pizza Factory (pizza)
910 Main Street
(208) 245-5515
Inexpensive

ALSO WORTH SEEING IN NORTH IDAHO

Factory outlets
Post Falls

Brooks Sea Planes
Coeur d'Alene

Coeur d'Alene Tribal Bingo/Casino
Worley

Crystal Gold Mine Museum
Kellogg

Heyburn State Park
Plummer

North Central Idaho

In Idaho, geography has decreed that there are simply some places where roads cannot go—or where travelers can pass only with much effort. In North Central Idaho, nature has made the rules and humans play along as well as we're able. Consequently there is only one east-west road, U.S. Highway 12, across this region—and it was not completed until 1962. The major north-south route, U.S. Highway 95, also evolved according to geography.

It's 196 miles from Moscow to McCall, but you're not going to make this trip in four hours. Between long hill climbs and river-hugging curves, it's slow, scenic going wherever you travel in North Central Idaho. The main routes are alluring enough, but plan to explore some of the secondary roads, too. The Lolo Highway, the Elk City Wagon Road, and the climb to the Hells Canyon Rim at Heaven's Gate are just a few of this region's many great byways.

For more North Central Idaho travel information, call (800) 473-3543; write the North Central Idaho Travel Association, P.O. Box 2018, Lewiston 83501; or see www.northcentral idaho.info.

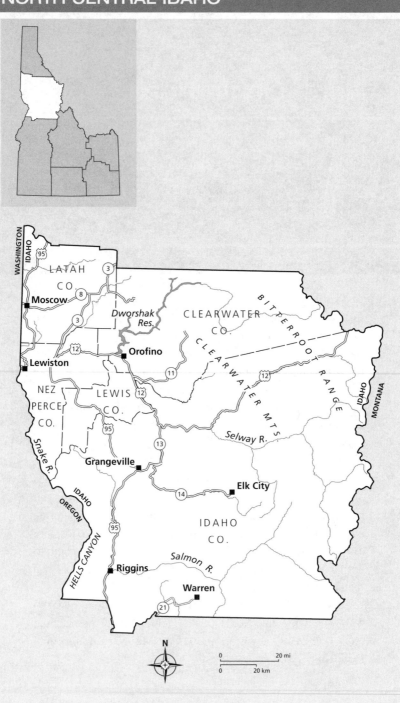

Palouse and Clearwater Country

North Central Idaho is a land of contrast, and nowhere is this fact more visible than in Latah and Clearwater Counties, where rolling farmlands seamlessly give way to dense forests. This is the Palouse (pronounced pah-LOOSE), a rich agricultural region that spills across the Idaho-Washington border. And there are few better places to start a tour of the area than **Mary Minerva McCroskey State Park.** To get there from Moscow, drive 25 miles north on US 95, and watch for the Skyline Drive sign atop a hill not far north of the state rest area. Turn left, or west, and follow the road through thick pine forests into the preserve, such as it is.

Although it's among Idaho's largest and oldest state parks, McCroskey is also the state's most forgotten, until recently going unmentioned on most maps and parks literature. Virgil T. McCroskey grew up looking at this ridge from his boyhood home at the base of Steptoe Butte, just over the Washington state line. He later bought the land, turned it into a parkway in honor of his mother, and sought to donate it to the state of Idaho. The state wasn't too interested, but it finally took charge after McCroskey agreed to put up money for maintenance until his death. Since then, the park—or state reserve, as it's sometimes called—has remained undeveloped, but its 18 miles of road and 32 miles of trails afford many good views of the Palouse. You'll find a few picnic areas and primitive campsites scattered along the drive. The road isn't recommended for vehicles of more than 28 feet in length.

Moscow, home to the University of Idaho, took its name not from the city in Russia but from a community in Pennsylvania. In its early years, Moscow had an even more unusual name: Hog Heaven, so called because farmers saw their pigs munching merrily on the camas bulbs so prevalent in the area. In

JULIE'S FAVORITES IN NORTH CENTRAL IDAHO

Lolo Motorway
North of Highway 12

Nez Perce National Historic Park
regionwide

Wolf Education and Research Visitor Center—Winchester

Dog Bark Park
Cottonwood

Heaven's Gate
west of Riggins

Backcountry B&B
Warren

1889 Moscow was named the site of Idaho's federal land-grant college. It may seem odd that the state's namesake university is so far from Idaho's population center in Boise, but despite or perhaps even because of its remoteness, Moscow is the quintessential college town—a blend of funky charm and high-tech attitude and more liberal than anywhere else in the state, with the possible exception of Boise and Sun Valley/Ketchum.

The U of I is blessed with a beautiful campus that includes the nineteen-acre **Shattuck Arboretum,** one of the oldest university arboretums in the western United States. Planted from 1910 to 1917, the arboretum is a pleasant place for a stroll amid native Idaho trees, as well as those introduced from other regions. Just across Nez Perce Drive from Shattuck Arboretum, the sixty-three-acre University of Idaho Arboretum and Botanical Garden was planted during the 1980s. It showcases trees and shrubs from around the world grouped by their geographical origin. For self-guiding brochures to both arboretums, visit the campus information center on Pullman Road (Highway 8) and Line Street. Guided tours may be arranged by calling (208) 885-6250.

Idaho's state horse, the Appaloosa, is best known by the spots on its rump. Learn everything you ever wanted to know about Appaloosas and more at the **Appaloosa Museum and Heritage Center** in Moscow. Exhibits recount the evolution of the Appaloosa, historical aspects of the breed, and its importance to the Nez Perce Indians. The museum is on Moscow's western edge at 2720 West Pullman Road, and it's open from 10:00 a.m. to 5:00 p.m. Tuesday through Friday and from 10:00 a.m. to 4:00 p.m. on Saturday year-round. Admission is free, but donations are welcome. Call (208) 882-5578 for more information.

Dig This

Idaho is not the first place that comes to mind when you think about jazz. So fans of America's indigenous music are pleasantly surprised to learn that Idaho has a rich and growing jazz scene. In Moscow, the University of Idaho is the setting for the annual **Lionel Hampton International Jazz Festival,** one of the premier events of its kind. Held during the last weekend in February in the university's Kibbie Dome, the festival has recently featured Russell Malone, Roy Hargrove, Jane Monheit, and dozens of other top jazz stars. Leonard Feather, jazz critic for the *Los Angeles Times*, called it "the number one jazz festival in the world." The festival also serves as a work-shop for thousands of music students who travel to Moscow to play with the pros. For ticket and schedule information, call (888) 8UIDAHO or see www.jazz.uidaho.edu.

TOP ANNUAL EVENTS IN NORTH CENTRAL IDAHO

Lionel Hampton Jazz Festival
Moscow (late February)

Dogwood Festival
Lewiston (late April)

Renaissance Faire
Moscow (early May)

Border Days
Grangeville (early July)

Chief Looking Glass Days
Kamiah (mid-August)

Lumberjack Days
Orofino (mid-September)

Moscow's restaurant scene isn't on a par with many other college towns, but *Red Door,* at 215 South Main, is one of the more interesting eateries you'll find. Open for dinner Tuesday through Saturday, Red Door specializes in creative cuisine and a fun decor featuring lots of local art. The menu changes often, but recent entrees include wild Alaskan salmon with a Creole crabmeat sauce, elk medallions with a Korean barbecue glaze, and Basque-style meatballs. Call (208) 882-7830 for reservations for parties of five or more. If you're early, do some window shopping across the street at *Wild Women Traders,* an eclectic, locally owned store featuring all kinds of cool clothes and home accents at 210 South Main.

Moscow also has a good downtown coffeehouse scene. *BookPeople,* one of Idaho's best independent bookstores, doubles as an espresso joint in its spacious location at 521 South Main. It also has a regular calendar of readings and other special events you can access at www.bookpeople.net.

MaryJane Butters has occasionally been described as "the Martha Stewart of the West." She prefers to call herself a farm girl. Either way, she has an arresting personality and is building quite an empire on her *Paradise Farm* south of Moscow, including a booming mail-order organic foods business, a magazine, a book, and "Pay Dirt Farm School" classes for people who want to learn how to grow their own food. A bed-and-breakfast experience is available at select times of the year. To learn about all things MaryJane, visit her Web site, www.maryjanesfarm.org, or call (888) 750-6004.

When you're wandering on the Palouse, keep an eye out for *Cowgirl Chocolates.* These sweet and spicy treats are just another form of art for creator Marilyn Lysohir, who is also a noted sculptor. The Moscow-based company ships its habanero truffles, caramel corn, and more worldwide. Learn more at www.cowgirlchocolates.com.

Elk River, at the tail end of Highway 8 east of Moscow, serves as the north gateway to Dworshak Reservoir. It's a great place to camp, pick huckleberries, fish, hunt, snowmobile, cross-country ski, and enjoy the Idaho outdoors. The **Elk River Lodge & General Store** has hostel-style rooms for rent starting at $35, plus two fancier suites with private bathrooms and a bunkhouse that sleeps up to ten for $150. Call (208) 826-3299 or see www.elkriverlodge.net for information.

Before you leave Elk River, take a walk around town. It's the kind of place where every family has its members' names posted on the welcome sign. There's also a handsome old schoolhouse built in 1912, perched on a hill overlooking the town. It's no longer used, but a nearby church built the same year is still in operation. For a more vigorous workout, consider a hike up 5,824-foot **Elk Butte,** where a panoramic view awaits all who make it to the top.

Several other natural attractions are within easy drives of Elk River. Just west of town **Elk Creek Falls**—actually three separate falls—are reached via a set of short trails that run along what was once the old route to Orofino. If you have time to visit only one of the cascades, make it Middle Falls, at 90 feet the highest of the three. Along the way hikers pass the site of Elk Creek Falls School, which operated between 1910 and 1930. The forest has reclaimed the building, but its gateposts still stand.

Some of Idaho's oldest and tallest trees may be seen north of Elk River. A giant Western red cedar, estimated at more than 3,000 years old, is accessed via Forest Road 4764, a branch off Road 382. At 177 feet tall and 18 feet in diameter, this is the largest tree in Idaho. Not far away, following Forest Roads 382 and 1969, is the Old Growth Cedar Grove. The eighty-acre stand is one of the few remaining old-growth cedar groves in Idaho, with trees estimated to be at least 500 years old.

The Dent Road leads from Elk River to Dworshak Dam and Reservoir. **Dworshak Dam** is notable because at 717 feet tall, it's the highest straight-axis, concrete gravity dam in the Western world and the largest ever built by the U.S. Army Corps of Engineers. A visitor center overlooks the dam; call (800) 321-3198 to check hours.

US 12 west and southeast of Orofino is known as the **Northwest Passage Scenic Byway,** and it's here where the velvety brown hillsides of the Inland Northwest meet the mountains and forests of the Rockies, sometimes intercepted by vast plateaus and prairies. Take Highway 11 east of Greer for a scenic drive across this changing landscape.

From Greer the highway climbs a dizzying grade onto the Weippe Prairie. Weippe, a town of about 500 people, has one of Idaho's best pizza parlors. **Weippe Pizza and Cafe** at 118 North Main Street specializes in some unusual combinations with such toppings as German sausage, jalapeño peppers, and sauerkraut. Pizza tops the menu, but soup, sandwiches, salads, and even breakfast are all available, too. The restaurant is open Tuesday through Sunday. Call (208) 435-4823.

It's about 12 miles from Weippe to Pierce, site of the **Pierce Courthouse,** the first public building in Idaho. The Pierce area boomed in the early 1860s after the discovery of gold, and the courthouse was built in 1862 to serve what was then Shoshone County, Washington Territory. (The Idaho Territory was established a year later, and Pierce is now in Clearwater County.) The mining boom led to the 1863 redrawing of Nez Perce reservation boundaries to exclude Pierce and other areas of mineral wealth. As a result, the Nez Perce were left with a reservation that was a tenth the size they'd agreed to just eight years before. The courthouse and nearby **Bradbury Logging Museum** are generally open 9:00 a.m. to 6:00 p.m. June through September; visitors can call OutBack Adventures at (800) 538-1754 to make an appointment at other times. From Pierce, travelers can retrace their route back to Weippe or continue north to Headquarters, Idaho, and the North Fork Adventure Road, a backcountry route to Superior, Montana.

Weippe can also be a jumping-off spot for the Lolo Trail, the famous path trod first by Indians and later by Lewis and Clark on their trek across the continent. It was just outside Weippe, in fact, that the Corps of Discovery (as President Thomas Jefferson dubbed the Lewis and Clark party) met the Nez Perce, who were to become indispensable to the white men's survival.

The Lolo Trail

Lewis and Clark had been told the Lolo Trail crossing could be made in five days, but it took the corps twice that time, and they almost froze and starved en route. An early snow blanketed the mountains, and—with no game to be found—the explorers were reduced to eating horse meat and candle wax. Finally, on September 20, 1805, Clark and an advance party of six other men dragged themselves out of the Bitterroot Mountains and onto the Weippe Prairie. Their route over the mountains can still be traced over the Lolo Motorway, accessible from the west via Weippe or Kamiah, or from the east via Forest Roads 569 (Parachute Hill) or 107 north from US 12. The **Lolo Motorway**—also known as Forest Road 500—is one of the roughest roads you'll encounter anywhere, but it's well worth the time and effort it takes to travel. The route is usually accessible only from mid-July through mid-

September. Four-wheel drive isn't a must, but a vehicle with good clearance is essential. For updated information see the Clearwater National Forest's Web page at www.fs.fed.us/r1/clearwater/, or call (208) 926-4274.

Castle Butte Lookout, a former working fire tower situated near the motor-way, is a wonderful place to get away from civilization for awhile. The lookout is about 15 feet square and is perched on a stone foundation about 20 feet high. Visitors are treated to sweeping views in all directions, but especially to the south, where the Selway-Bitterroot Wilderness stretches beyond the Lochsa River and east into Montana. The river itself is barely visible thousands of feet below this ridge.

Castle Butte Lookout

Castle Butte Lookout is fur-nished with a double bed, single cot, table with two chairs, pro-pane stove, and several chests of drawers. It's a great place to read, write, nap, and day-dream. Visitors also can amuse themselves by learning to use the firefinder (a device consist-ing of a map and a sighting instrument used to determine the location of a forest fire), exploring the local terrain, or rummaging through artifacts left by previous lookout tenants: a copy of *The Smokechaser,* a memoir by former fire lookout Carl A. Weholt; a deck of playing cards; old magazines; a Western novel. The lookout is available for rent from mid- to late summer; for information write to the Clearwater National Forest's Lochsa Ranger District Office, Route 1, Box 398, Kooskia 83539; call (208) 926-4274; or book online at www.recreation.gov.

Several Lolo Trail landmarks are a short hike or drive from Castle Butte. To the east are the Sinque Hole, where Lewis and Clark camped September 17, 1805, and the Smoking Place, where the returning explorers stopped in June 1806 to share a pipe with their Nez Perce guides. To the west, the dry camp of September 18, 1805, was where Captain Clark moved ahead with six hunters to look for game. And from nearby Sherman Peak, the captains first glimpsed the distant prairies. The corps called this spot Spirit Revival Ridge, realizing that their toilsome mountain travel was almost behind them.

US 12, the road the explorers' route paralleled, has many interesting sights of its own. Up near Lolo Pass, the **Packer Meadows** area is especially beautiful in mid-June when the purple camas are in bloom. Packer Meadows is also an excellent spot for cross-country skiing. The picnic area near milepost 165 on US 12 is known as the **DeVoto Memorial Cedar Grove,** named in honor of Bernard DeVoto, a noted writer and historian. Western red cedars tower here over the spot DeVoto often camped at while editing the Lewis and Clark journals, well before US 12 was completed in 1961. DeVoto's ashes were sprinkled over the grove after his death in 1955.

Powell, a little outpost along the highway, is the last place to buy gas until Lowell, about 50 miles west. The **Lochsa Lodge** has been feeding and lodging travelers since 1928, with accommodations ranging from about $45 to $115. Call (208) 942-3405 or visit www.lochsalodge.com for rates and information.

Colgate Licks and **Jerry Johnson Hot Springs,** both located near US 12 west of the Wendover-Whitehouse campgrounds, are among the most popular stops along US 12. At Colgate Licks deer, elk, and other animals are attracted by the springs' saltiness. Take the loop trail from the parking lot to reach the springs. The Jerry Johnson site is accessed by a mile-long trail up Warm Springs Creek. The **Lochsa Historical Ranger Station,** with one of the West's best collections of Forest Service memorabilia, is also worth a stop. It's located across from the Wilderness Gateway campground, among the most pleasant along US 12.

At Lowell, Idaho, the Lochsa and Selway Rivers meet to form the Middle Fork of the Clearwater River. This is an area well-known to the folks at River

Lolo Trail Area Tours

Whether you're interested in horseback riding, mountain biking, hiking, or interpreted scenic drives, guided tours are a good way to experience Lewis and Clark history in North Central Idaho. Much of the country here is wild and remote, and guides can ensure you have a safe, trouble-free trip.

The Clearwater National Forest has approved half a dozen outfitters for trips on and near the Lolo Trail. Horseback riding specialists include Triple "O" Outfitters, (208) 464–2349, www.tripleo-outfitters.com; Weitas Creek Outfitters, (888) 983–WEST, www.idahooutfitter.com; and Lost Lakes Outfitters, (866) LST–LAKE, www.lostlakes outfitters.com. Mountain biking and hiking trips are offered by Lewis & Clark Trail Adventures, (800) 366–6246, www.trailadventures.com. Western Spirit Cycling, (800) 845–2453, www.westernspirit.com, specializes in bicycle trips.

River Dance Lodge

Odysseys West (ROW), who've been offering river trips here and across Idaho and beyond since 1979. ROW opened the **River Dance Lodge** a few miles down Highway 12, in the hamlet of Syringa in 2005. Six handcrafted log cabins sleep four to ten people. Each has its own front deck and hot tub. Rates start at $195 in July and August, with discounts available in spring and fall. In summer, River Dance becomes the base for family adventure camps that feature raft and kayak trips, fishing, mountain biking, and more. Budget tent camping is available, too, for $8 per person per night, including access to showers. River Dance also has taken over the long-beloved Syringa Cafe, adding Mediterranean dishes to its traditional Idaho fare. For more information or reservations, see www.riverdancelodge.com or call (800) 451-6034. Use the same number or Web site to check ROW's statewide menu of river trips.

Travelers looking for the hospitality of a bed-and-breakfast combined with the privacy of a motel will enjoy staying at **Reflections Inn** (formerly known as the Looking Glass Inn). This is one of the most restful, friendly accommodations in North Central Idaho. The one-time guest ranch is perched on a hillside above the Clearwater River about 11 miles east of Kooskia. Each of the seven rooms has its own entrance and bathroom and is individually decorated in casually elegant style. A communal kitchen/family room makes this a good spot for reunions and small-group retreats. Outside there's a barbecue grill, hot tub, and ten wooded acres to explore. Rates run $79 to $119 double occupancy, including a gourmet breakfast. For more information call (888) 926-0855; write HCR 75 Box 32, Kooskia 83539; or see www.reflectionsinn.com.

Land of the Nez Perce

The Nez Perce people—or Nimiipuu, as they call themselves—have played a substantial role in the history of what is now Idaho, as well as that of the United States as a whole. For more than a century, history students have been moved by the words of Nez Perce leader Chief Joseph who, upon his tribe's capture in Montana, made his famous "I will fight no more forever . . ." speech. Those words, uttered just 42 miles short of refuge at the Canadian border, marked the end of a 1,000-mile march punctuated by the battles of the Nez Perce War.

The war was precipitated by the discovery of gold on the Nez Perce reservation, which—by the original treaty signed in 1855—included most of the tribe's traditional homeland. When the gold was found, however, the U.S. government redrew the reservation's boundaries to exclude the areas of mineral wealth. One Nez Perce leader known as Lawyer accepted the new boundaries and signed a new treaty. But other members of the tribe, led by Old Joseph, did not agree, and soon there were two bands of Nez Perce: the "treaty" and "nontreaty."

Soon after Lawyer signed the treaty in 1867, the government launched a campaign to move all Nez Perce to the new reservation. The nontreaty Nez Perce ignored the government's orders, and for a time they were able to live peaceably. But by 1877 the government was ready to force the nontreaty Nez Perce to move, and a June 14 deadline was set.

In the meantime Young Joseph had succeeded his father. He did not wish to move, nor did he wish to wage war, so he moved his followers toward the reservation. Before they made it, however, three young Nez Perce men—angry at the forced move and seeking revenge for the death of one of their fathers—killed four white settlers by noon on June 14. Over the next few days, other Nez Perce joined in and an additional fourteen or fifteen whites were slain. The Nez Perce War was on.

Although the Nez Perce trail crosses through several states, North Central Idaho and adjacent areas in Oregon and Washington comprise the tribe's ancestral homeland. For that reason the ***Nez Perce National Historic Park*** was established in the Gem State. Unlike most national park sites, however, the Nez Perce park isn't one specific place. Instead it includes thirty-eight sites scattered across this region. Two of the most interesting are located near US 12 on the way to Lewiston.

Just outside Kamiah, a basaltic formation known as the ***Heart of the Monster*** explains how the Nez Perce came to be. According to tribal legend, Coyote—a mythical figure central to much Native American literature—killed a great monster near here. The Nez Perce and other tribes were created, each as parts of the monster fell to the earth. An audio station at the site retells the legend, first in the Nez Perce's native tongue, then in English. Kamiah is also the site of the annual Chief Looking Glass Days festival held the third weekend of August. This traditional powwow features descendants of Chief Looking Glass, a Nez Perce leader, participating in dancing and other cultural activities. Call (208) 935-2525 for more information.

The Nez Perce National Historic Park headquarters are at Spalding, just east of Lewiston on US 95. This is where Henry and Eliza Spalding established their mission to the Nez Perce in the 1830s. A Presbyterian missionary, Spalding believed it was his duty to Christianize the Indians. "What is done for the poor Indians of this Western world must be done soon," he said. "The only thing that can save them from annihilation is the introduction of civilization."

The ***Spalding Site,*** as the headquarters are sometimes called, features an excellent visitor center that catalogs the changes—both good and bad—this philosophy wrought for the Nez Perce. Exhibits include a Book of Matthew printed in the Indians' language, a case full of beautiful beadwork, and a silk ribbon and silver friendship medal presented to the Nez Perce by Lewis and Clark. Another highlight is a 32-foot canoe made in 1837 from a single cottonwood log. The visitor center is open daily from 8:00 a.m. to 5:00 p.m. Memorial Day through Labor Day and until 4:30 p.m. the rest of the year.

Lewiston is the largest city in North Central Idaho, and it has more than 15 miles of trails for joggers, cyclists, walkers, and strollers. Many of these paths are on the Lewiston Levee, which was constructed by the U.S. Army Corps of Engineers to protect Lewiston after the completion of Lower Granite Dam down the Snake River.

Visit the West End of Lewiston's charming downtown for one of the city's most interesting attractions. ***Morgan's Alley*** at 301 Main Street is a collection of specialty shops, restaurants, and a banquet facility. The "alley" is actually four old buildings linked together by thirteen stairways and seventeen brick arches.

Interspersed among the Alley's seventeen shops are numerous artifacts from area history. Hidden Treasures Antiques & Country House features the front of the U.S. Postal Service substation, which came from the post office in Pomeroy, Washington, circa 1888. An old-fashioned gas pump marks the entrance to Bojacks, a steak-and-seafood eatery and cocktail lounge. Sets of doors came from the local sheriff's office and the Lewiston National Bank. And so on.

Do the Twist

For a different perspective on Lewiston and environs, check out the famous *Spiral Highway* north of town. This twisting two-lane with sixty-four curves climbs 2,000 feet to the top of Lewiston Hill. It was completed in 1917 at a cost of $100,000—about twice the projected tab. Until 1979 the Spiral Highway was the only route from Lewiston to the Palouse region above. It's still open to traffic, but most motorists now use the newer four-lane section of US 95. Either way, stop at the overlook at the top of the hill for a great view of Lewiston, neighboring Clarkston, Washington, the confluence of the Clearwater and Snake Rivers, and the rolling farmland all around.

Lewiston history is also the focus at the ***Nez Perce County Museum,*** at Third and C Streets. The museum sits on the site occupied by one of Lewiston's first buildings, the Luna House Hotel. After serving as a hotel, the building also functioned as a courthouse for a few years in the late 1880s. Today's museum is home to a collection of Nez Perce and pioneer artifacts, along with a striking trio of paintings by Dan Piel portraying the Indian leader Chief Joseph in his youth, maturity, and old age. The museum is open from 10:00 a.m. to 4:00 p.m. Tuesday through Saturday, March through December. Admission is by donation. Call (208) 743-2535 for more information. Elsewhere downtown the ***Lewis-Clark Center for Arts & History*** at 415 Main Street has an interesting permanent exhibit, "Chinese at the Confluence," featuring artifacts from the city's nineteenth-century Chinese temple. Call (208) 799-2243 for hours or more information.

Lewiston has several interesting spots to get a meal or a quick snack. For fine dining, ***Macullen's*** at 1516 Main Street is a good choice, with steaks, seafood, pastas, and more. It's open for lunch and dinner Monday through Friday and dinner only on Saturday. Call (208) 746-3438 for reservations.

Lewiston doesn't have much of a coffeehouse scene, but you can get good java at ***Yo! Espresso.*** The cart parks on the Main Street sidewalk between Brackenbury Square and the Liberty Theatre. Not far away at 704 Main Street, ***Kling's*** is an office supply and stationery store that also has the best caramel corn in town, often piled high in its front window.

If you're looking to spend a night or longer in Lewiston, ***The York House*** is an interesting choice. This bed-and-breakfast at 504 Sixth Avenue on the campus of Lewis-Clark State College is named for the man known only as York, an African-American slave who accompanied the Lewis and Clark Expedition across the continent, and is run by LCSC students majoring in hospitality management. The York House actually includes four suites in two separate homes, the Lewis Home and the Clark Home. All have access to wireless Internet, cable TV, a fitness center, and your choice of a continental breakfast delivered to your room or a full breakfast in the dining room. Rates range from $60 to $90 per night. Call (208) 792-2900 or visit www.theyorkhouseatlcsc.com for reservations or more information.

Lewiston spends much of the month of April celebrating the arrival of spring with the annual *Dogwood Festival*, named for the hundreds of dogwood trees and perennial plants that burst forth in bloom that time of year. Events typically include Art Under the Elms, an outdoor art festival on the LCSC campus; the Confluence Grape & Grain microbrew and wine festival; a quilt show; athletic competitions; and a concert. Call (208) 799-2243 for information.

Lewiston is also the northern gateway for *Hells Canyon,* the deepest gorge in North America. Hells Canyon National Recreation Area straddles the Snake River south of Lewiston and includes parts of Oregon's Wallowa-Whitman National Forest and the Nez Perce and Payette National Forests of Idaho. More than thirty outfitters offer jet boat or rafting trips through the canyon. For a list contact the Hells Canyon National Recreation Area headquarters in Clarkston at (509) 758-0616 or see www.fs.fed.us/hellscanyon. One of our favorites, *Snake River Adventures,* offers overnight accommodations, meals, and good fishing at its Kirby Creek Lodge. For information call (800) 262-8874 or see www.snakeriveradventures.com.

Private rafters and jet-boaters also may travel the river, but a Forest Service permit is required before launching. Many river trips leave from Hells Canyon Dam northwest of Cambridge, Idaho; see the Southwestern Idaho chapter for more details on those.

South of Lewiston, US 95 cuts across the Nez Perce Indian Reservation, with the aforementioned National Historic Park site and the tribal headquarters at Lapwai. Just outside Winchester, the tribe—in a partnership with the Wolf Education and Research Center (WERC)—has established a twenty-acre enclosure that is home to a small pack of wolves. The "Sawtooth Pack-Wolves of the Nez Perce," as they are known, originally lived north of Sun Valley, Idaho, under the care of WERC founder and photographer/filmmaker Jim Dutcher. The pack was relocated to Winchester in 1996 and serves as ambassadors for their wild cousins now being reintroduced in Idaho and elsewhere in the Rocky Mountain region.

The *Wolf Education and Research Visitor Center* is open from 9:00 a.m. to 5:00 p.m. daily in summer. The small center features beautiful doors created by Nez Perce artist John Wilson, plus a small gift shop and exhibits. There's no charge for the center or for the viewing platform immediately outside, which overlooks the wolf enclosure, the main attraction. For $5 ($3 for children ages six to twelve), visitors can take a short self-guided tour that ends at a closer viewing platform about 50 yards from the enclosure. Or visitors can plan to take a naturalist-guided tour, which goes inside the outer perimeter of the enclosure, where wolves can sometimes be seen within a few feet. Since early mornings or evenings are the best times to see wolves and hear them howl, these tours are scheduled most summer days at 7:30 a.m. and 7:00 p.m. Tours cost $10 for ages twelve and up; younger children are admitted free. Private tours can also be arranged in the off-season by calling (208) 924-6960. For more information visit www.wolfcenter.org.

The wolf center is near Winchester State Park, a popular place for camping and fishing in summer and cross-country skiing, ice fishing, and ice-skating in winter. The park has three yurts available for rent year-round. Equipped with electricity and heat and big enough to sleep five, the yurts cost $45 to $55 per night. They can be reserved by calling (208) 924-7563 or visiting their Web site at www.idahoparks.org/parks/winchesterlake.aspx.

South of the Nez Perce reservation border on US 95, near the town of Cottonwood, you can't miss the sight of Sweet Willy, a 30-foot-high beagle looming over **Dog Bark Park.** Look closer and you'll see Sweet Willy actually doubles as a guest house that can comfortably sleep a family of four. The house has a queen bed, small kitchen, and bathroom in the main quarters and a loft for kids up in the dog's head. This clever idea was the brainchild of Dennis J. Sullivan, who with his wife, Frances Conklin, has already found some measure of fame as a chain saw artist specializing in dogs. (A gift shop at the site features their work, and there's also a picnic area and visitor information center for passersby. And if you need a restroom? Look for the 10-foot-high fire hydrant!) Sweet Willy is available April through October for $92 a night, double occupancy ($8 each for extra

Dog Bark Park

people), including continental breakfast. For more information or a reservation, call (208) 962-3647 or see www.dogbarkparkinn.com.

Also near Cottonwood, the **Monastery of St. Gertrude** sits high on a hill overlooking the Camas Prairie. The monastery is well worth a visit for its stone chapel and a most impressive museum.

St. Gertrude's Chapel was built in 1924 of blue porphyry stone quarried nearby. Each stone was individually chiseled and placed by hand, with the nuns themselves doing much of the work. The resulting Romanesque structure and its 97-foot twin towers may be seen for miles around. The tower's bells are rung daily to call the Benedictine sisters of St. Gertrude's to prayer or to Mass, but they're also sounded at times of severe storms as a prayer for protection. The chapel's interior is equally striking, most notably the German altar at the front. In deference to the pain Jesus Christ felt when he was hung on the cross, not one nail was used to make the altar; each part was mortised and glued. A self-guiding tour brochure is available inside the chapel.

The Historical Museum at St. Gertrude is also quite a sight, particularly the Rhoades Emmanuel Memorial Gallery, added in 1988. This section houses the collection of Samuel Emmanuel, who gave the museum a treasure trove of artistic pieces ranging from Ming ceramics to a French cabinet that appeared in the 1896 World's Fair in Chicago to a Czechoslovakian chandelier bedecked with more than 1,000 crystals. This European finery may seem out of place on the prairies of Idaho, but plenty of local lore is represented, too, most notably an exhibit about the life of Polly Bemis. Having been sold into slavery as a young girl in China, this fascinating woman was nineteen years old when she arrived in the Warren mining camps of Idaho. She wound up marrying saloon-keeper Charlie Bemis and running a boardinghouse.

The Historical Museum at St. Gertrude is open 9:30 a.m. to 4:30 p.m. Tuesday through Saturday year-round. Admission is $5 for adults and $2 for children ages seven to seventeen. The museum holds an annual Raspberry Festival the first Sunday of August. This popular fund-raiser has food, live music, a craft show, and more. For additional information or to arrange a group tour, call (208) 962-2050 or see www.historicalmuseumatstgertrude.com.

At the north entrance of Grangeville, it's worth a brief stop to check out the **mammoth exhibit** in Eimer's Park. In 1994, a heavy-equipment operator working at the bed of Tolo Lake 6 miles west of Grangeville discovered what turned out the be the thigh bone of a male Columbian mammoth. The Idaho Museum of Natural History from Pocatello led digs at the site in the summer of 1995 and found bones from at least nine mammoths. The glassed-in pavilion here in Grangeville features a full-size mammoth replica, as well as a mural by

The Deepest Canyon?

Name the deepest gorge in North America. In Idaho, you'll frequently hear the claim that the obvious choice—the Grand Canyon—is not it and that Hells Canyon on the Idaho-Oregon border is actually deeper. But in his book, *The Snake River,* author Tim Palmer says that's wrong. "Sorry, Idahoans, but you still see this error all the time, propagated by regional, state, and private tourism promoters. Even the official Idaho highway map calls it the deepest canyon," *Idaho Statesman* reporter Dana Oland wrote recently. Palmer says that Kings Canyon in California's Sierra Nevada Mountains is even deeper because Spanish Mountain is 8,240 feet above the Kings River, while Idaho's He Devil Mountain is 7,900 feet above the Snake River. By contrast the Grand Canyon of the Colorado is a mere 4,000 to 5,500 feet deep from rim to river.

Plenty of sources—including the federal Hells Canyon National Recreation Area Web site—still call Hells Canyon the deepest river gorge in North America. The current Idaho state highway map lists He Devil with an elevation of 9,393 feet, and the Hells Canyon National Recreation Area Web site says that at its east rim the canyon is 8,043 feet above the river—but that's still shy of the 8,240 feet at Kings Canyon. Measured from He Devil Mountain, however, Hells Canyon would be deeper.

Whatever the statistics say, Hells Canyon is an awesome place. Visit or call the Hells Canyon National Recreation Area office in Riggins for maps and detailed directions into the canyon. The phone number is (208) 628–3916, and the Web site is www .fs.fed.us/hellscanyon/. (Also see the Southwestern Idaho chapter for information on trips from Hells Canyon Dam west of Cambridge.)

local artist Robert Thomas depicting what the Tolo Lake area may have looked like about 12,000 years ago when mammoths were on the scene. Tolo Lake, meanwhile, has refilled and is a popular spot for fishing and bird-watching.

When Grangeville got going back in 1876, the Grange Hall was the first building in town, which is how the city got its name. The hall later fell to fire, but a new building went up in 1909 and still stands on the northeast corner of Main and Hall Streets. The place is now home to **Oscar's Restaurant,** one of the region's best. At breakfast the "Egg-static" features eggs scrambled with diced ham and a pile of hash browns, while kids might want to order a "Teddy Cake" flapjack done up like a bear. For lunch there are homemade soups, salads, and fourteen sandwiches. Dinner choices include steak, prime rib, seafood, and chicken, with almost everything on the menu between $10 and $18. The dessert specialties include Kentucky Pie, with chocolate chip filling. For a nightcap, walk next door to **Brodock's Saloon,** where booths, tables, and even couches are grouped for easy conversation and where Albert

Bierstadt prints and Thomas Moran artwork grace the walls. Oscar's, at 101 East Main, is open from 7:00 a.m. to 9:00 p.m. Monday through Saturday and 8:00 a.m. to 2:00 p.m. Sunday; hours are shorter in winter. The phone number is (208) 983-2106.

The town of Harpster, east of Grangeville on Highway 13, serves as the gateway to another historic roadway off the beaten path. The **Elk City Wagon Road** was developed in the late nineteenth century as a route to the gold mines of central Idaho. Earlier still, the Nez Perce on their seasonal rounds used the trail as a way from the Camas Prairie to the Bitterroot Valley in Montana. The 53-mile, mostly unpaved road doesn't appear much different now than it did a hundred years ago. Today, however, drivers can expect to traverse it in four to six hours instead of the two days (in summer) or five days (in winter) it took in the old days.

The Elk City Road is generally open June through September. To find it, look for Wall Creek Road by a group of mailboxes in Harpster and head east. Make sure your vehicle is in good condition, and fuel up before you go—there are no filling stations along the way, although gas and other services are available in Elk City. The return trip from Elk City to Harpster via Highway 14, itself quite scenic, is 50 miles and takes about an hour and a half to drive. For more information on road conditions and a self-guiding brochure on the Elk City Wagon Road, stop at the Nez Perce Forest Service office in Grangeville or Elk City or call (208) 983-1963 or 842-2245.

Elk City also offers access to Dixie and Red River Hot Springs. If you want to get seriously off the beaten track in North Central Idaho, you can't get much more remote than these two communities. Red River Hot Springs, about 25 miles off Highway 14, is a year-round resort with rooms and cabins, priced from $50 to $120, and pools for swimming and soaking. Call (208) 842-2587 or see www.redriverhotspringsresort.com for information or reservations. There are no restaurants at Red River Hot Springs, but the resort's rooms have cooking facilities. Stock up in Elk City before making the drive. Dixie, 32 miles south of Elk City—with all but the last 4 miles paved—caters to hunters, anglers, and snowmobile enthusiasts. Many people stay in the area's primitive Forest Service campgrounds, but indoor lodging and food are available. For more information on activities and accommodations in the Elk City–Red River Hot Springs–Dixie area, see www.elkcityidaho.com.

Back on US 95, the **White Bird Grade** south of Grangeville is one of Idaho's most notable highway achievements. Before it was completed in 1975, it took thirteen hours to drive from Boise to Grangeville—a distance of 197 miles. The grade replaced a tortuous old road that took 14 miles to climb 2,900 feet. (An Idaho historical marker overlooking the old road notes that if all the old route's curves and switchbacks were placed together, they'd make thirty-seven complete circles.) Yet the old White Bird Road was itself an engineering marvel, built from 1915 to 1921 at a cost of $400,000 to replace a wagon road. The old route—the only road linking Northern Idaho to the state capital—was finally paved in 1938. In 1974, the year before its replacement opened, the grade was added to the National Register of Historic Places.

The old White Bird Road is easily seen east of the present highway, which takes just over 7 miles to climb 3,000 feet. Stop at the pullout for a sweeping view of White Bird Canyon. This was the site of the opening battle in the Nez Perce War, described earlier. As you'll recall, several young nontreaty Nez Perce seeking revenge for the death of one of their fathers and angered by their forced move to the reservation killed a number of white settlers. In response General Oliver Otis Howard dispatched ninety-nine men led by Captain David Perry to confront the Indians at the Salmon River near here. Although they were poorly armed and outnumbered by the white men, the Nez Perce successfully turned back the Army while suffering no casualties of their own. From here the tribe started the three-and-a-half month, 1,000-mile retreat that finally ended with Chief Joseph's surrender in Montana.

White Bird Summit Lodge & Guest Ranch perches in the high country just a mile from US 95, on the LocKey U Ranch. Unlike a lot of guest ranches, this one is easy to get to *and*—also unlike many ranches—offers short-term overnight accommodations. Rooms rent from about $115, including breakfast, swimming in an indoor pool, access to a barbecue area, and amazing views. Of course trail rides, guided hunts, and other outdoorsy pursuits are available, too. For more details or reservations, call (208) 983-1802 or visit www .lockeyu.com.

The small towns of Lucile and Riggins serve as outfitting stops for the Salmon River as well as for treks into Hells Canyon National Recreation Area and the Hells Canyon Wilderness. For an inspiring, top-down look at the region, turn west off of US 95 onto Forest Road 517 for the 18-mile road to **Heaven's Gate.** This road, generally open from the Fourth of July until early October, can be managed by any passenger car (although trailers shouldn't make the climb). The first 8 miles are easily traversed; after that, the road gets washboarded, but the views make it all worthwhile. At Windy Saddle follow the signs for Heaven's Gate. A 350-yard trail climbs to a vista point at 8,429-feet elevation with dead-on views of the Seven Devils Range and the rest of the surrounding countryside. On a clear day you might see all the way into Montana. Unfortunately, the lookout at Heaven's Gate is only occasionally staffed by volunteers, and the interpretive signs could be better, but these are among the most memorable views in the Northwest.

US 95 in Riggins is lined with businesses catering to the traveler, but it seems just as many locals as visitors wind down at the **Seven Devils Saloon & Steakhouse.** Lunch is available Monday through Saturday, and dinner is served seven nights a week year-round. There's outdoor seating when the weather allows it. Seven Devils is at 312 South Main (US 95), and the phone number is (208) 628-3351.

Some of Idaho's most luxurious guest ranches can be found along the Salmon River east of Riggins. Ten miles from the highway on the south side of the river, the **Lodge at Riggins Hot Springs** is on a site revered by the Nez Perce for the water's healing properties. The resort features ten cushy rooms, fine dining, an impossibly beautiful pool, and a near-wilderness setting. The lodge recently shifted its focus to become a small-group reunion, wedding, and retreat center. The per-night price is $1,200 for up to six people; $1,500 for seven to fifteen people; $1,875 for between sixteen and twenty-two guests; and $2,200 for between twenty-three and twenty-nine people. Reservations are a must. For more information call (208) 628-3785; write the Lodge at Riggins Hot Springs, P.O. Box 1247, Riggins 83549; or see www.rhslodge.com.

Farther east you can't drive to the **Shepp Ranch** (located about 45 miles from Riggins), but they'll either send a jet boat to pick you up or arrange a charter flight from Boise. Once at Shepp Ranch, guests enjoy boating, rafting, trail riding, fishing, and hiking. Meals served family style feature the bounty of Idaho—trout, berries, vegetables from the ranch garden, and homemade bread, pies, and cakes. For more information call (801) 573-6096; write Shepp Ranch, HC 83 Box 8000, Cascade 83611; or see www.sheppranch.com.

A spur off US 95 south of Riggins leads to Pollock, a small community along the Little Salmon River. Pollock is the headquarters for **Northwest Voyageurs,** which, in addition to running river trips and multisport adventures, operates the Little Salmon Lodge, with river and mountain views. Rooms cost from $105 to $145 for two people, including breakfast; extra people in the same room cost $20 each, or $15 each for children ages six to fifteen. Northwest Voyageurs also runs international trips to such locales as Costa Rica and the Galapagos Islands. For more information call (800) 727-9977; write Northwest Voyageurs, HC2 Box 501, Pollock 83547; or see www.voyageurs.com.

US 95 continues along the Little Salmon clear to New Meadows. At that point, we've crossed over into what Idaho's tourism office calls Southwestern Idaho, but that's necessary to reach our final North Central Idaho destinations: the towns of Burgdorf and Warren.

At New Meadows turn onto Highway 55. Just before you reach Payette Lake and McCall, hang a left to head north on the Warren Wagon Road. The road is paved nearly to the Burgdorf turnoff (Forest Road 246, to the north), then it turns into gravel. Allow about an hour for travel to Warren, which sits about 44 miles from the highway. The route passes through a lot of timberland ravaged by forest fires in 1994, but signs of renewed forest growth can be seen, too.

Burgdorf Hot Springs, about 30 miles from McCall, is a popular soaking spot dating back to 1870. There are two pools—a large one, 5 feet deep, in which the temperature ranges from 98°F to 104°F, and a small children's wading pool—plus several hot tubs. The pools look inviting enough, and the managers even have a supply of 300 extra bathing suits and 150 towels available for rent for anyone who came unprepared. But once you hear how they wash those suits and towels in a nearby stream, beating them with rocks to get 'em clean, you may wish you'd brought your own, home-laundered suit and towel. Pool admission is $5.30 for adults and $2.65 for children ages five to twelve.

The resort accommodates overnight visitors. Fourteen cabins, most built between the 1870s and 1930s, sleep from two to sixteen people. Rates (which include pool privileges) are about $38 per adult per night and $11 per child ages five to twelve. The cabins come equipped with woodstoves, beds, kerosene lamps, and outhouses, but guests need to bring their own bedding, food, and utensils. No tents or RVs are allowed, but there are several Forest Service campgrounds nearby, one right next door. You can buy a few supplies

In Plane View

Here's how a Payette National Forest brochure tells it: On January 29, 1943, flying from Nevada back to Tacoma, Washington, a B-23 bomber made an emergency landing on frozen Loon Lake near Warren. The "Dragon Bomber" slid across the ice and 150 feet into the nearby trees, both its wings sheared off. All eight men aboard survived, with a broken kneecap the only injury.

But the crew had no radio, and they were stranded. After waiting five days for rescue, they decided to send three men for help. The trio, carrying a shotgun and chocolate, hiked about 42 miles over two weeks through waist-deep snow before reaching the Lake Fork Guard Station. Once there, they were able to contact the Forest Service in McCall, which sent assistance. Today, hikers can still see the **B-23 Dragon Bomber wreckage** near the south side of the lake. The Forest Service brochure gives detailed directions. For more information call (208) 634–0400 or write the McCall Ranger District, P.O. Box 1026, McCall 83638.

(snacks, cold drinks, coffee, and a smattering of groceries) at Burgdorf, but it's wise to stock up ahead of time. All prices at Burgdorf are cash only.

Although the road from McCall closes between November and mid-May, people come to Burgdorf all year long, usually by snowmobile, sometimes by cross-country skis. (There are 38 miles of groomed x-c trails in the area.) Year-round this is an excellent spot to see wildlife: deer, elk, moose, and even the occasional black bear and mountain lion. For more information call (208) 636-3036 or write Burgdorf Hot Springs, McCall 83638.

Return to the Warren Wagon Road for the final 13 miles toward Warren. On the way the road passes through a community of private homes known as Secesh Meadows. *Secesh* is short for *secessionist*; seems there were quite a few Southern sympathizers among those mining here in the mid-nineteenth century. The Secesh Stage Stop sells gasoline, meals, and snacks to people passing through the area. Nearby, the Forest Service's Chinook Campground is a trailhead for the Secesh to Loon Lake Trail, part of the Idaho Centennial Trail. Aside from being a fairly easy trail, the path provides access to a fascinating and little-known artifact from Idaho history: the wreckage of a B-23 bomber. (See sidebar.)

Warren isn't literally the end of the road, but it's darn close. From here it's just a few bumpy miles to the edge of the Frank Church–River of No Return Wilderness, largest in the lower forty-eight United States. About a dozen people live year-round in Warren, maybe three times that number in summer. Once a year on the Fourth of July, they stage a "Spotted Owl Shoot" to raise money for community projects (the town water system is a recent beneficiary) and poke a bit of fun at environmentalists. No, they don't really shoot endangered wildlife—just targets. Warren has no electricity, but it did get phone lines in 1995.

Warren may not have many people, but it has plenty of history. Established in 1862 with the discovery of gold, this is one of Idaho's oldest towns. In its first boom, Warren had 2,000 people. By 1870 many of these first miners had left, but more than a thousand Chinese miners had moved in to try their luck. (Chinese mining artifacts can be seen at the Forest Service's Warren Guard Station and at the Winter Inn.) Warren had another population boom in the 1930s when dredging resumed. Although modern Warren was again threatened by a 1989 forest fire in the nearby Whangdoodle Creek drainage (and by yet another nearby fire in 2007), the town survived, and many of the standing buildings are more than one hundred years old. Stop by the Forest Service's Warren Guard Station for a Warren walking tour booklet.

For a memorable stay in Warren, you can't beat the ***Backcountry B&B,*** run by Betty and Leland Cavner on the far edge of town about a quarter-mile from the Forest Service compound. The Cavners, who had been visiting Warren since the 1950s, built this lodge themselves in the early 1990s, even logging and milling the logs. Models of self-sufficiency, the Cavners run their washing machine and television on solar power and heat their home with a huge stove made by Betty's father. Betty also made the quilts in the four guest rooms, and she's just as much a whiz in the kitchen, baking homemade bread and creating such luscious treats as nectarine cobbler and apple dumplings. She's a gifted decorator, too: Check out the shelf above the stairway, with its sweet collection of dolls, bears, and books—many from Betty's own childhood.

The downstairs living room is as welcoming as can be, for both its comfortable country furnishings and the Cavners' gift for making visitors feel immediately at home. Upstairs, travelers can relax with a game of pool or Scrabble. The Cavners have built a wonderful second-story deck, too, perfect for viewing the deer, moose, and foxes that may happen by at sunrise or twilight.

Rooms at the Backcountry B&B go for $95 double occupancy including breakfast, $75 for one person. The four rooms share two baths. The inn is open year-round, though visitors must arrive by snowmobile or a long cross-country ski trek in wintertime. Smoking is allowed outdoors only. Children are welcome, and Betty adds, "If they're good kids, the price is reasonable. If they're bad, they pay full price." But chances are your kids—and you—will be enchanted by this house. For more information call (208) 636-6000 or write Backcountry B&B, P.O. Box 77, Warren 83671.

Places to Stay in North Central Idaho

MOSCOW

America's Best Value Inn & Suites
414 North Main Street
(208) 882-7557
Inexpensive–Moderate

Best Western
University Inn
1516 Pullman Road
(800) 325-8765
Moderate

LaQuinta Inn
185 Warbonnet Drive
(208) 882-5365
Moderate

ELK RIVER

Elk River Lodge
(208) 866-3299
(see text)
Inexpensive–Moderate

Huckleberry Condos & RV Park
(208) 826-3405
fax: (208) 826-3284
Inexpensive–Moderate

OROFINO

Konkolville Motel
2000 Konkolville Road
(208) 476-5584
Inexpensive

Riverside Motel
10560 Highway 12
(208) 476-5711
Inexpensive

PIERCE

OutBack Adventures
Main Street
(208) 464-2171
Inexpensive–Moderate

Pierce Motel
509 Main Street
(208) 464-2324
Inexpensive

POWELL

Lochsa Lodge
(208) 942-3405
Inexpensive–Moderate

LOWELL

Three Rivers Resort
(208) 926-4430
fax: (208) 926-7526
Inexpensive–Moderate

SYRINGA

River Dance Lodge
(800) 451-6034
fax: (208) 667-6506
(see text)
Moderate–Expensive

KOOSKIA

Reflections Inn
US 12 east of town
(888) 926-0855
(see text)
Moderate

KAMIAH

Clearwater 12 Motel
US 12 at Cedar
(800) 935-2671
Inexpensive

Hearthstone Lodge
US 12, milepost 64
(877) 563-4348
Moderate–Expensive

Lewis Clark Resort
US 12 east of town
(208) 935-2556
fax: (208) 935-0366
Inexpensive

LEWISTON

Comfort Inn
2128 Eighth Avenue
(800) 228-5150
Moderate

Guesthouse Inn & Suites
1325 Main Street
(800) 806-7666
fax: (208) 746-7955
Inexpensive

Kirby Creek Lodge
(in Hells Canyon)
(800) 262-8874
Moderate–Expensive

Red Lion Hotel
US 12 and Twenty-first
Street
phone/fax: (208) 799-1000
Moderate–Expensive

The York House
504 Sixth Avenue
(208) 792-2900
(see text)
Inexpensive–Moderate

ELK CITY

Prospector Lodge and
Cabins
(208) 842-2597
Inexpensive

Red River Hot Springs
(208) 842-2589
Inexpensive–Moderate

COTTONWOOD

Dog Bark Park
(208) 962-3647
(see text)
Moderate

GRANGEVILLE

Downtowner Inn
113 East North Street
(208) 983-1110
Inexpensive

Elkhorn Lodge
822 Southwest First Street
(208) 983-1500
Inexpensive

Gateway Inn
700 West Main Street
(877) 983-1463
Inexpensive

WHITE BIRD

Hoots Motel
US 95
(208) 839-2265
Inexpensive

HELPFUL WEB SITES IN NORTH CENTRAL IDAHO

Regional tourism
www.northcentralidaho.info

Moscow community site
www.moscow.com/

Lewiston community site
www.lewiston.com/

Nez Perce National Historic Park
www.nps.gov/nepe/

Grangeville/Camas Prairie area
www.grangevilleidaho.com

**White Bird Summit Lodge
& Guest Ranch**
Atop White Bird Summit
(208) 983-1802
Moderate

RIGGINS

**Best Western Salmon
Rapids Lodge**
1010 South Main Street
(877) 957-2743
fax: (208) 628-3834
Moderate

Big Iron Motel
515 North Main Street
(888) 517-3005
Inexpensive

Riggins Motel
615 South US 95
(800) 669-6739
Inexpensive–Moderate

WARREN

Backcountry B&B
(208) 636-6000
(see text)
Moderate

Places to Eat in North Central Idaho

MOSCOW

**Archie's on the Square
(comfort food)**
100 West Fourth Street
(208) 892-2724
Inexpensive-Moderate

**The Breakfast Club
(breakfast)**
501 South Main Street
(208) 882-6481
Inexpensive

**Red Door
(eclectic)**
(208) 882-7830
(see text)
Moderate–Expensive

WEIPPE

**Weippe Pizza & Cafe
(American)**
118 North Main Street
(208) 435-4823
(see text)
Inexpensive

POWELL

Lochsa Lodge (American)
(208) 942-3405
Inexpensive–Moderate

LOWELL

**Ryan's Wilderness Inn
Cafe (American)**
US 12
(208) 926-4706
Inexpensive

KOOSKIA

**Idaho Backroads Cafe
(American)**
118 South Main
(208) 926-4304
Inexpensive

KAMIAH

**Hearthstone Bakery & Tea
House (American)**
502 Main Street
(208) 935-1912
Inexpensive

**Jilinda's Family Dining
(American)**
(208) 935-1158
Inexpensive

OROFINO

**Dining on the Edge
(American)**
625 Main Street
(208) 476-805
Inexpensive–Moderate

**Ponderosa Restaurant
(American)**
220 Michigan Avenue
(208) 476-4818
Inexpensive–Moderate

LEWISTON

**Bojack's Broiler Pit
(steaks)**
311 Main Street
(208) 746-9532
Moderate–Expensive

**Macullen's
(steaks/seafood)**
1516 Main Street
(208) 746-3438
(see text)
Moderate–Expensive

**Meriwether's
(American)**
in the Red Lion Hotel
(208) 799-1000
Moderate–Expensive

**Rowdy's Texas
Steakhouse and Saloon
(American)**
1905 Nineteenth Avenue
(208) 798-8712
Moderate

Thai Taste (Thai)
1410 Twenty-first Street
(208) 746-6192
Inexpensive–Moderate

**Waffles 'N' More
(American)**
1421 Main
(208) 743-5189
Inexpensive

Zany's (American)
2006 Nineteenth Avenue
(208) 746-8131
Inexpensive–Moderate

ALSO WORTH SEEING IN NORTH CENTRAL IDAHO

McConnell Mansion
Moscow

Hells Gate State Park
Lewiston

Dworshak National Fish Hatchery
Orofino

Meacham Mills
Lewiston

Clearwater River Casino
Lewiston

Camas Pairie Winery
Moscow

COTTONWOOD

Country Haus
(American)
407 Foster Street
(208) 962-3391
Inexpensive–Moderate

GRANGEVILLE

Camas Cafe
(American)
123 West Main
(208) 983-1019
Inexpensive

Oscar's Restaurant
and Espresso
(American)
101 East Main
(208) 983-2106
(see text)
Moderate

RIGGINS

Back Eddy Grill
(American)
533 North Main
(208) 678-9233
Inexpensive

Seven Devils Saloon
& Steak House
(American)
312 South Main
(208) 628-3351
(see text)
Inexpensive–Moderate

WARREN

Winter Inn (American)
(208) 636-4393
Inexpensive–Moderate

Southwestern Idaho

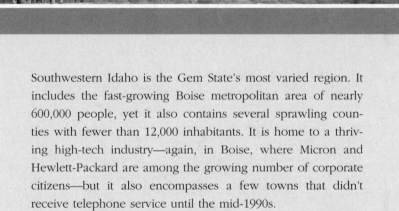

Southwestern Idaho is the Gem State's most varied region. It includes the fast-growing Boise metropolitan area of nearly 600,000 people, yet it also contains several sprawling counties with fewer than 12,000 inhabitants. It is home to a thriving high-tech industry—again, in Boise, where Micron and Hewlett-Packard are among the growing number of corporate citizens—but it also encompasses a few towns that didn't receive telephone service until the mid-1990s.

Because of this variety and the sheer sweep of backcountry, there is no one best way to explore Southwestern Idaho, and it could easily take a week or more to cover the region. But here's one possibility, the option you'll see used in this chapter:

Start on the shores of Payette Lake near McCall and New Meadows, the region's most popular resort area. Head southwest on U.S. Highway 95 to Cambridge, then west to explore the Hells Canyon Scenic Byway and the upper reaches of North America's deepest gorge. After backtracking to Cambridge and New Meadows, you might want to head east from McCall into the wilderness areas near Yellow Pine and Warm Lake (and Burgdorf and Warren, covered in the North Central Idaho chapters but most accessible from McCall). After returning to

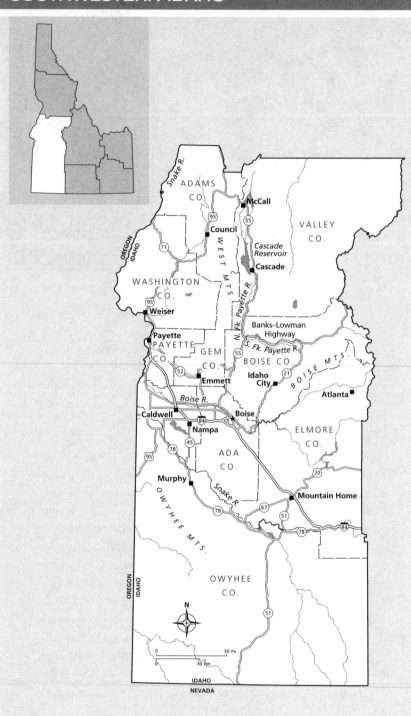

Highway 55, we'll veer off onto the back roads once again to survey the Boise Basin, rich in mining history. Adjacent to Interstate 84 we'll visit the capital city of Boise, the Treasure Valley of suburbs and fast-disappearing farmland west of Boise, and the high desert outback of Owyhee and Elmore Counties.

For more Southwestern Idaho travel information, call (800) 635-5240; write the Southwest Idaho Travel Association, P.O. Box 2106, Boise 83701; or see www.swita.org.

Wilderness Gateways

McCall has been called Idaho's most complete resort town, and with a regionally noted ski area and a spacious lake at hand, it's difficult to argue. Many who come to enjoy these recreational riches stay at the venerable *Hotel McCall* overlooking Payette Lake. Opened in 1904, the inn recently underwent major renovations. The funky old rooms are gone, but the hospitable touches remain, including free DVD rentals, fresh flowers, and warm homemade cookies each evening. Guests also have access to a well-stocked library and a new indoor pool. Rates range from $135 for a room with two queen beds to $350 for a two-bedroom condominium. For more information or reservations, call (866) 800-1183 or write Hotel McCall, 1101 North Third Street, McCall 83638.

Hotel McCall guests don't have to go far for a fine meal. *Rupert's,* the hotel restaurant, features fine Northwest cuisine and a patio with a view of the lake. It's open for breakfast, lunch, weekend brunch, and dinner. Call (208) 634-8108 for reservations.

Among McCall's other restaurants, the *Mill Supper Club* is one of the oldest and most interesting spots in town. The menu includes steak, prime rib, and seafood, and the decor features lots of antiques and what may be the

JULIE'S FAVORITES IN SOUTHWESTERN IDAHO

Hells Canyon Scenic Byway
West of Cambridge

Boise Greenbelt
Boise

World Center for Birds of Prey
south of Boise

Bruneau Dunes State Park
near Hammett

Idaho Anne Frank Human Rights Memorial
Boise

largest collection of beer taps anywhere in the United States—thousands of 'em displayed all over the restaurant and adjacent bar. Dinner is served seven nights a week starting at 5:30 p.m. The restaurant is at 324 North Third Street (Highway 55). Call (208) 634-7683 for reservations.

No matter what season you visit McCall, you're bound to have a good time outdoors. Late spring through early fall, boats and watercraft of all kinds flit across the sparkling surface of Payette Lake. For one of Idaho's most sublime paddling experiences, try canoeing or kayaking the gentle North Fork Payette River, accessed via the North Beach area along the Warren Wagon Road. The put-in is about 6.5 miles from Highway 55. **Backwoods Adventures** rents canoes and kayaks at North Beach by the hour ($8 to $11) or half day (four hours; $25 to $35) during the summer months. Call (208) 469-9067 for reservations or more information.

Ponderosa State Park—one of the state's most popular—is a favorite for camping, hiking, biking, and boating in the warm months and cross-country skiing once the snow falls. Occupying a thousand-acre peninsula just across Payette Lake from McCall (as well as the North Beach area mentioned above), Ponderosa is named for the tall pine trees that hug the lakeshore and cover the nearby mountainsides. It's just as rich in wildlife and wildflowers. For camping and recreation information, call (208) 634-2164 or see www.idahoparks.org/parks/ponderosa.aspx.

Despite the opening of the high-profile Tamarack Resort to the south, **Brundage Mountain**—located 8 miles northwest of McCall via Highway 55—continues to attract a loyal following for its affordable prices and good variety of terrain. Full-day lift tickets run about $48 for adults and $22 to $34 for children and seniors, with discounts after 1:00 p.m. One of the lifts offers scenic rides in summer, too. Call (800) 888-7544 for the ski report, or see www .brundage.com for more information.

The biggest winter event in Southwestern Idaho—possibly the entire state—is the **McCall Winter Carnival.** Each year the festival draws about 100,000 people. A snow-sculpting competition is the big attraction, and there are also fireworks, a full-moon cross-country ski tour, dogsled races, wine tasting, and more. Winter Carnival takes place in late January or early February each year. For information phone the McCall Chamber of Commerce at (208) 634-7631.

About 16 miles northwest of McCall, Highway 55 ends at US 95 in New Meadows. Turn south on US 95 to reach Cambridge, best known as the jumping-off spot for the Hells Canyon Scenic Byway. Although there are a few other ways to access Hells Canyon by vehicle, the byway is the only one usually open year-round. From Cambridge, Highway 71 crosses into Oregon

TOP ANNUAL EVENTS IN SOUTHWESTERN IDAHO

McCall Winter Carnival
(late January–early February)

National Oldtime Fiddlers Championship
Weiser (third week of June)

Idaho Shakespeare Festival
Boise (June–September)

Yellow Pine Harmonica Fest
(first full weekend of August)

Western Idaho Fair
Garden City (late August)

Art in the Park
Boise (early September)

Idaho Steelheads Hockey
Boise (October–March)

at Brownlee Dam and back into the Gem State at Oxbow Dam. From Oxbow Dam, the Hells Canyon Scenic Byway—an Idaho Power–owned road open to the public—runs north to its terminus (and back into Oregon) at Hells Canyon Dam. There's some fine camping along the reservoirs behind these dams. Sites are first come, first served. Call (800) 422-3143 for information.

Many boat trips launch from below Hells Canyon Dam. Choose from either a rafting expedition or, if your time and pocketbook are pressed, a jet-boat ride. For a raft trip of three to six days, choices include Hughes River Expeditions at (800) 262-1882, Northwest Voyageurs at (800) 727-9977, or Mackay Wilderness River Trips at (800) 635-5336. Jet-boat trips ranging from two hours to two days (with an overnight in Lewiston) are run by Hells Canyon Adventures, which also does one-day white-water rafting/jet-boat combo trips. For a complete list of outfitters traveling in Hells Canyon, contact the Hells Canyon National Recreation Office at (509) 758-0616 or write P.O. Box 699, Clarkston, WA 99403.

Hells Canyon Adventures' two- and three-hour trips are just long enough to give riders a taste of the canyon's scenery and history; they're also good choices for families with young children who aren't yet ready to brave big white water on the rafts. (HCA is fond of saying even babies and grandmas enjoy these trips.) Highlights include an up close, bottom-up view of Hells Canyon Dam; a stop at an area known for its Indian pictographs; and an interpretation of early homestead life in Hells Canyon. A few of the stories you may hear verge on tall-tale territory, but all in all, this is an enjoyable and scenic trip.

The two-hour trip begins at 2:00 p.m. Pacific time with a cost of $35 per adult, $15 per child under twelve, or a $100 family rate that covers two adults and up to six kids. The three-hour ride, which includes a riverside picnic lunch, starts at 10:00 a.m. Pacific time and costs $45 for adults and $20 for children under twelve. Allow about two and a half hours for the winding, 64-mile drive from Cambridge to Hells Canyon Dam. For more information on these tours or other Hells Canyon Adventures, call (800) 422-3568; see their Web site at www.hellscanyonadventures.com; or write Hells Canyon Adventures, P.O. Box 159, Oxbow, OR 97840.

Aside from its role as Hells Canyon base camp, Cambridge is an interesting little town in its own right. If you plan to spend the night, consider the *Hunters Inn Motel.* Rates range from $45 (for old-fashioned rooms in the 1920s Cambridge House) to $70 for kitchenettes. Call (208) 257-3325 for reservations. Check out the *Cambridge Museum* at the junction of US 95 and Highway 71 for fascinating exhibits such as one detailing the journey of Edith Clegg, who went upriver through Hells Canyon in 1939. The museum is open May 15 through September 15 from 10:00 a.m. to 4:00 p.m. Wednesday through Saturday and 1:00 to 4:00 p.m. Sunday, or you can call (208) 257-3541 or 257-3485 for an appointment.

Two other scenic day trips out of the McCall area lead to some of Idaho's most cherished yet accessible backcountry destinations. North of McCall, the Warren Wagon Road leads to Burgdorf Hot Springs and the former mining town of Warren. (See the end of the North Central Idaho chapter for details on this route.) Another route leading east from McCall travels to Yellow Pine and Warm Lake before looping back to Highway 55 at Cascade. The road from McCall to Yellow Pine, Forest Road 48, is a rough but scenic route passable by any vehicle in good condition driven by a motorist using care. The road runs alongside boulder fields and immense rock outcroppings, along with areas where extensive wildfire damage is visible; this region is among those most heavily damaged by forest fires in recent years.

A few spots along the way are worth noting. The *Duck Lake Trail,* just a mile long, is among the easier high-country paths you'll find in these rugged parts. It's not far east of Lick Creek Summit, and the trailhead is well signed. And near the junction of Road 48 and the Salmon River Road (Forest Road 674), there's an exhibit that explains the history of the Chinese miners who toiled in the area a century ago. From 1870 through 1900, in fact, the Chinese miners had a three-to-one majority among prospectors working the Warren mining district.

Yellow Pine, with a year-round population of about fifty, is surprisingly bustling despite its remote location. Yellow Pine folks also have a nifty sense of humor: Witness the University of Yellow Pine sign on the town's one-room schoolhouse. Most Idaho towns have an annual community bash or two, and Yellow Pine is no exception. The *Yellow Pine Harmonica Fest,* held the first full weekend of August, typically attracts between thirty and thirty-five contestants and about 1,200 spectators who crowd the tiny town for the mouth harp competition and other musical events, as well as barbecues, breakfasts, community potlucks, and a street fair. If you want to attend the festival, odds are you'll be camping out. The **Yellow Pine Lodge** has twelve rooms priced from $45 to $65 and home-cooked meals. Innkeeper Darlene Rosenbaum will pack you a sack lunch if your plans for the day will keep you out of town over the noon hour. To reach the lodge call (208) 633-3377 or write P.O. Box 77, Yellow Pine 83677.

Nine miles south of Yellow Pine on Forest Road 413, **Wapiti Meadow Ranch** is the oldest dude ranch in Idaho and one of the oldest in the Northwest. Long run by Lafe and Emma Cox, the ranch is now owned by Diana and Barry Bryant. Wapiti Meadow specializes in horseback riding and fly-fishing trips into the adjacent wilderness areas; hiking and cross-country skiing are popular, too. And Wapiti Meadow is no misnomer: Guests really are likely to see plenty of elk, especially in springtime, along with deer, moose, coyotes, and maybe a black bear.

The center of the ranch is its spacious stone and pine lodge, warmly furnished with antiques and comfortable furniture, like the big leather sofa sitting before the ample hearth. Four guest cabins plus two pond-side suites in a log lodge are outfitted with living rooms as well as sleeping quarters. Each of the guest quarters has a woodstove (along with modern baseboard heating), and each comes graced with fresh flowers, a coffeemaker, a refrigerator stocked with soft drinks, a fruit basket, and other snacks.

You might not have room for those goodies, however, once you've had your fill of Diana's cooking. The ranch specializes in "hearty gourmet" fare, and some guests have been known to book vacations at the ranch strictly for the food. The buffet-style breakfasts include such fare as mushroom and cheddar omelets and hot blueberry muffins. Breast of turkey on fresh croissants and homemade tomato bisque are among the luncheon selections. And dinners range from filet of beef served by candlelight to a game meal featuring New Zealand elk tenderloin, rack of lamb, and Madeira-poached duck breast.

Wapiti Meadow offers a wide range of packages, depending on activities selected. Guided fly-fishing trips, riding vacations, photography tours, wildlife viewing, and more are offered. Contact the lodge for current pricing. For more information or reservations, call (208) 633-3217 or write 1667 Johnson Creek Road, Cascade 83611. You can also reach the lodge via fax at (208) 633-3219 or via the Internet at www.wapitimeadowranch.com.

Forest Road 413 continues south from Wapiti Meadow to Landmark, site of a Boise National Forest ranger station. From there a good paved road takes a steep and winding plunge through heavily timbered country to Warm Lake, a resort and summer home area.

The ***Warm Lake Lodge*** has been catering to backcountry adventurers since 1911. In summertime, fishing and hiking are big draws, while hunters pack the cabins come fall and snowmobilers and cross-country skiers arrive in winter. Warm Lake Lodge has nine cabins, some with cooking facilities, priced from about $30 to $160, based on double occupancy, with additional people a few extra bucks per night. The restaurant serves such fare as Idaho trout, breast of chicken, and homemade pies, and includes a lounge and a general store. If you're an angler, make sure to ask about Tule Lake, a trophy cutthroat fishery southwest of Warm Lake. Warm Lake Lodge is open year-round. Reservations may be made by calling (208) 632-3553 or writing Warm Lake Lodge, Warm Lake 83611. If this lodge is full, the nearby North Shore Lodge has similarly priced cabins and services in the summertime. There's also camping nearby.

The Warm Lake Road ends up back in Cascade, which—together with its neighboring town to the north, Donnelly—sits at the epicenter of one of Idaho's biggest modern-day land rushes. The opening of the posh ***Tamarack Resort*** along the west side of Lake Cascade is having a big impact on these

Soaking up the Outdoors

Idaho has plenty of hot springs—but not many come ready equipped with bathtubs. ***Molly's Tubs,*** on the South Fork of the Salmon River just a few miles west of Warm Lake, is one such site.

Look for Forest Road 474 on the south side of the Warm Lake Road, then drive 1.3 miles to a small pullout on the right-hand side. A short but somewhat steep path leads down to an array of real bathtubs, hauled to the site for your soaking pleasure amid the cathedral of pines. A hose has been rigged up from the spring to fill the tubs. The water is too hot to sit in, but a big bucket sitting nearby may be used to haul cold water from the Salmon until just the right temperature is achieved.

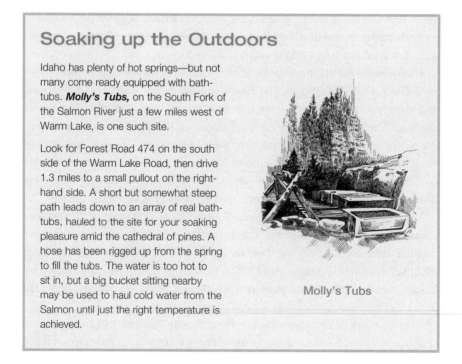

Molly's Tubs

two towns, especially Donnelly, which used to be a real blink-and-you've-missed-it spot. Now retirees, vacation-home buyers, and a fair number of land speculators are snapping up every available piece of real estate, and the times, they are a-changin'.

Tamarack has been billed as the first four-season resort community built from scratch in North America in more than twenty years. Tamarack offers top-notch skiing, golf, and boating on Lake Cascade, as well as an array of new homes that range from modest to extravagant in scale. (None are modestly priced by local standards, however.) Top to bottom, the resort is run by people who love playing in Idaho's outdoors. They're eager to help guests have a great time, and a wide menu of recreational choices and special packages make a Tamarack experience accessible to middle-class Idaho locals. The downside is that the development is very much still a work in progress, so there are still plenty of bulldozers on the scene. For more information on things to do and see, visit www.tamarackidaho.com or call (877) TAM-RESORT.

Even with Tamarack's arrival, a few places in the Cascade-Donnelly area are staying pretty much the same. Just 1 mile east of Donnelly off of US 95, the **Roseberry General Store** is a terrific old-time store and museum restored and run by local historian (and Valley County Commissioner) Frank Eld. Nearby, some of Frank's kin operate the **Hap and Florence Points Sleigh Rides** each winter, giving families a chance to ride close to wintering elk in the Gold Fork River valley. (Hap was the man who, years ago, started feeding the elk. It was either that or see his cattle starve, since the elk would run the cattle off and eat their hay.) The sleigh rides typically run from late December through mid-March; call (208) 325-8876 or (208) 325-8783 for more information or reservations. **Gold Fork Hot Springs** is another special spot far enough from the highway to deter crowds. Although it's commercially owned (charging about $8 for adults, $6 for children; closed Tuesday), the pools are in a lovely rock-rimmed setting. A yurt is available for overnight rentals. Call (208) 890-8730 for updates and directions.

Railroad buffs may want to schedule a trip with the **Thunder Mountain Line,** a historic railway that runs several routes along the Payette River. The "Cabarton Flyer" travels between Cascade and Smiths Ferry, and the "Horseshoe Bend Express" runs from its namesake town to Banks. Either excursion lasts two-and-a-half hours and costs $24.50 for adults, $23.00 for seniors age sixty and up, and $15.00 for children twelve and under. The Thunder Mountain Line has a wide range of specialty trips for holidays, plus excursions that feature dinner, wine tasting, and even Wild West–style entertainment with a simulated train robbery and shoot-out. Call (877) 432-7245 or (208) 793-4425 in the Boise area for reservations, or see www.thundermountainline.com for more details.

The Thunder Mountain Line also works in conjunction with **Cascade Raft and Kayak** to run summertime "Rivers and Rails" trips combining a train trek from Horseshoe Bend to Banks with a raft trip down the Payette River. These cost $59 for adults, $57 for seniors, and $40 for children under twelve. For reservations or more information, call Cascade Raft and Kayak at (800) 292-7238.

South of Cascade, the Payette River can't help but command the traveler's attention, with plenty of handy pullouts for fishing, picnicking, or even taking a dip on a scorching summer day. Keep the camera handy, too: The graceful yet sturdy Rainbow Bridge south of Cascade is one of Idaho's most picturesque. Hang a left at Banks for a trip into the Boise Basin, a former mining hotbed still rich in scenic wealth.

The Boise Basin

The two-lane Banks-Lowman Highway leads through scenic Garden Valley. This road wasn't even paved until the early 1990s, but locals now say it's the best road in Boise County. It's no slouch on scenery either; the South Fork of the Payette, which had its headwaters near Grandjean, tumbles far below the road.

Eight miles east of Banks, turn left off the highway to travel a mile to the hamlet of Crouch, which is the commercial heart of Garden Valley. You'll find several down-home restaurants and shops here, along with the **Starlight Mountain Theatre,** which presents Broadway musicals outdoors each summer. Tickets run $10 to $25, with dinner served Thursday through Saturday for an extra $17 to $25. For more information call (208) 462-5523 or see www .starlightmountaintheatre.com. Four miles north of Crouch, **Terrace Lakes Resort** features a challenging golf course, a geothermal pool, a restaurant, and overnight lodging priced from $50 to $125. Call (208) 462-3250 or see www .terracelakes.com.

At Lowman, Highway 21 treks north to Stanley and south to Idaho City. A short spur off the northern stretch leads to Grandjean. This tiny town on the western slope of the Sawtooth Mountains is just outside the Sawtooth Wilderness Area boundaries. Grandjean was named for the Boise National Forest's "grandfather," Emile Grandjean, first supervisor of the forest from 1908 to 1919.

Grandjean is home to the **Sawtooth Lodge.** More accurately you could say the Sawtooth Lodge *is* Grandjean. The lodge serves meals from 8:00 a.m. to 8:00 p.m., with hearty mountain fare topping the bill. No-frills log cabins heated by wood stoves sleep from two to four people at prices ranging from about $60 to $100 a night. (The least–expensive cabins share bathroom facilities.)

Outdoors, guests are free to enjoy a warm mineral-water plunge pool, wildlife viewing, hiking, and fishing. RV and tent-camping facilities are available, too, and it also should be noted that Grandjean makes an ideal vacation destination for folks with disabilities; one of the Sawtooth Lodge's cabins is outfitted for people with disabilities, and a mile-long nature trail is wheelchair accessible.

Sawtooth Lodge usually opens Memorial Day and closes in late October. For current rates, reservations, or other information, call (208) 259-3331 in Grandjean or (208) 344-2437 during the off-season. The mailing address is 130 North Haines, Boise 83712. Sawtooth Lodge also is home to **Sawtooth Wilderness Outfitters,** which provides horses and guides for trail rides and pack trips into the wilderness area. For more information call (208) 462-3416; write P.O. Box 81, Garden Valley 83622; or see www.sawtoothadventures.com.

Although not as well known as the '49ers' rush to the California gold fields or the boom in the Yukon, Idaho miners had glory days all their own. During the 1860s more gold was mined from the mountains northeast of Boise than from all of Alaska. In fact Idaho City was once the largest city in the Northwest, and like most mining towns, it had a reputation as a wild place. It's been reported that only 28 of the 200 people buried in the town's Boot Hill died a natural death. These days, however, it's much more calm—even peaceful—with a small selection of visitor services and abundant recreation nearby. The areas around Idaho City are justly famous for great hiking and cross-country skiing.

Stop by the town visitor center at the corner of Highway 21 and Main Street for a leaflet describing notable Idaho City buildings. Among them, the old 1867 post office now serves as the **Boise Basin Museum,** open Monday through Saturday from 11:00 a.m. to 4:00 p.m. and Sunday from 1:00 p.m. to 4:00 p.m. Memorial Day through Labor Day and weekends in May and September. Museum visitors can buy a gold-panning kit or arrange a guided walking tour of Idaho City. (Tours also can be set up by calling Barbara Frentress at 208-392-4550 or 392-4447. Cost is $3.50 per person or $2.00 for seniors and kids six to twelve, with a $30.00 per-group minimum.)

For a meal in Idaho City, try **Trudy's Kitchen** at 419 Highway 21. This locally popular restaurant serves hearty breakfasts, bodacious hamburgers, and a house salad drizzled with huckleberry vinaigrette dressing. Sandwiches range in price from about $5 to $8, with dinner entrees priced from about $7 to $15. Trudy's is open daily at 7:00 a.m. and closes at about 8:00 p.m. The phone number is (208) 392-4151.

The area around Idaho City is known for some of the best cross-country skiing in the state: Eighteen miles north of town on Highway 21, the Whoop-Um-Up Park N' Ski area has 6.6 miles of marked trails, with sections suitable for all skier levels. Another 2 miles north, Gold Fork Park N' Ski accesses 21.4 miles of groomed trails, with terrain best for advanced beginners to serious skiers. Banner Ridge Park N' Ski, 3.5 miles from Gold Fork, has 22 miles of groomed trails for intermediate and expert skiers, plus off-trail bowl skiing. Gold Fork and Banner Ridge both have yurts available for rent. For more information call the Idaho Department of Parks and Recreation at (208) 334-4199 or see http://parksandrecreation.idaho.gov.

Another side trip off of Highway 21 leads to *Atlanta,* a late bloomer among Idaho's mining districts and a scenic little town well worth the long drive. On one hand, several roads in the Boise Basin head toward Atlanta. On the other hand, none of them is easy—and some (notably Forest Road 126, the way from Rocky Bar) are sort of scary. The most popular routes are the heavily rutted, 68-mile Middle Fork Road (Forest Road 268) from Lucky Peak Reservoir near Boise and the 40-mile combination of the Edna Creek (384), North Fork Boise River (327), and Middle Fork Boise Roads. Check with the Forest Service office in Idaho City at (208) 392-6681 for information on road conditions. Logging trucks often work these highways, so monitor Channel 19 if you have a CB and always be an attentive, cautious driver.

The www.atlantaidaho.org Web site has updates on the handful of area businesses, as well as turn-by-turn road directions from Boise and Mountain Home. Be sure to have a full tank of gas before you head out for Atlanta since no fuel is available.

Atlanta doesn't have tourist attractions, but that's the point: People come here to relax and escape the pace and clutter of modern life. Much of the town is on the National Register of Historic Places. A tiny museum in what used to be the town jail displays historic photos, and a restored log cabin and pioneer cemetery are other interesting spots to see.

Two nearby hot springs beckon bathers. To find *Atlanta Hot Springs,* drive a mile east of town and look for the little parking area on the right-hand side of the road just past the big green pond. (No, the pond is not the hot spring!) The choice spot, *Chatanooga Hot Springs,* is much nicer, sitting below a waterfall in a rock pool on the Middle Fork of the Boise River. But it's also a bit harder to find—and to get there, you have to cross land owned by Pinnacle Peaks Sawtooth Lodge (see below), although the resort's current owners realize it is futile to keep bathers at bay. To get there, look for the spur road just west of Atlanta Hot Springs (but on the other side of the road) and follow it about ³⁄₁₀ of a mile north. The road ends at the top of a bluff. Cross a small stream and hike down the bluff to the hot springs. The road leading to the bluff is marked PRIVATE PROPERTY, but locals say that if you stay on the road and refrain from rowdiness, you're OK.

Pinnacle Peaks Sawtooth Lodge is Atlanta's secret showplace. Once the private playground of Herman Coors (of the Colorado brewing family), Pinnacle Peaks now caters to upscale vacationers, reunions, and business retreats with its handsome 500-acre spread between the Middle Fork of the Boise River and the southernmost stretch of the Sawtooth Wilderness Area. With 9,317-foot Greylock Mountain as a backdrop, guests can ride horseback, swim or soak in the geothermally heated pool and hot tub, play tennis, fish, golf, hike, bike, or do nothing. Winter activities include cross-country skiing, ice-skating, snowshoeing, and snowmobiling. Meals are ample and include lots of Idaho-grown produce. They are served indoors in the great room or outside when weather permits. Guests can bring their own alcohol, but smoking is allowed outdoors only.

Pinnacle Peaks has eighteen rooms with a variety of bed configurations. Rates range from $175 to $250 per person, per night, with all meals and many activities included. Children ages five through thirteen stay half-price; kids four and under stay free. Minimum group sizes apply; call for details. For reservations or more information, call (208) 864-2168; write 1 Greylock Lane, Box 39, Atlanta 83601; or see www.pinnaclepeaks.com.

From Atlanta, you can either backtrack along the Forest Service roads to Highway 21 or take the southern routes (Forest Service Roads 126 or 156) to Rocky Bar and the Featherville-Pine-Trinity Lakes area. (See the "Snake River Vistas" section later in this chapter for more information on this region.)

When Highway 21 intersects with I-84, it's just a few miles west to Boise. First, however, you might want to head east for a few miles to get your first look at Idaho's capital city as our forebears did, from ***Bonneville Point.*** This was the spot from which mountain men and Oregon Trail pioneers first spied the verdant Boise River Valley below. Boise got its name, in fact, when a party of French trappers visited Bonneville Point in 1833. For weeks the trappers had seen nothing but lava and sagebrush. Now, far below but after less than a day's walk, they saw a verdant river valley, the stream bank lined with trees. "*Les bois, les bois, voyez les bois*" ("The trees, the trees, look at the trees"), the trappers supposedly cried in joy. To this day Boise is known as the "City of Trees."

To find Bonneville Point, take exit 64 off I-84 and follow the signs north. The Bureau of Land Management has placed an interpretive kiosk at the site, and a long stretch of wagon-wheel ruts may be seen nearby, along with a good look at Boise and its foothills. "When we arrived at the top we got a grand view of the Boise River Valley," emigrant Cecilia E. M. Adams noted in her diary. The trees they saw, she added, were "the first we have seen in more than a month." Likewise, explorer John Frémont, who mapped the West, wrote of his joy in seeing the Boise River, "a beautiful rapid stream, with clear mountain water" and noted he was "delighted this afternoon to make a pleasant camp under fine old trees again."

City of Trees

With a 2006 population of about 570,000, the Boise metro area is among the fastest growing in the United States. The Treasure Valley—as the whole area is known—has been discovered by young professionals who want to cap off a day of work with a microbrew or a mountain bike ride; by families seeking a city environment that still feels "small town"; and by retirees who like the lively but livable pace.

Boise may be growing, but its downtown remains wonderfully compact, with many of its most interesting sites within walking distance. Looming over all is the **State Capitol,** which would usually make a logical spot to start explorations, except it is closed for extensive renovations. Plans call for the expanded capitol to reopen in time for the legislative session beginning in January 2010; in the meantime, project updates and a virtual tour can be found online at www.capitolcommission.idaho.gov/.

The area southeast of the statehouse, known as Old Boise, is one of the city's busiest nightlife districts, and it has an array of restaurants and stores, too. **Flying M,** at 500 West Idaho Street, is a popular coffeehouse with strong local flavor and a quirky gift shop. (Flying M now has a "coffee garage" in Nampa, too, at 1314 Second Street South.) **Ceramica**—another block south at 510 Main Street—is a drop-in, paint-your-own pottery shop where you can indulge your creative side.

Mortimer's, downstairs in the handsome Belgravia building at the corner of Fifth and Main Streets, is one of the city's best fine-dining options. (Others include **Milky Way** at 205 North Tenth Street, **Andre's** at 816 West Bannock Street, **Bungalow** at 1520 North Thirteenth Street in Hyde Park, and **Café Vicino** at 808 West Fort Street.) Entrees run mostly $20 to $30 per person, or you can try the seven-course tasting menus for about $40 to $50 per person. Call (208) 338-6550 to reserve a table. For less-fancy fare, try the southwest corner of Sixth and Main, where **Pair** (downstairs) and **Reef** (upstairs) are both good choices. Pair specializes in small plates of food for sharing; Reef is an island-themed bar and restaurant that often has live music.

The ages-old **Pengilly's Saloon** at 513 West Main Street has been written up everywhere from *Esquire* to *Cosmo,* but it's anything but a meat market. Adult-friendly acoustic, blues, and jazz music and a no-smoking policy make this a great place to enjoy a drink and soak in a little history. Call (208) 345-6344 to find out who's playing.

Find Good Eats in Boise

You'll find a dozen or so Boise-area restaurants briefly noted in this chapter. The fact is, however, the establishments mentioned here are just a taste of what awaits. Boise is rich in great breakfast joints, locally owned lunch counters, neighborhood pizzerias, and enticing ethnic eateries that range from simple to high concept. For the latest dining news, your two best sources are **Boise Weekly**—which has ample listings and sends two critics to check out new restaurants—and the **Idaho Statesman**'s weekly **Scene** magazine. Both are widely available for free in newsstand boxes around town. Both are also good resources for local arts and entertainment offerings.

West of Capitol Boulevard along several blocks of Eighth Street, the *Capital City Market* is held each Saturday morning from mid-April through October. Vendors from all over Southwestern Idaho line the sidewalks to sell fresh food, plants, arts and crafts, and more. (While you're strolling, be sure to look at the mural on the side of the escalator leading from the street to the second floor of the Capitol Terrace building between Main and Idaho Streets.) The market often spills out onto the Grove, Boise's largest downtown plaza, which is also the site of Alive After Five, a summer concert series that runs on Wednesday evening May through August. The *Brick Oven Bistro* on the Grove's northwest side is another casual-dining favorite with lots of open-air seating. Continue south across Front Street to access *BoDo,* which features shops and restaurants (plus a hotel and movie multiplex) amid some of the city's oldest warehouses. *The Flicks* at 646 Fulton Street is another classic Boise institution, serving light cafe fare and screening independent and foreign films.

Idaho has the nation's highest percentage of people hailing from Euzkadi, or the Basque homeland that straddles the border of Spain and France. Although pockets of Basque culture can be found throughout the state, Boise, by virtue of its size, is probably the state's true Basque capital. A 1-block area of Boise's downtown is an especially rich site of Basque heritage and culture. Take a stroll down Grove Street between Sixth and Capitol for a look at what's known as Boise's *Basque Block.*

The block's centerpiece, the *Basque Museum and Cultural Center,* at 611 Grove, has many fascinating exhibits on all aspects of Basque history and culture. Here you can learn, for example, about famous people of Basque heritage, including Simón Bolivar, Francisco Goya, Balboa, and Juan de la Cosa, who served as Columbus's navigator. Another Basque mariner was responsible for guiding Magellan's ship home after the explorer was killed in the Philippines following the first circumnavigation of the globe.

Visitors discover that most Idaho Basques trace their heritage to the province of Vizcaya in the northwest section of the Basque homeland. Here, too, are history lessons about Gernika, Boise's sister city and the ancient Vizcayan capital and spiritual homeland of the Basques. It was the bombings here during the Spanish Civil War of 1936–1939 that inspired Pablo Picasso's *Guernica* painting, one of his most famous. Gernika is also home to an oak tree that symbolizes Basque liberty; a model of the tree and its surroundings sits in the museum. Next door at 607 Grove Street, the **Cyrus Jacobs–Uberuaga House** has recently been renovated as part of the museum. Built in 1864, this is the oldest brick building still standing in Boise. It was the site of the city's first indoor bathtub and the wedding of Senator William Borah. The building served as a Basque boardinghouse for much of the twentieth century. The Basque Museum is open from 10:00 a.m. to 4:00 p.m. Tuesday through Friday and from 11:00 a.m. to 3:00 p.m. Saturday. Suggested donation is $1 for adults and 50 cents for children and senior citizens. Call (208) 343-2671 for more information.

The **Fronton Building** at 619 Grove was built in 1912 and, although it has housed businesses over the years, none has ever altered the fronton, or handball court, inside. It is the largest covered court of its kind in the Northwest, and it is still used by sporting Basques today. This building also served as a boardinghouse for a time.

Gernika Basque Pub and Eatery, at the corner of Grove and Capitol, was established in 1991. The menu here includes several Basque-inspired dishes, such as a Solomo sandwich (marinated pork loin topped with pimientos and served on a French roll) or a cheese plate accompanied with fresh bread and grapes. Espresso and microbrews are available, too. Gernika is open from lunch until late daily except Sunday. The phone number is (208) 344-2175.

At the opposite end of the Basque Block at 117 South Sixth Street, **Leku Ona**—which means "the good place" in Basque—is proving a worthy bookend to Gernika. Leku Ona features a wide menu of traditional Basque fare, including squid, cod, beef, and lamb. There's also a boardinghouse-style boutique hotel with rooms priced from $65 to $85. Ask for a room away from the noise on Sixth Street. Call (208) 345-6665 for more information or reservations.

Not far from the Basque Block, Julia Davis Park is home to the Boise Art Museum, the Idaho Historical Society, and the **Idaho Black History Museum** at 508 Julia Davis Drive. Less than 1 percent of Idaho's population is African American, and visitors often wonder whether the state has any blacks at all, but this museum sets the record straight. Located in the former St. Paul's Baptist Church, the museum has featured exhibits on everything from Idaho's jazz heritage to the history of the state's African Americans in the military. The museum is open Saturday only, 11:00 a.m. to 4:00 p.m., or by appointment for groups. Admission is by donation. For more information call (208) 433-0017 or see www.ibhm.org.

Boise is also the unexpected home of a moving tribute to one of the twentieth century's most famous teenagers. Dedicated in 2002, the **Idaho Anne Frank Human Rights Memorial** features a life-size statue of Frank, the teenage diarist who documented her family's efforts to evade the Nazis during the Holocaust. Visitors will also find reflecting ponds, waterfalls, and walls engraved with the full text of the United Nations' Universal Declaration of Human Rights and dozens of quotes from human-rights leaders past and present. The memorial plaza is located behind the Boise Public Library and the Log Cabin Literary Center and along the Greenbelt.

The Linen District—on the west edge of downtown along Grove Street at Fifteenth Street—is a good destination for breakfast, with hearty eats at **Donnie Mac's Trailer Park Cuisine,** 1515 West Grove Street, and lighter fare at the always-jumping **Big City Coffee**, 1416 West Grove Street. With a few tattoo parlors, a "gentlemen's club," and a skate park sprinkled amid a growing number of more upscale galleries and shops, the Linen District is about as gritty as it gets in Idaho.

In recent years Boise has become famous among sports fans as home of the Boise State University Broncos, a highly successful college football

Idaho Anne Frank Human Rights Memorial

team that plays (and usually wins) its home games on blue turf. The Broncos shocked the sporting world on New Year's Day 2007 with their unlikely Fiesta Bowl win over Oklahoma in what many people believe was one of the greatest college gridiron games ever played. The BSU campus is just across the Boise River from downtown, between Capitol and Broadway Avenues. The **World Sports Humanitarian Hall of Fame** is located at Boise State; look for the entrance behind the big bronco statue on the southwest side of Bronco Stadium. This little-heralded museum includes tributes to and memorabilia from such athletes as Roberto Clemente, Arthur Ashe, Mary Lou Retton, and David Robinson—jocks known as much for their philanthropic and community activities as for their sporting heroics. The hall of fame is open weekdays from 8:00 a.m. to 5:00 p.m. and weekends by appointment. For more information call (208) 343-7224 or see www.sportshumanitarian.com.

Boise's lodging choices have gotten a lot more varied in the past few years, with rooms ranging from chic and sleek to warm and historic. In the first category, the retro-cool **Modern Hotel & Bar,** 1314 West Grove Street, provides a suitably hip base camp for the Linen District (and the rest of downtown, about 5 blocks away, though if you want big-city cool right in the heart of the action, **Hotel 43** is a better bet). The Modern, with its cocktail lounge, patio, and upscale in-room amenities, has rooms starting at about $100 for weekends, $130 for weekdays. Add about $100 to that for suites. For more information or reservations, call (866) 780-6012 or see www.themodernhotel.com.

On the other hand, visitors seeking a bed-and-breakfast stay should consider the **Idaho Heritage Inn** at 109 West Idaho, close to both downtown and the Warm Springs neighborhood of gracious old homes. Built in 1904 for Henry Falk, one of Boise's early merchants, the home was bought by Idaho governor Chase Clark in 1943. Later, Clark's daughter, Bethine, and her husband, the beloved Senator Frank Church, used the home as their Idaho residence during Church's Senate tenure. The home remained in the Clark/Church family until 1987, when Tom and Phyllis Lupher bought it with an eye toward opening a bed-and-breakfast.

The Idaho Heritage Inn offers guests a choice of six rooms in the main house and two in a restored 1912 fire station ranging in price from $79 to $120 for two. Each has a private bath and telephone, making this a good spot for business travelers. Room rates also include a breakfast featuring fresh-squeezed juice and fresh fruit in season along with an entree: Baked German pancakes, apricot cream cheese–stuffed French toast, and apple skillet cake are among past offerings. Call (800) 342-8445 or (208) 342-8066; write the Idaho Heritage Inn, 109 West Idaho, Boise 83702; or see www.idheritageinn.com for more information or reservations.

East of downtown on the opposite end of the Warm Springs district, the **Old Idaho Penitentiary** housed inmates from 1870 through 1973. More than 13,000 convicts did time behind its gates, including Harry Orchard, who killed former Idaho governor Frank Steunenberg in 1905 in the aftermath of mining unrest in North Idaho, and Lyda Southard, sentenced to the pen in 1921 after she killed her fourth husband (and maybe her previous spouses, too) with a slice of arsenic-laced apple pie. Visitors can tour the Old Pen on their own or with a guide; some guides earlier served as guards or inmates at the facility. The museum also houses the J. Curtis Earl Collection, a treasure trove of historic arms and military memorabilia. The collection, valued at $3 million, is among the largest of its kind.

The Old Pen is open seven days a week from 10:00 a.m. to 5:00 p.m. Memorial Day to Labor Day. It's open from noon to 5:00 p.m. the rest of the year, except state holidays. Admission is $5 for adults and teens, $4 for seniors, and $3 for children ages six through twelve. (Kids under age six are admitted free.) For recorded information call (208) 368-6080.

Hyde Park in Boise's North End ranks among the city's hippest addresses. Centered at Thirteenth and Eastman Streets, this historic district has a good selection of restaurants and specialty shops. One of the most interesting, **Ten Thousand Villages,** sells crafts, toys, jewelry, and decorative items from around the world. Most of the goods are made by disadvantaged artisans

Urban Oasis

Ask many Boiseans what they love most about their city, and chances are they'll mention the **Greenbelt.** More than 20 miles long, this network of paths reaches from Sandy Point Beach east of the city past Glenwood Street, with more mileage planned for the future.

On a warm weekend day, the Boise Greenbelt could hardly be considered off the beaten path since it sometimes seems half the city is out there walking, running, bicycling, or blading. Even then, however, it's possible to lose the crowds by venturing away from the crowded downtown corridors (near the Boise State University campus and Julia Davis and Ann Morrison Parks) to less-traveled sections. The western stretch from Willow Lane to Americana Boulevard is a good bet, as is the area east of downtown.

A few Greenbelt sections are limited to pedestrian use only, including Kathryn Albertson Park and a stretch bordering the south banks of the Boise River just west of Barber Park. For more information on the Boise River Greenbelt, call (208) 384–4240 or write the Boise Parks & Recreation Department, 1104 Royal Boulevard, Boise 83706.

from Third World nations—people who would otherwise be jobless or under-employed. All in all, a cool and fun place to shop. Ten Thousand Villages is at 1609 North Thirteenth Street, and its phone number is (208) 333-0535. Hours are 11:00 a.m. to 5:00 p.m. Tuesday through Saturday.

Camel's Back Park, just north of the Hyde Park neighborhood, has one of Boise's best playgrounds. Past the park, Thirteenth Street veers into Hill Road, which soon intersects with Bogus Basin Road, the route to Boise's back-yard ski resort of the same name. Near this intersection a nondescript building opposite the Bogus Basin Shopping Center might look like a dentist's office, but it's really home to *Highlands Hollow Brewhouse.* Quench your thirst with one of the beers brewed on-site, and get some good grub, too; menu items include tasty barley breadsticks and the "mess-o-chops" (thinly sliced pork chops, lightly marinated and charbroiled). Highlands Hollow is open daily from 11:00 a.m. The address is 2455 Harrison Hollow. Call (208) 343-6820 for more information.

Continue up Bogus Basin Road to *Bogus Basin Mountain Resort,* just 16 miles from downtown. In addition to more than fifty downhill runs over 2,600 acres, the resort has a tubing hill with an 800-foot slide and a tow to take tubers back to the top. Ski-lift tickets (available at the mountain) run from $20 to $46. Two-hour tubing passes cost $9. The ski hill is open nightly in winter (with tubing on weekends), which makes Bogus an after-work hot spot for Boiseans. During the summer months Bogus offers hiking, horseback riding, mountain biking, and disc golf. For more information call (208) 332-5100 or see www.bogusbasin.org.

The Rest of the Treasure Valley

If Boise is the City of Trees, the communities to its west are its fast-growing branches. One-time farm towns like Meridian, Star, Eagle, and Kuna have become full-fledged suburbs, while the cities of Nampa and Caldwell form a mini-metropolis of their own. Even outlying towns stretching to the Oregon border have become bedroom communities for Boise and its suburbs. We'll explore the area in counterclockwise fashion from Boise's western city limits.

Meridian has two faces: the rampant commercial development along I84 and its feeder roads, and the much slower pace of an old-time downtown centered around Main Street and Pine Avenue. Near the center of the latter, the *Library Coffeehouse* at 141 East Carlton Avenue in Meridian is a great place to take a break. Its name is no misnomer; there really are about 4,000 books to browse and lots of comfy chairs in which to perch. Enjoy a full menu of coffee drinks, pastries, sandwiches, and more. The Library features live music several nights each week, along with wireless Internet. Hours are 7:00 a.m. to 9:00 p.m. Monday through Friday and 8:00 a.m. to 2:00 p.m. Saturday and Sunday. Call (208) 288-1898 or see www.librarycoffeehouse.com.

Both Meridian and Eagle—the upscale community to its north—are starting to rival Boise as top southwestern Idaho dining destinations. One of Meridian's longtime standouts is *Epi's—A Basque Restaurant* in an old house at 1115 North Main Street. Squid rolls, shrimp, crab cakes, and lamb loin chops are among the tasty items on the menu. Call (208) 884-0142 for more information or reservations.

In Eagle, *SixOneSix* won the *Idaho Statesman*'s "Best New Restaurant" nod in 2006. Look for such creative dishes as pistachio-crusted venison and maple bourbon pork loin—not to mention luscious deserts including lemon meringue ice-cream pie and donuts with dipping sauces. SixOneSix is at 1065 Winding Creek Road (a block from State Street). Call (208) 938-3010 for reservations, or see menus and more at www.restaurantsixonesix.com.

Eagle Island State Park is one of only two state parks in the Boise metropolitan area. (The other is Lucky Peak, out Warm Springs Road east of Boise. Neither park allows camping.) Eagle Island offers a swimming area with a waterslide, riverside walking paths, and more than 5 miles of trails for horseback riding. The park also is the site for the Eagle Island Experience Festival, held in mid-May every year. The three-day event focuses on environmental sustainability and features an Enchanted Forest of cool interactive fun for the young and young at heart. Eagle Island is located at 4000 West Hatchery Road, off Linder Road west of Eagle. Park admission is $4 per vehicle per day. For more information call (208) 939-0696 or see http://parksandrecreation.idaho.gov/parks/eagleisland.aspx.

Idaho is horse country, and the *R. C. Bean Saddlery* at 7100 Star Road west of Eagle caters to the Western equestrian with beautiful handmade saddles and a wide selection of other tack. The Bean family has been in the ranching business since the 1950s, and R. C. "Rick" Bean started making saddles around 1979. There's a two-year waiting list for his custom-made, hand-tooled models, which start at $3,300 and average about $5,000. Some particularly ornate saddles can command much more. The Beans also stock quality saddles made elsewhere, with prices starting at $1,000. It's worth a stop just to smell the leather. The shop is open from 9:00 a.m. to 5:30 p.m. Monday through Friday and 10:00 a.m. to 4:30 p.m. Saturday. The phone number is (208) 286-7602, or you can see 'em on the Web at www.rcbean.com.

Nestled in a sheltered valley where Highway 16 meets Highway 52, Emmett is fast becoming a bedroom community for commuters who don't mind a scenic drive of up to an hour to their Boise workplaces. The foothills outside

Emmett provide a striking location for **Frozen Dog Digs,** an oddly named bed-and-breakfast inn with equally unusual amenities. The inn, run by former English teacher and technical writer Jon Elsberry, may be the only one in Idaho with its own racquetball court. A major sports fan, Elsberry also has created a fun "sports bar" room featuring an overstuffed baseball mitt chair and lots of New York Yankees memorabilia. The library resembles a one-room schoolhouse, complete with original Dick and Jane posters and desks salvaged from local classrooms. The newest addition is a bi-level guest suite complete with a kitchenette and jetted tub. The suite, decorated in an Asian motif, opens onto a Japanese garden. Throughout the house Elsberry has made an effort to use local woods and other materials for the custom-built furnishings and decor.

Frozen Dog Digs' four guest rooms rent for $69 to $189 double occupancy, including a full gourmet breakfast. For reservations or more information, call (208) 365-7372; write Frozen Dog Digs, 4325 Frozen Dog Road, Emmett 83617; or see www.frozendogdigs.com.

On fine autumn days—which includes most of them in Southwestern Idaho—the towns of New Plymouth, Fruitland, and Payette make a great scenic-drive destination. Watch for roadside markets piled with fat orange pumpkins and tart, crisp apples, and stock up on some tasty seasonal produce while enjoying some of the state's loveliest fall foliage.

Weiser, located north of Payette, is the most interesting town in this neck of the woods, best known as the site of the annual **National Old-Time Fiddlers Contest.** As much a family reunion as a competition, the fiddle fests have been going on in Weiser since 1914. The town became host to the Northwest Mountain Fiddlers Contest in 1953, and the national championship was inaugurated in 1963, Idaho's territorial centennial. The contest is held the third full week of June, drawing about 300 contestants ages four to ninety and more than 10,000 spectators.

Year-round, Weiser is home to the **Fiddlers Hall of Fame,** located in the old Oregon Short Line depot at the end of State Street. Stop by to see photos of past champions, including noted bowman Mark O'Connor. If you miss the Old-Time Fiddlers Contest, try to time your Weiser visit to the second or fourth Thursday September through June, when local fiddlers come to jam. For more information on the contest, call (208) 414-0525 or see www .fiddlecontest.com.

Down the block at 30 East Idaho Street, the Knights of Pythias built an impressive temple to Pythianhood back in 1904. Cross the street for a good view of the **Pythian Castle,** which was built for $9,000 using sandstone quarried on the nearby Weiser River. Inside, the building has a vaulted pressed-tin ceiling that may be the finest of its kind in the Northwest. The castle is open during special events, or it can be seen by appointment. To arrange a tour, call Steve Clausen at (208) 549-1844 or Tony Edmondson at (208) 549-0211.

Chocoholics, don't miss a stop at **Weiser Classic Candy** at 449 State Street in Weiser. The business was started by Fawn Olsen out of her home. Today new co-owners Keith Bryant and Patrick Nauman and their crew continue to ship hand-dipped chocolates and homemade candies nation-wide and even around the world. In addition to its tempting candy counter, Weiser Classic Candy serves muffins, bagels, coffee, ice cream, soups, and sandwiches. The shop is open from 9:00 a.m. to 7:00 p.m. Monday through Friday and 10:00 a.m. to 7:00 p.m. Saturday. Call (208) 414-2850 or see www .weiserclassiccandy.com.

The small town of Parma, south of I-84 on U.S. Highway 20/26, is home to a replica of the Hudson's Bay Company's **Fort Boise,** built in 1834 and one of two nineteenth-century forts so named. (The town of Boise grew up around the other, a U.S. Army cavalry post erected in 1863.) The original Fort Boise was situated on the east bank of the Snake River about 8 miles north of the mouth of the Boise River. Although it was built as a fur-trading post, Fort Boise soon switched its emphasis to serving emigrants on the Oregon Trail, and it was a most welcome sight after 300 miles of dry and dusty travel from Fort Hall.

Flooding extensively damaged Fort Boise in 1853, and historians believe any attempts to rebuild it were probably thwarted by increasingly hostile relationships with the Shoshone Indians. Tensions culminated with the 1854 Ward Massacre, in which eighteen emigrants (out of a party of twenty) died; a monument marking the event may be seen in a park south of Middleton, Idaho. Hudson's Bay Company abandoned Fort Boise two years later, and the land on which it originally stood is now a state wildlife management area.

The Fort Boise Replica in Parma sits 5 miles southeast of the original fort site. In addition to the emigrant story, the Fort Boise Replica has artifacts and displays from Southwestern Idaho history. One room features a desk built in 1891 by a boy whose family was traveling to Oregon when their money ran out and they decided to stay. Another exhibit tells how Parma is the only Idaho town to have produced two Gem State governors: Clarence Baldridge, a Republican, and Ben Ross, a Democrat. Visitors also may view a video on Fort Boise history.

A statue and historical marker on the Fort Boise grounds also are worth noting. They tell of Marie Dorian, an Iowa Indian married to Pierre Dorian who came to the area with Wilson Price Hunt's party of Astorians in 1811. Three years later Marie and her two children were the sole survivors of a midwinter battle with Bannock Indians at a nearby fur-trading post. They set out with two horses on a 200-mile journey through deep snow and after three months were finally rescued by a Columbia River band of Walla Walla Indians in April.

The Fort Boise Replica is open from 1:00 to 3:00 p.m. Friday, Saturday, and Sunday during June, July, and August, but if you want to see it during off-hours, you can call (208) 722-5138 or (208) 722-7608 at least a day in advance to make arrangements. The park adjacent to the fort replica includes a small campground with showers and a dump station, as well as shady picnic spots, a playground, and a drive-in restaurant next door. Parma celebrates its role in pioneer history late each May with the Old Fort Boise Days celebration.

Caldwell got its start as a railroad town, and it's an interesting stop for Idaho history buffs. Dearborn Street—one block south of Cleveland Boulevard (Caldwell's main drag)—is the center of the **Steunenberg Residential Historic District,** packed with lovely old homes reflecting many architectural styles. The southeast corner of Dearborn and Sixteenth Street was the site of the 1905 assassination of former Idaho governor Frank Steunenberg. The historic district is within walking distance of the lovely campus of the College of Idaho, a small liberal-arts school.

Idaho's vineyards may never become as well-known as those in California's Napa Valley, but the Gem State has more than twenty **wineries,** with the largest concentration in the state's southwestern region. In fact in 2007 the Snake River Plain was designated as an American Viticultural Area. Warm days, cool nights, and rich soil make valleys along the Snake River just right for growing wine grapes. Ste. Chapelle at 19348 Lowell Road near Caldwell is probably Idaho's best known winery, drawing many visitors for its summer jazz concert series. Other Treasure Valley vineyards worth a visit include Sawtooth Winery, at 13750 Surrey Lane south of Nampa, with its panoramic view and annual Mother's Day Wine and Food Festival, and Hells Canyon Winery, 18835 Symms Road, Caldwell. Ste. Chapelle is open daily for tours, and Sawtooth and Hells Canyon wineries welcome visitors on the weekends. You can pick up a brochure on Idaho wineries at many visitor centers and some finer restaurants, or get information online at www.idahowines.org.

If you're traveling along I-84 when the hungries hit, you could pull off almost any Treasure Valley exit into a wide selection of chain fast-food eateries. Or you could wander a bit farther from the freeway for the homemade fare served by the **Little Kitchen** at 1224 First Street South in downtown Nampa. This darling restaurant, open daily for breakfast and lunch, is a great place for families. (How many restaurants keep kids entertained with Cheerios as well as paper and crayons?) The hamburgers are especially excellent, and the service is friendly. Call (208) 467-9677.

After your meal, wander across the street to visit the **Yesteryear Shoppe,** a huge used bookstore that's one of the best in Idaho. In addition to recent used books of all sorts, Yesteryear stocks rare volumes, vintage vinyl record albums, and other treasures from decades gone by. Beware: It's easy to lose all track of time in the stacks here. Hours are 11:00 a.m. to 5:30 p.m. Monday through Saturday at 1211 First Street South. Call (208) 467-3581.

The Little Kitchen and Yesteryear Shoppe are near the Belle District, centered at Thirteenth Avenue and First Street South. Thjs once-rundown historic area is being extensively renovated and filled with hip new shops including **Market Limone,** an upscale food and kitchen store at 112 Thirteenth Avenue South, and **Ewephoria,** a yarn and fiber emporium at 1225 First Street South. The Treasure Valley's only outdoor urban skating rink, the **Nampa Ice Factory,** is set to open fall 2008. For the latest additions to the district, see www.belledistrict.com. The Nampa Farmers' Market is downtown, too, with local produce on sale from 9:00 a.m. to 1:00 p.m. each Saturday May through October.

Budget travelers, international vagabonds, and others who want inexpensive or nontraditional accommodations in the Boise metro area will enjoy **A Country Place–Hostel Boise,** currently the only hostel in southern Idaho. The hostel is in a rural setting at 17322 Can Ada Road, about 2 miles north of I-84 exit 38. Facilities include a kitchen, barbecue grill, common area, covered patio, big yard, and free wireless Internet access. Typical dorm-style hostel beds are $19. One private room is available; it costs $34 for one person, $40 for two people, or $45 for three. Check-in is between 5:00 p.m. and 10:30 p.m., but once you've checked in, there's no curfew.

From the hostel, it's about a fifteen-minute drive to Boise. Travelers coming via Greyhound will want to get off the bus in Nampa, not Boise, and take a cab. Get more information by calling (208) 467-6858 or at www.hostelboise.com.

The Snake River Canyon in Southwestern Idaho is home to the world's largest concentration of nesting eagles, hawks, and prairie falcons. There are two ways to discover this raptor kingdom: tour the **Snake River Birds of Prey Conservation Area** and visit the Peregrine Fund's **World Center for Birds of Prey** near Boise.

The conservation area encompasses more than 482,000 acres along 81 miles of the river, and it's best reached via the Swan Falls Road south of Kuna. The Bureau of Land Management has established an interpretive area near Swan Falls Dam, and visitors may catch a glimpse of raptors soaring through the canyon or nesting in its cracks, crevices, and ledges. Early morning and late afternoon mid-March through mid-June are the best times to visit. Bring binoculars, a bird field guide, water and food, sunscreen, a jacket, and a hat.

Because the raptors can be difficult to see, many visitors take a guided tour. **Birds of Prey Expeditions** offers a variety of land and boat tours ranging from $35 to $105 per person. Guides help participants identify bird species and locate the raptors' nesting areas. For more information or trip reservations, call (208) 658-9980; write Birds of Prey Expeditions, 4519 North Mountain View Drive, Boise 83704; or see www.birdsofpreyexpeditions.com.

Scientists study raptors because, like humans, they are near the top of the food chain—and what happens to them could very well happen to us. Four decades ago the peregrine falcon (for which the Peregrine Fund is named) had almost been wiped out in the United States. Through research it was learned that falcons ate smaller birds that had in turn ingested insects exposed to DDT, and the chemical made the falcons' eggshells so thin that the baby birds could not survive.

DDT is now banned in the United States, and the peregrine falcon has made an impressive comeback on our continent. But the chemical remains legal in some other nations; that fact, coupled with other environmental woes, has endangered or threatened nearly a quarter of the world's 300 raptor species. So the Peregrine Fund continues to study birds of prey and their status as environmental indicators, and much of this fascinating and important work takes place at the World Center for Birds of Prey and its Velma Morrison Interpretive Center, sitting high on a windswept hill south of Boise. Take I-84 exit 50 and drive 6 miles south to 5668 West Flying Hawk Lane.

Visitors to the center can walk around on their own or join a guided tour. Through films, lectures, and displays visitors learn how the Peregrine Fund breeds raptors in captivity, then sets them free in their natural habitat. The odds against survival can be high: All peregrines, whether captive bred or born in the wild, face a 50 percent mortality rate during their first year of life. Another 20 percent die in their second year. But those who survive two years usually go on to live an average of fifteen years. At the end of each tour, visitors are often treated to a visit with a live falcon. The World Center for Birds of Prey is open daily from 9:00 a.m. to 5:00 p.m. March through October and from 10:00 a.m. to 4:00 p.m. Tuesday through Sunday the rest of the year. Admission is $5 for adults, $4 for senior citizens ages sixty-two and up, and $3 for children ages four through sixteen. Call (208) 362-8687 for more information or see www.peregrinefund.org.

The Owyhee Outback

Owyhee County deserves its own section in any book about Idaho's lesser-known places, simply for its sheer size and remoteness. It isn't Idaho's biggest county—Idaho County takes that honor with 8,497 square miles. But Owyhee County, tucked into the state's corner, is mostly unexplored and unknown.

At 7,643 square miles, it's larger than New Jersey, but with about one-eight-hundredth the population!

Nearly half the county's 11,100 residents live in the Homedale-Marsing area along the Snake River southwest of Caldwell. Lucky people, they can eat at the **Sandbar River House Restaurant** anytime they want. This classy yet casual eatery in Marsing attracts people from Boise and beyond in search of some of Idaho's best dining. House specialties include prime rib (served Friday, Saturday, and Sunday), pork chops, and beef en brochette. Seafood and chicken are also on the menu, and patrons are invited to make a combo dinner by adding such side orders as shrimp scampi, fresh mushroom topping, or a rock lobster tail to their main dish. A deck beckons for guests who want to dine outside overlooking the river. The Sandbar is open for lunch and dinner from 11:00 a.m. to 9:00 p.m. Tuesday, Wednesday, and Thursday and from 11:00 a.m. to 10:00 p.m. Friday and Saturday. Dinner only is served from noon to 8:00 p.m. Sunday, and the restaurant is closed Monday. Call (208) 896-4124 for reservations, which are recommended.

While in Marsing, look for **Lizard Butte,** the volcanic formation looming over town. Waterfall lovers may wish to travel west of Marsing to see **Jump Creek Falls.** The falls, a silver ribbon cascading into a placid pool, are part of the Bureau of Land Management's Jump Creek Special Recreation Management Area, an area of desert plateau and canyonlands. Look for the Jump Creek Road sign west of the intersection of Highway 55 and US 95.

Givens Hot Springs, 12 miles from Marsing, got its start as a campground on the Oregon Trail. Pioneers frequently stopped here to wash their clothes; one emigrant said the water was "sufficiently hot to boil eggs." Before that, Native Americans used the area as a base camp. Milford and Martha Givens, pioneers themselves, had seen the springs on their way west. Once they got where they were going, however, they decided they liked Idaho better and came back.

The first Givens Hot Springs bathhouse was built way back in the 1890s, and a hotel stood on the grounds for a while as well. Givens Hot Springs is still a campground, with an enclosed year-round swimming pool, private baths, picnic grounds, softball and volleyball play areas, horseshoe pits, cabins, and RV camping. For more information call (208) 495-2000 or see www.givenshotsprings.com.

If you enjoy old mining towns but find most far too bustling for your tastes, don't miss **Silver City.** Although fairly well-known, Silver, as the locals call it, is decidedly off the beaten path, an often rough and winding 23-mile drive southwest of Highway 78. Look for the sign and War Eagle Mines historical marker near milepost 34 east of Murphy, and drive carefully. The road is generally open from Memorial Day through late October.

Tucked away in the Owyhee Mountains, Silver was a rollicking place from 1864 through the early 1900s. Not only was it county seat for a vast reach of territorial southern Idaho, Silver was also home to the territory's first telegraph and the first daily newspaper. Telephones were in use by the 1880s, and the town was electrified in the 1890s. Silver City had its own doctors, lawyers, merchants . . . even a red-light district. During its heyday the town had a population of 2,500 people and seventy-five businesses, all made possible by the fabulous riches on War Eagle Mountain.

All this seems unlikely—even unbelievable—today. Silver City isn't technically a ghost town, since about sixty families maintain part-time residences in the vicinity. But there are just a handful of telephones to the outside world; within town, about two dozen more run on the town's magneto crank system, reportedly the last in Idaho. There's no local mail delivery and no electricity. It's not even the county seat anymore, since that honor went to Murphy in 1934. (The Idaho legislature finally made the change official in 1999.) Needless to say, there's no gas station, either.

Silver City's charm is that it has barely enough amenities to make an overnight or weekend stay possible, yet it hasn't become nearly as commercialized as many other Western "ghost towns." The best way to enjoy Silver is simply to walk its dusty streets, survey the many interesting buildings, and try to imagine what life was like here more than a hundred years ago. The second weekend after Labor Day marks the town's open house, when about ten buildings not normally open to the public may be seen for a nominal fee. Proceeds help pay the town watchman. The Fourth of July is another fun, but busy and crowded, time, with family activities including a parade and games. If you want solitude, you'd be better off visiting another time.

Murphy's Law

Murphy, the seat of Owyhee County, has a sense of humor. Why else would there be a lone parking meter in front of the county courthouse? This town of about fifty people is also home to the Owyhee County Museum, housed in a building that also includes the local library. The museum features varied displays of early county artifacts ranging from Indian tools to cowboy gear. Visitors also learn about life in the early mining towns, seen from several perspectives including that of the many Chinese miners who lived and worked in Idaho during the nineteenth century.

The museum is open from 10:00 a.m. to 4:00 p.m. Tuesday through Saturday year-round. Admission is by donation. Call (208) 495–2319 for more information or current operating hours.

The *Idaho Hotel* serves as Silver City's focal point. Gorgeous antiques—an ice chest, slot machine, and pianos—vie for attention with whimsical signs and racks of guidebooks. The hotel was originally built in nearby Ruby City in 1863 and moved to Silver in 1866. Although many visitors simply stop in for a cold drink, short-order meal, books, or postcards, it's still possible to stay overnight in the Idaho Hotel, and the current owners have welcomed guests from all over the world. Rates range from $55 to $125 per room. The hotel can also provide full family style meals, with about a week's advance notice, to nonguests as well as guests.

The Empire Room may be the inn's finest. Used on occasion as a honeymoon suite, it is named for the style in which it is furnished, with some pieces dating from the Late Empire era of the 1840s. Woodstoves provide heat, and kerosene and twelve-volt lamps shed light. The bedrooms are too small and historic to accommodate full baths, so there are toilets, sinks, and showers in other rooms down the hallways.

Rooms in the Idaho Hotel are available from Memorial Day until mid-October; after that, the city water system is turned off for the winter. Reservations are advised. For more information from May through October, call (208) 583-4104 or write The Idaho Hotel, P.O. Box 75, Murphy 83650-0075. (Call instead of writing if time is of the essence, since it often takes a week or more for mail to reach Silver City from Murphy.) In the off-season, you can call (208) 853-2161 for information. The Bureau of Land Management also has a small campground at Silver City, and its sites are free.

Back on Highway 78 watch for the signs to Oreana. Located in a scenic valley 2 miles south of the highway, Oreana has a population of seven, maybe eight, according to the sign at the "city limits." It's also the setting for *Our Lady, Queen of Heaven Catholic Church,* a striking stone building that started life as a general store. Mike Hyde, an area rancher, built the store from native stone in the late 1800s. When only its walls were completed, word was heard around Oreana that a war party of Indians was on its way to the town. All the local folks reportedly took refuge behind the stone walls, expecting an attack. But the Boise-based militia arrived first, and the Indians were deterred.

The store served the Oreana area well into the twentieth century, but by 1961 it had been empty and unused for some time. That year, Albert Black—on whose land it stood—gave the old building to the Catholic Diocese in Nampa. The diocese encouraged local Catholics to turn the store into a church, and Our Lady, Queen of Heaven, was the result. The small belfry atop the church houses the bell that originally hung at Our Lady of Tears in Silver City. The bell survived a 1943 flood and still rings to herald occasional services at the church. Unfortunately the church is not open for tours, but it's still worth a look from the outside if you're in the area. Masses are held several times a year. Call (208) 466-7031 for dates.

Snake River Vistas

For a pleasant riverside picnic or some good home cooking, consider a stop at Grand View, located at the intersection of Highways 78 and 67. The town's small park has fishing access, a nature trail, and several tables overlooking the Snake River. Grand View's small city center has an old-fashioned Western boardwalk.

Just outside Grand View, Jack and Belva Lawson have created one of the state's most unusual tourist attractions at ***Lawson's EMU-Z-Um.*** Here, on the land they've worked since 1967, the Lawsons have set up a replica of an 1860s town, complete with the contents of the Silver City Schoolhouse Museum. Visitors also see a silver mine replica, model trains, pioneer and Native American artifacts, and one of the area's first hand-built automobiles.

EMU-Z-Um—it got its name from the emus the Lawsons raise—is open from 9:00 a.m. to 5:00 p.m. Saturday and Sunday March 1 through October

Antique egg-vending machine at Lawson's EMU-Z-Um

15, or by appointment the rest of the week spring through fall. Admission is $5.00 for ages thirteen and up and $2.50 for children ages six to twelve. To get there, look for the sign between mile markers 52 and 53 on Highway 78. For more information, or to make an off-season appointment, call the Lawsons at (208) 834-2397.

Mountain Home, 23 miles from Grand View via Highway 67, is an Air Force town and a popular stop for travelers on I-84. Few visitors make it past the clot of gas stations and restaurants at exit 95, but those who do will find a few interesting places in town.

The military's presence is unmistakable in Mountain Home: Look no farther than **Carl Miller Park,** possibly the only place in the United States where you can picnic in the shadow of an F-111 fighter jet. The park was established in 1919 as a memorial for the first local soldier killed in World War I. This is also the site of Mountain Home's annual **Air Force Appreciation Day,** held the Saturday after Labor Day weekend each year. About 10,000 people turn out annually for the parade and free barbecue.

Mountain Home also has a growing collection of murals, mostly done by local painter Randall Miller. The largest, 49 feet by 8 feet, is on the side of the NAPA Auto Parts store at 295 East Jackson Street. It depicts Commodore Jackson, who staked a claim on what would become the Mountain Home town site in the 1880s. Stop at the visitor center on the southeast side of exit 95 to get a brochure listing the murals, or see Miller's Web site at http://web.mac.com/thinkq for more information.

Mountain Home is the main gateway for trips to **Anderson Ranch Reservoir** and the **Trinity Lakes** area. Anderson Reservoir dams the South Fork of the Boise River, and while the human-made lake isn't especially scenic, it does have plenty of inlets and bays that provide visual relief from the high-and-dry hills all around. At one of the prettiest coves, **Fall Creek Resort and Marina** (on the reservoir's west side, 8 miles from the dam) offers ten rooms priced at $65 and up double occupancy, which includes use of a sauna, hot tub, and exercise equipment. A restaurant and lounge serve up breakfast, lunch, dinner, and karaoke. Other amenities include swimming and fishing and an RV park. Call (208) 653-2242 for more information. A few other little resorts dot Anderson Reservoir's east side near the settlements of Pine and Featherville.

From Fall Creek north it's 17 miles to Trinity Mountain. (Take Forest Service Roads 123 and 129. The steep, rough route is passable by most vehicles, but forget towing a trailer.) If the scenery was ho-hum around Anderson Reservoir, it is sublime here in the highlands. Stake a spot at one of four campgrounds, or rent the Forest Service's Big Trinity Cabin, which sleeps six for $30 per night. It can be reserved by calling (877) 444-6777. For other information call (208)

587-7961 or write the Mountain Home Ranger District, 2180 American Legion Boulevard, Mountain Home 83647.

Not surprisingly the Trinity Lakes region is popular with hikers and other recreationists. The 4-mile, pedestrians-only *Rainbow Basin Trail* takes trekkers into a subalpine cirque basin dotted with nine lakes and populated by lots of critters including elk, deer, mountain lion, and black bear. From Trinity Mountain you can follow more forest roads over to Featherville or Atlanta (see the Boise Basin section), or turn around for the descent back to Mountain Home.

Southeast of Mountain Home, the top attraction is *Bruneau Dunes State Park.* Most sand dunes form at the edge of a natural basin, but these form at the center, making them unique in the Western Hemisphere. The Bruneau complex also includes the largest single structured sand dune in North America, with its peak 470 feet high. The combination of sand and a natural trap has caused sand to collect here for about 15,000 years, and the prevailing wind patterns—from the southeast 28 percent of the time and from the northwest 32 percent—ensure the dunes don't move far. The two prominent dunes cover about 600 acres.

Hiking, camping, and fishing are favorite activities at the Bruneau Dunes. Hiking to the top of a sand dune is an experience unlike any other. Once there, many hikers simply linger a while to savor the view before walking the crest of the dunes back to terra firma. Others use the dunes' inside bowl for sledding, sand skiing, or snowboarding. Bass and bluegill thrive in the small lakes at the foot of the dunes, and the campground—with one of the longest seasons in Idaho—has a steady stream of visitors March through late fall. Bruneau Dunes State Park has a good visitor center featuring displays of wildlife and natural history. There's also an observatory that features astronomy programs at dusk Friday and Saturday evenings, spring through fall. Take I-84 exit 95 or 112 to the dunes. A $4-per-vehicle park entrance fee is charged, and observatory programs are $3. For more information call (208) 366-7919; write Bruneau Dunes State Park, HC 85, Box 41, Mountain Home 83647; or see the Web site at http://parksandrecreation.idaho.gov/parks/bruneaudunesstatepark.aspx.

At what is now *Three Island Crossing State Park,* pioneers traveling west on the Oregon Trail faced the most difficult river crossing of their 2,000-mile journey. Many chose not to ford the river and continued along the south bank of the Snake River through the same country we've just traversed. But about half the emigrants decided to brave the Snake to the shorter, easier route on the river's north side. It's still possible to see the islands used in the crossing, as well as scars worn by the wagon wheels.

The crossing is re-enacted in one of Idaho's most popular annual festivals, usually held the second Saturday each August. Although the Snake isn't as mighty as it once was, fording it remains dangerous. Wagons sometimes capsize, and livestock occasionally drown. It's hard for spectators to rest easy until every man, horse, and wagon has made it across safely. Once all have, however, everyone flocks to the festival's other attractions: food, arts and crafts booths, entertainment, and the park itself. If you can't make it at crossing time, you can still enjoy the park's year-round Oregon Trail History and Education Center and recreational activities, including camping, fishing, swimming, and picnicking. The park even rents cabins at a cost of $45 per night for up to five people. Three Island Crossing State Park is reached via exit 120 off of I-84. Drive south into Glenns Ferry and follow the signs to the park. For more information call (208) 366-2394 or visit the park Web site at http://parksandrec reation.idaho.gov/parks/threeislandcrossing.aspx

End your visit to Glenns Ferry with a stop at *Carmela Winery,* right next door to Three Island Crossing State Park. Located in a building that looks like a cross between a medieval castle and a French chateau, Carmela's tasting room is open daily, with tours available by request. You can also sample the wines with a meal in the on-site restaurant, which has a beautiful panoramic view. The restaurant is open from 11:00 a.m. to 9:00 p.m. Monday through Saturday, and from 10:00 a.m. to 8:00 p.m. Sunday. After your meal browse the adjacent gift shop's good selection of artwork, books, and Idaho products.

Carmela may very well be the only winery with a golf course right on the premises, too. Weekend summertime greens fees are $15 for nine holes and $23 for eighteen holes, with gas and pull carts available. If Three Island's campground is full, try the RV park adjacent to Carmela. For more information on the winery, call (208) 366-2313.

Places to Stay in Southwestern Idaho

MCCALL

Best Western McCall
415 North Third Street
(800) 528-1234
fax: (208) 634-2967
Moderate

Hotel McCall
1101 North Third Street
(866) 800-1183
(see text)
Moderate–Expensive

The Hunt Lodge–Holiday Inn Express
210 North Third Street
(208) 634-4700
Moderate–Expensive

Scandia Inn Motel
401 North Third Street
(208) 634-7394
Inexpensive

Whitetail Club
501 West Lake Street
(208) 634-2244
fax: (208) 634-7504
Expensive

NEW MEADOWS

Hartland Inn & Motel
Highway 55 and US 95
(208) 347-2114
fax: (208) 347-2535
Inexpensive–Moderate

Meadows Motel
US 95
(208) 347-2175
Inexpensive

CAMBRIDGE

Frontier Motel & RV Park
(208) 257-3851
Inexpensive

Hunters Inn Motel
US 95
(208) 257-3325
(see text)
Inexpensive

COUNCIL

Starlite Motel
102 North Dartmouth
(208) 253-4868
Inexpensive

YELLOW PINE

Yellow Pine Lodge
(208) 633-3377
(see text)
Inexpensive

WARM LAKE

North Shore Lodge
(800) 933-3193
Inexpensive–Moderate

Warm Lake Lodge
(208) 632-3553
(see text)
Inexpensive–Moderate

CASCADE

Ashley Inn
500 North Main Street
(866) 382-5621
Moderate–Expensive

Mountain View Motel
(208) 382-4238
fax: (208) 382-4713
Inexpensive

Pinewood Lodge Motel
& RV Park
900 South US 95
(208) 382-4948
Inexpensive

DONNELLY

Boulder Creek Inn &
Suites
629 Highway 55
(866) 325-8638
Moderate

Tamarack Resort
2099 West Mountain Road
(208) 325-1000
Expensive

LOWMAN

Sourdough Lodge
& RV Resort
(208) 259-3326
Inexpensive–Moderate

GRANDJEAN

Sawtooth Lodge
(208) 259-3331
(see text)
Inexpensive–Moderate

IDAHO CITY

Idaho City Hotel/
Prospector Motel
(208) 392-4290
fax: (208) 392-4505
Inexpensive

One Step Away Bed &
Breakfast
112 Cottonwood Street
phone/fax: (208) 392-4938
Inexpensive–Moderate

ATLANTA

Beaver Lodge
(208) 864-2132
Inexpensive

Pinnacle Peaks Sawtooth
Lodge
(208) 864-2168
(see text)
Expensive

HELPFUL WEB SITES FOR SOUTHWESTERN IDAHO

Boise Convention & Visitors Bureau
www.boise.org/

Idaho Statesman (Boise daily
newspaper)—www.idahostatesman
.com

McCall Area Chamber of Commerce
www.mccallchamber.org/

Idaho Press–Tribune (Nampa/
Caldwell–area newspaper)
www.idahopress.com/

**Mountain Home Chamber of
Commerce**
www.mountain-home.org/chamber

BOISE

Best Western Vista Inn
2645 Airport Way
(800) 727-5006
fax: (208) 342-3060
Moderate

Cambria Suites
2970 West Elder Street
(208) 344-7444
Moderate

Grove Hotel
245 South Capitol
Boulevard
(208) 333-8000
fax: (208) 333-8800
Moderate–Expensive

Hampton Inn & Suites
495 South Capitol
Boulevard
(208) 331-1900
Moderate

Harrison Plaza Suite Hotel
409 South Cole Road
(800) 376-3608
fax: (208) 376-3608
Moderate–Expensive

Hotel 43
981 Grove Street
(208) 342-4622
fax: (208) 344-5751
Moderate–Expensive

Idaho Heritage Inn
109 West Idaho
(208) 342-8066
(see text)
Moderate

J. J. Shaw House
Bed & Breakfast Inn
1411 West Franklin Street
(877) 344-8899
Moderate

Leku Ona
117 South Sixth Street
(208) 345-6665
(see text)
Inexpensive–Moderate

The Modern Hotel
1314 West Grove Street
(208) 424-8244
(see text)
Moderate–Expensive

Motel 6
2323 Airport Way
(800) 466-8356
Inexpensive

Super 8
2773 Elder Street
(800) 800-8000
fax: (208) 344-8871
Inexpensive

MERIDIAN

Best Western Rama Inn
1019 South Progress
Avenue
(800) 937-8376
fax: (208) 887-7600
Moderate

Mr. Sandman Inn & Suites
1575 South Meridian Road
(800) 959-2230
Moderate

EAGLE

Hilton Garden Inn
145 East Riverside Drive
(208) 938-9600
Moderate

STAR

**The Maples Bed &
Breakfast**
10600 West State Street
(208) 286-7419
Moderate

EMMETT

Frozen Dog Digs
Bed & Breakfast
4325 Frozen Dog Road
(208) 365-7372
(see text)
Moderate–Expensive

Holiday Motel & RV Park
1111 South Washington
Avenue
(208) 365-4479
Inexpensive

WEISER

Colonial Motel
251 East Main Street
(208) 549-0150
Inexpensive

**Indianhead Motel &
RV Park**
747 US 95
(208) 549-0331
Inexpensive

State Street Motel
1279 State Street
(208) 549-1390
Inexpensive

PARMA

The Court Motel
712 Grove Street
(208) 722-5579
Inexpensive

CALDWELL

Holiday Motel
512 Frontage Road
(208) 453-1056
Inexpensive

La Quinta Inn
901 Specht Avenue
(800) 531-5900
fax: (208) 454-9334
Inexpensive–Moderate

Sundowner Motel
1002 Arthur Street
(208) 459-1585
fax: (208) 454-9487
Inexpensive

NAMPA

Budget Inn
908 Third Street South
(208) 466-3594
Inexpensive

A Country Place–
Hostel Boise
17322 Can Ada Road
(208) 467-6858
(see text)
Inexpensive

Nampa Super 8
624 Nampa Boulevard
(800) 800-8000
fax: (208) 467-2888
Inexpensive

Shilo Inn–Nampa Suites
1401 Shilo Drive
(800) 222-2244
fax: (208) 465-5929
Moderate

SILVER CITY

Idaho Hotel
(208) 583-4104
(see text)
Inexpensive–Moderate

MOUNTAIN HOME

Best Western Foothills
Motor Inn
1080 US 20
(800) 528-1234
fax: (208) 587-5774
Moderate

Motel Thunderbird
910 Sunset Strip
(208) 587-7927
Inexpensive

Sleep Inn
1180 US 20
(800) 753-3746
fax: (208) 587-7382
Inexpensive–Moderate

ANDERSON RANCH
RESERVOIR AREA

Fall Creek Resort and
Marina
(208) 653-2242
(see text)
Inexpensive

Featherville Motel
(Featherville)
(208) 653-2310
Inexpensive

Nester's Mountain Motel
(Pine)
(208) 653-2210
Inexpensive–Moderate

GLENNS FERRY

Redford Motel
601 West First Avenue
(208) 366-2421
Inexpensive

Places to Eat in
Southwestern Idaho

MCCALL

Lardo's Grill & Saloon
(American)
600 West Lake Street
(208) 634-8191
Inexpensive–Moderate

The Mill Supper Club
(American)
324 North Third Street
(208) 634-7683
(see text)
Moderate

The Pancake & Christmas
House (American)
209 North Third Street
(208) 634-5849
Inexpensive

Romano's Ristorante
(Italian/American)
downtown on the lake
(208) 634-4396
Moderate

Rupert's (Northwestern)
1101 North Third Street
(at Hotel McCall)
(208) 634-8108
Moderate–Expensive

ALSO WORTH SEEING IN
SOUTHWESTERN IDAHO

Boise Art Museum

Idaho State Historical Museum
Boise

Zoo Boise

Discovery Center of Idaho
Boise

Morrison-Knudsen Nature Center
Boise

Warhawk Air Museum
Nampa

Roaring Springs Water Park
Meridian

NEW MEADOWS

Sagebrush BBQ
(American)
210 Virginia Avenue
(208) 347-2818
Inexpensive–Moderate

CAMBRIDGE

Bucky's Cafe (American)
US 95
(208) 257-3330
Inexpensive

DONNELLY

Flight of Fancy (coffee-
house-bakery)
282 North Main Street
(208) 325-4432
Inexpensive

YELLOW PINE

Yellow Pine Lodge
(American)
(208) 633-3377
(see text)
Inexpensive

WARM LAKE

North Shore Lodge
(American)
(800) 933-3193
Inexpensive–Moderate

Warm Lake Lodge
(American)
(208) 632-3553
(see text)
Inexpensive–Moderate

CASCADE

Route 55 Cafe (family)
806 South Main Street
(208) 382-4496
Inexpensive

GRANDJEAN

Sawtooth Lodge
(American)
(208) 259-3331
(see text)
Inexpensive–Moderate

IDAHO CITY

Trudy's Kitchen
(American)
419 Highway 21
(208) 392-4151
(see text)
Inexpensive–Moderate

ATLANTA

Beaver Lodge (American
(208) 864-2132
Inexpensive–Moderate

BOISE

Brick Oven Bistro
(home-style cooking)
801 Main Street
(208) 342-3456
Inexpensive

Cottonwood Grille
(upscale)
913 West River Drive
(208) 333-9800
Moderate–Expensive

Donnie Mac's Trailer Park
Cuisine (American)
1515 West Grove Street
(208) 384-9008
(see text)
Inexpensive

Flying Pie Pizzaria (pizza)
6508 Fairview Avenue
(208) 345-0000
Inexpensive

Gernika Basque Pub
& Eatery
202 South Capitol
Boulevard
(208) 344-2175
(see text)
Inexpensive

Leku Ona (Basque)
117 South Sixth Street
(208) 345-6665
(see text)
Moderate

Milky Way (fine dining)
205 North Tenth Street
(208) 343-4334
(see text)
Moderate–Expensive

Mortimer's
110 South Fifth Street
(208) 338-6550
(see text)
Expensive

Pair (eclectic American)
601 Main Street
(208) 855-9877
(see text)
Inexpensive–Moderate

Reef (Island/Northwest)
125 South Sixth Street
(208) 287-9200
(see text)
Inexpensive–Moderate

MERIDIAN

Epi's (Basque)
1115 North Main Street
(208) 884-1142
Moderate

The Library Coffeehouse
(light fare)
141 East Carlton Avenue
(208) 288-1898
(see text)
Inexpensive

Louie's (Italian)
2500 East Fairview Avenue
(208) 884-5200
Moderate

EAGLE

Eagle Rib Shack
(barbecue)
360 East State Street
(208) 938-0008
Inexpensive–Moderate

Franco Latino
(European-Latin)
775 South Rivershore Lane
(208) 938-2850
Moderate

SixOneSix (fine dining)
1065 Winding Creek Road
(208) 938-3010
(see text)
Moderate–Expensive

WEISER

Idaho Pizza Company
1255 State Street
(208) 549-8765
Inexpensive

Weiser Classic Candy
(sandwich shop)
449 State Street
(208) 414-2850
(see text)
Inexpensive

EMMETT

The Timbers (American)
300 Highway 16
(208) 365-6915
Inexpensive–Moderate

NAMPA

Copper Canyon
(fine dining)
113 Thirteenth Avenue
South
(208) 461-0887
Moderate–Expensive

House of Kim (Chinese)
1226 First Street South
(208) 466-3237
Inexpensive

Little Kitchen (American)
1224 First Street South
(208) 467-9677
(see text)
Inexpensive

Say You Say Me
(American)
820 Nampa–Caldwell
Boulevard
(208) 466-2728
Inexpensive

CALDWELL

Creekside Grill (fine dining)
2805 Blaine Street
(208) 455-0100
Moderate

Fiesta Guadalajara
(Mexican)
420 North Tenth Avenue
(208) 455-8605
Inexpensive

Sage Cafe (American)
2929 Franklin Road
(208) 454-2084
Inexpensive–Moderate

MARSING

Sandbar River House
Restaurant (American)
Highway 78
(208) 896-4124
(see text)
Inexpensive–Moderate

MOUNTAIN HOME

Martin Family Mexican
Restaurant
145 North Second East
(208) 587-922
Inexpensive

Smoky Mountain Pizza &
Pasta (Italian)
1465 American Legion
Boulevard
(208) 587-2840
Inexpensive

ANDERSON RANCH
RESERVOIR AREA

Deer Creek Lodge
(American)
Pine-Featherville Road
(208) 653-2454
Inexpensive–Moderate

Fall Creek Resort and
Marina (American)
(208) 653-2242
(see text)
Inexpensive–Moderate

GLENNS FERRY

Carmela Winery
(American)
(208) 366-2313
(see text)
Inexpensive–Moderate

South Central Idaho

To the casual traveler along Interstate 84, South Central Idaho seems an arid, apparently barren expanse on the way to somewhere else—most likely Boise or Salt Lake City. To many visitors the best show seems to be in the sky, where clouds roll over wide vistas hemmed by distant mountain peaks.

This big landscape hides its treasures well, but they're not hard to find if you get off the freeway. U.S. Highway 30, a slower and more scenic alternative to I-84, crosses the region from Bliss east to Heyburn (near Burley) before returning to the freeway; Twin Falls, the region's largest city and crossroads to points north and south, is about midway, offering a good beginning and end to loop day trips. From Twin Falls, U.S. Highway 93 drops south over high desert into Nevada, while Highway 75 climbs north over rugged lava fields to Sun Valley and the rest of mountainous Central Idaho. From these spokes, small byways and farm roads provide the passport to fertile farmland, abundant recreation, and one of the world's great canyons.

For more South Central Idaho travel information, call (800) 255-8946; write the Southern Idaho Tourism, P.O. Box 5155, Twin Falls 83303-5155; or see their Web site at www.visitsouth idaho.com.

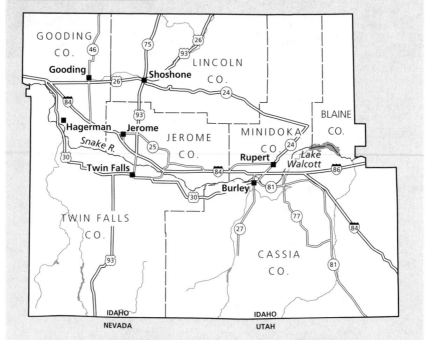

GOODING CO.
46

Gooding
26

75
26

93

Shoshone
LINCOLN CO.
24

84

93

Hagerman
Jerome
JEROME CO.
MINIDOKA CO.
BLAINE CO.

Snake R.
25
24
Rupert
Lake Walcott

30
Twin Falls
84
86

30
Burley
81

TWIN FALLS CO.
77
84

27

93
CASSIA CO.
81

IDAHO
NEVADA
IDAHO
UTAH

N

0   20 mi

0   20 km

In many cases, South Central Idaho's best-kept secrets are just a few miles off the interstate. In the case of Malad Gorge, the highway literally passes right overhead.

The Big Wood River and Little Wood River become the Malad River, tumbling into a canyon 250 feet deep and just 140 feet wide at Malad Gorge. This area, called the Devil's Washbowl, is part of the recently created ***Thousand Springs State Park,*** which includes five units near Hagerman. All of them are just a short drive from I-84, but Malad Gorge is the closest, making it a handy spot for a break from the interstate. To get there take exit 147 at Tuttle. *Malad* is French for "sick," and Malad Gorge got its name when nineteenth-century fur trappers became ill after eating beaver caught nearby. The Malad River itself is thought to be one of the world's shortest, running just 12 miles before being swallowed up by the mighty Snake River downstream. A short trail from the main parking area leads to a footbridge over the plunge. Wagon-wheel ruts from the Kelton Road, an old freight route from Utah to Idaho, may be seen nearby, as may traces of the old stage stop. Park staff discovered these several years ago while cleaning up a local garbage dump. Malad Gorge has facilities for hiking and picnicking, but no camping is permitted. The park's roads are excellent for walking, jogging, or bicycling; indeed this is the site of a popular annual run/walk event held the Saturday before each St. Patrick's Day. Most days, however, you'll likely have the place to yourself. For more information on Malad Gorge and the other Thousand Springs State Park units (which include Billingsley Creek, Box Canyon, Ritter Island, and Niagara and Crystal Springs), call (208) 837-4505 or check the park Web site at http://parksandrecreation.idaho.gov/parks/thousandsprings.aspx.

From Malad Gorge it's a short drive to the ***Gooding Hotel Bed & Breakfast.*** A historic inn built in Ketchum and moved to its current site in 1888, twenty years before the town of Gooding was even founded, the hotel is now owned by Dean Gooding, the great-great-nephew of former Idaho gover-

JULIE'S FAVORITES IN SOUTH CENTRAL IDAHO

City of Rocks National Reserve
south of Burley

Herrett Center for Arts & Science
Twin Falls

Shoshone Falls
east of Twin Falls

Snake River Canyon
Twin Falls

The South Hills (Sawtooth National Forest)—south of Hansen

Thousand Springs Preserve
west of Wendell

nor and U.S. Senator Frank Gooding, and Dean's wife, Judee. Gooding was an old railroad town, and the hotel is hard by the tracks. Then as now its location was ideal, within walking distance of restaurants, bars, and shops. Ten rooms are available, priced at $57 to $82 including breakfast. Most have their own bathroom. Ask about gift certificates and "pamper me" packages. The hotel also has a visitor information center. For more information or reservations, call (208) 934-4374 or (888) 260-6656. If you're in Gooding in midsummer, don't miss the annual Basque Picnic, usually served the third Sunday of July at the Gooding County Fairgrounds. The event includes a barbecue of lamb chops, chorizos (a highly seasoned pork sausage), beans, rice, and more, plus dancing, music, and games.

Northwest of town off Highway 46, the **Gooding City of Rocks** and **Little City of Rocks** offer panoramas of highly eroded canyon lands, Native American petroglyphs, and spring wildflowers. Both areas are located west off of Highway 46, and they're particularly appealing to kids, who will have a ball exploring the fantastic rock formations—but keep your eyes open for rattlesnakes and the elk herds who live on the high desert lands nearby. Highway 46 continues north to a sweeping vista of the Camas Prairie, its blue flowers usually in bloom shortly before Memorial Day.

South of Gooding the town of Wendell provides access to both sides of the Snake River Canyon and to the Hagerman Valley, where recreation and relaxation are a way of life. But since Snake River crossings are few and far between here, we'll first take a look at some north- and east-rim attractions that are best accessed from I-84.

TOP ANNUAL EVENTS IN SOUTH CENTRAL IDAHO

Western Days
Twin Falls (late May/early June)

Jazz in the Canyon
Twin Falls (mid-June)

Idaho Regatta
Burley (last weekend in June)

Twin Falls City Band Concerts
(each Thursday June through early August)

Sagebrush Days
Buhl (Fourth of July week)

Gooding Basque Picnic
(third Sunday in July)

Twin Falls County Fair and Magic Valley Stampede
Filer (six days ending Labor Day)

Thousand Springs Festival of the Arts, Hagerman Valley (late September)

Ritter Island is the centerpiece of what was until recently the Nature Conservancy's Thousand Springs Preserve on the Snake River. The island is now a unit of Thousand Springs State Park and the site of one of the state's best arts festivals, held in late September; see www.thousandspringsfestival. org. There's excellent bird-watching, canoeing, and kayaking nearly year-round. To get there take I-84 exit 155 from Wendell. Turn right and drive 3 miles. Take a left onto 1500 East, drive 2.5 miles, then turn right onto 3200 South. Take this road 2 miles. You will see a sign. Turn right at the sign and then take a quick right.

Hagerman is accessible via US 30 south from Bliss or north from Buhl and via the Vader Grade west from Wendell. With its year-round mild climate and abundant recreation, the Hagerman Valley offers many pleasures, and it's easy to enjoy several diversions on any given day. Fishing is a major lure, with some of the state's most productive waters—the Snake River, Billingsley Creek, Oster Lakes, and the Anderson Ponds—located nearby. Floating is another popular pastime, and rafters often can take to the Snake as early as April 1 (and as late as Halloween), with the area just below the Lower Salmon Falls Power Plant the most popular spot to put in. Many people navigate this stretch on their own, but at least two companies—*High Adventure River Tours* at (208) 837-9005 and *Idaho Guide Service* at (208) 734-4998—offer guided white-water floats. *Thousand Springs Tours* specializes in scenic floats and dinner cruises on calmer waters in the area. Call (208) 837-9006 for information.

A float trip below Lower Salmon Falls is the best way to sneak a peak at *Teater's Knoll,* the only Idaho structure designed by Frank Lloyd Wright. The home and studio, which are perched high above the Snake, were built for Western artist Archie Teater and his wife, Patricia, who lived there part-time from the late 1950s through the 1970s. The home, later purchased and restored by modern-day Idaho architect Henry Whiting, is on the National Register of Historic Places. It is currently inaccessible to the public.

For a good meal in Hagerman, try the Snake River Grill at State and Hagerman Streets. Meals include catfish, sturgeon, pasta, and wild game. Many locals and day-trippers drop in for the yummy catfish sandwiches, but classically trained Chef Kirt Martin also is known for creating specially prepared feasts with all sorts of wild game. (So now you know what to do with that venison or elk roast your brother-in-law brings over every hunting season. Call 208-837-6227 to make arrangements.)

As if all this wasn't enough to entice visitors to Hagerman, the town is host to an unusual archaeological find. The *Hagerman Fossil Beds National Monument* marks the spot where an area farmer discovered fossils that turned out to be those of the zebralike Hagerman Horse, now the official Idaho state fossil. In the 1930s the Smithsonian Institution sent several expeditions to collect specimens of the horse. Archaeologists unearthed 130 skulls and 15 skeletons of an early, zebralike horse that dated back to the Pliocene Age, about 3.4 million years ago. Other fossils in the area preserved early forms of camel, peccary, beaver, turtle, and freshwater fish.

The monument has a visitor center at 221 North State Street in Hagerman, open from 9:00 a.m. to 6:00 p.m. daily Memorial Day weekend through late August and 9:00 a.m. to 5:00 p.m. Thursday through Monday the rest of the year. Stop there to see the exhibits and get directions to other monument areas open to the public; opportunities include several hiking trails and interpretive areas. The monument also occasionally has tours and special programs, mostly on Saturday in summer. For more information or a schedule, call (208) 837-4793 or see www.nps.gov/hafo.

Hagerman celebrates ***Fossil Days*** each year over Memorial Day weekend. On Saturday of that weekend, there's a classic small-town parade, both provincial and poignant. In recent years a local nursing home's wheelchair drill team and a horse painted like the famous prehistoric zebra have been among the crowd-pleasing entries.

South of Hagerman, US 30 enters Twin Falls County. The highway here is known as the ***Thousand Springs Scenic Route,*** taking its name from the

Sage, Wind, and Stone

A few weeks after our daughter, Natalie, was born in 1994, my husband and I took a Sunday-afternoon drive to the Snake River between Hagerman and Bliss. We'd come to watch kayakers negotiate a new stretch of rapids created by a rock slide a year or so before.

We parked our car and walked the narrow dirt path down to the river, our child cradled in a baby carrier against my chest. Along the way, I picked a sprig of sagebrush and held it to Natalie's nose. Her tiny nostrils flared at the sweet, pungent scent. "This is what Idaho smells like," I told her.

At that moment, I realized my own Idaho walks have given me an intimate knowledge of the place where I live—things I would never know if I never left my car. What freshly picked sage smells like, for example, and how south winds blow much warmer than west winds, and how lava rock ranges from smooth and sinewy to rough and jagged. I have adopted this state, and so I came to this understanding as an adult. For my little native Idahoan, however, these facts were the fabric of her childhood. No matter where she may live, Natalie will have immutable memories of sage, of wind, and of stone.

white cascades that gush from the black basalt of the Snake River Canyon. At one time there probably were truly a thousand springs, give or take a few. Today there are far fewer, but the sight remains impressive.

Where do the springs originate? Many have traveled underground from near Arco, where the Big Lost River and several other streams abruptly sink underground. From there the water moves ever so slowly, possibly just 10 feet a day, through the Snake River Aquifer before bursting forth from the canyon walls. In other words, the water you see here entered the aquifer about the year 1800 and has been making its way across the underground aquifer ever since.

Hot springs also are abundant in the area, and several resorts line US 30 between Hagerman and Buhl. Most feature swimming, camping, and picnic facilities; at least two (***Banbury Hot Springs*** and ***Miracle Hot Springs***) boast private VIP baths, and Miracle also rents camping domes, some equipped with beds. ***Sligar's 1000 Springs Resort*** offers indoor swimming year-round in a spacious pool.

South Central Idaho produces a whopping 90 percent of the world's commercially raised trout, and ***Clear Springs Foods***—by far the largest of the trout processors—provides a glimpse of the fish business at its visitor center north of Buhl on the Snake River. Little kids in particular love to press their noses against the underground fish-viewing window, where trout swim by within inches and huge sturgeon can be seen dwelling in the murkier depths. The center has good picnicking grounds, too.

In Buhl itself, the little coffeehouse/bookstore ***Cosmic Jolt*** at 120 South Broadway provides a taste of the metaphysical in this unlikely farm-town setting. Check out the cool decoupaged tables, each with a different theme, where you can enjoy a latte or luscious muffin. ***Smith's Dairy,*** another local institution at 205 South Broadway, scoops up ice-cream cones. Enjoy one in the gazebo outside.

The Buhl Arts Council makes its headquarters in the ***Eighth Street Center.*** Set in a beautifully renovated landmark building, the center has outstanding programming that goes well beyond the arts to include such fare as intimate concerts and classes in everything from yoga to taxidermy to French cooking. Take time to walk the outdoor labyrinth. For more information or a list of upcoming programs, call (208) 543-2888; write the Buhl Arts Council, 200 North Eighth Street, Buhl 83316; or see www.buhlartscouncil.org.

A short drive southwest of Buhl leads to ***Balanced Rock,*** a curious geological formation that appears poised like a giant mushroom (or maybe a question mark?) against the blue Idaho sky. The landmark is just a few miles west of Castleford, and a nearby small county park along Salmon Falls Creek

Balanced Rock

provides another perfect spot for a picnic. To get there follow the signs out of Buhl for 16 miles.

Clover, a small farming community due east of Castleford, is the setting for one of Idaho's most beautiful country churches. *Clover Lutheran Church* has long served the families of the area, and the parishioners have given back to the church in equal measure, most notably through the stained-glass windows that grace the north and south sides of the sanctuary. These windows, done in traditional leaded stained-glass style, were made entirely by members of the congregation. The windows on the south side depict the local farming community, including sprigs of clover; those on the north are rich in Christian symbolism. The church also has its original ceiling of embossed tin.

Sunday morning would be the best time to see Clover Lutheran, hear its pipe organ, and visit with the congregation. But the church is worth a stop at any time. If no one's in the office on the building's northwest side, check at the parsonage, located at the ranch house just to the north. The church cemetery also is notable for its headstones, some of which are in the native German of the people who settled Clover. The oldest graves are in the cemetery's southwest corner.

Just east of Filer, US 93 swings south from US 30 for the Nevada border some 40 miles away. Just over the Nevada line, *Jackpot* serves as the gambling hub for Idaho (and, judging from license plates in the casino parking lots, for revelers from as far away as Montana, Manitoba, and Saskatchewan, too). The town's biggest draw is *Cactus Pete's,* a full-fledged resort with comfortable rooms, abundant dining options (including the Plateau Room, possibly the classiest restaurant in a 100-mile radius), and semi-big-name entertainment. But some folks prefer the down-home, distinctly non-Vegas atmosphere of the town's smaller casinos, especially *Barton's Club 93.*

US 93 is also the best jumping-off spot for the Jarbidge country, one of the West's most wild and remote areas, located about 60 miles southwest of Rogerson. (All but the last 17 miles are paved.) Although on the Nevada

The Filer Fair

Filer is home to the **Twin Falls County Fair and Magic Valley Stampede,** which the *Los Angeles Times* named one of the top ten rural county fairs in the United States. The "Filer Fair," as it's known locally, runs the six days up to and including Labor Day. It's big enough to draw top-name country singers and rodeo cowboys, yet small enough to retain a real down-home feel. For many Southern Idahoans, the fair recalls a reunion, high time to get caught up on gossip and marvel at how much the kids have grown.

The fair also provides a ready excuse to forget your diet for a while: For some of the most unusual fare, check out the Job's Daughters' elephant-ear scones (deep-fried dough topped with cinnamon sugar), the one-of-a-kind troutburgers served up by the Buhl Catholic Church, or the tater pigs—a link sausage stuffed inside an Idaho baked potato—offered by the Magichords, a local barbershop singing group. You'll also find everything from cotton candy and ice cream to homemade pies and gyros. Just remember to visit the carnival rides before you eat, not after!

border like Jackpot, Jarbidge's main attraction isn't gambling but natural splendor: The *Jarbidge Mountains* boast eight peaks higher than 10,000 feet, the highest concentration in Nevada, and campers, hikers, and horseback riders will swear they've found paradise. Casual visitors will find primitive campsites along the Jarbidge River or indoor accommodations at the Outdoor Inn, which also serves food. For people eager to explore the wilderness, Lowell Prunty's Jarbidge Wilderness Guide & Packing offers horse packing, backpacking, and hunting trips. For more information call (208) 857-2270 or see www.jarbidgeadventures.com. Have a look at *Nevada Off the Beaten Path* for more ideas on seeing the Silver State.

The Magic Valley

Back on US 30, the traveler reaches Twin Falls, the largest city in South Central Idaho, with a population of about 40,000. US 30 becomes Addison Avenue within the city; at Blue Lakes Boulevard you can either turn left (north) for the city's crowded commercial strip or south (onto Shoshone Street) to find charming downtown Twin Falls.

First, though, consider dropping in at the recently renovated *Twin Falls County Historical Museum,* west of town on US 30 in the old Union School. From fancy old hats to agricultural equipment, the museum has a bit of everything that made life tick in early Twin Falls. Of special note is the display on pioneer-era photographer Clarence Bisbee, a colorful character who chronicled the city's growth for many decades. Displays rotate every other month, so there's always something new to see. Museum hours are 10:00 a.m. to 5:00 p.m. Tuesday through Saturday (or by appointment), and admission is free, although donations are welcome. Call (208) 736-4675 for more information. If the small Bisbee exhibit here piques your interest, you can see more of his work at the Twin Falls Public Library, where his photo collection is stored. (Some of it can also be viewed online atwww.twinfallspubliclibrary .org/photo.html.)

Twin Falls is as Midwestern a town as you'll find anywhere in the western United States. The city throws a big **Western Days** celebration each spring, but make no mistake: This is a Jimmy Stewart sort of place, complete with a tree-lined downtown, open-air band concerts every Thursday night June through early August, and neat neighborhoods of mostly modest homes. But like the rest of Idaho, Twin Falls is growing, and the city's personality has started to mirror the new diversity with new culinary and cultural options.

Most of Twin Falls' best dining bets are found in and around downtown. **Rock Creek** is a first-class spot for steaks and seafood, though it's easy to miss amid the gas stations and motels along Addison Avenue West. (It's at 200 Addison Avenue West.) In downtown proper, **O'Dunken's Draught House,** a friendly, well-lit tavern at the intersection of Main Avenue and Shoshone Street, is the local version of Cheers, but with a decidedly Idaho flavor. O'Dunken's offers an excellent selection of beers and ales from the Northwest and beyond, and the walls—a veritable capsule history of Twin Falls—are a sight to see.

Travelers who are as interested in preparing food as they are in eating it will enjoy a stop at **Rudy's—A Cook's Paradise** at 147 Main Avenue West. From Dutch-oven gear to gourmet kitchenware, you'll find it here. There's also a good selection of fine wine and beer, as well as regular cooking classes taught by some of the region's most acclaimed chefs. On the first Friday of each month, look for live music and libations from 6:00 to 9:00 p.m. Regular hours are 9:00 a.m. to 7:00 p.m. Monday through Friday and 9:00 a.m. to 5:30 p.m. Saturday. Call (208) 733-5477 or see www.cooksparadise.com for more information on upcoming classes and events.

Also downtown and adjacent to the Magic Valley Arts Council office in the Main Street Plaza, 132 Main Avenue South, is the **Full Moon Gallery.** This artists co-op, which is managed by the Arts Council, showcases locally created fine artworks and contemporary craft items. Browse for paintings, pottery, photography, jewelry, and more. Hours are noon to 5:00 p.m. Tuesday through Friday and 11:00 a.m. to 3:00 p.m. Saturday. On the first Friday of each month, the gallery is open from 7:00 to 9:00 p.m., often hosting opening-night artist's receptions. The receptions are fun and free—with food and wine—and are open to the public. Exhibits change every two months. For more information call (208) 734-2787 or visit www.magicvalleyartscouncil.org.

One of Twin Falls's best assets is the **College of Southern Idaho,** one of the fastest-growing higher-education institutions in the state. On the north side of the pretty 300-acre campus, the **Herrett Center for Arts and Science** includes an anthropology museum of pre-Columbian artifacts, a contemporary, regional art gallery, a digital planetarium, and a public observatory. The 24-inch research-grade telescope is the largest handicapped-accessible telescope in the world. Free and low-cost public viewing events are scheduled regularly. The Herrett's rainforest archaeology exhibit features iguanas, snakes, lizards, and frogs, all showcased in twice-monthly "Mingle in the Jungle" educational programs. The Herrett Center is open Tuesday through Saturday; hours vary by season. Call (208) 732-6655 or visit the Web site at www.csi.edu/herrett.

Few towns can match Twin Falls for an impressive "front door," in this case, the majestic **Snake River Canyon.** The canyon was created by the Bonneville Flood, which came roaring from prehistoric Lake Bonneville through Southeastern Idaho's Red Rock Pass about 15,000 years ago. At its peak the flood spewed 15 million cubic feet of water per second, or three times the flow of the Amazon River, carving the massive canyon that now serves as Twin Falls's welcome mat. The gorge is spanned by the **Perrine Bridge,** a 1,500-foot-long engineering marvel standing 486 feet above the river. When the first Perrine Bridge was completed in 1927, it was the highest cantilever bridge for its length in the world. The present span was completed in 1976, and visitors can view the canyon from overlooks on either rim or from a walkway on the bridge itself. Don't worry if you see people leaping from the bridge. They are BASE jumpers (BASE stands for *bridge, antenna, span,* and *earth*), and Twin Falls is one of the most popular places in the world for enthusiasts of this extreme sport. In fact, the Perrine Bridge is the only spot in the United States where it's legal to jump year-round. Bear in mind, however, that BASE jumping is only for experienced sky divers who have the proper equipment and training.

The **Buzz Langdon Visitor Center** on the south rim is staffed by helpful senior-citizen volunteers who can guide you to local attractions. Also visible from the Perrine Bridge are two of America's prettiest golf courses: **Canyon Springs Golf Course** (which is open to the public) and **Blue Lakes Country Club** (which is private). Twin Falls is a great golfing and tennis town, with links and courts accessible nearly year-round.

The **Idaho Farm and Ranch Museum,** along US 93 north of Twin Falls at the I-84 interchange, is a good place to explore the history of high-desert

Evel Knievel Jumped Here

September 8, 1974, is arguably the most notable date in the history of South Central Idaho. On that day, in an event televised worldwide, motorcycle daredevil Evel Knievel attempted to leap the Snake River Canyon at Twin Falls on his rocket-powered Sky-Cycle X-2. After weeks of hype, the stunt proved a dud: Knievel's parachute malfunctioned and he plunged into the river, everything—even his monumental ego—surviving unscathed.

The Great Snake River Canyon Jump went awry, but few people have forgotten it. That's why most visitors to Twin Falls are only too happy to gape upriver from the Perrine Bridge at the dirt remains of **Evel Knievel's launch site** on the south rim, and why boaters scan the canyon's north wall for Knievel's supposed "target," still visible just below the rim. Robbie Knievel once sought permission to avenge his father's most spectacular failure, but local officials—memories of 15,000 marauding Knievel fans still fresh in their minds—were reluctant to let Knievel Jr. take a flying leap.

farming. Southern Idaho is one of the most productive agricultural areas in the United States, but it would be little more than a sagebrush flat were it not for the Snake River. Several massive irrigation projects fostered early in the twentieth century turned the desert's dry but fertile soil into rich agricultural land, just like "magic." That's how this part of Idaho, known as the Magic Valley, got its nickname. The Farm and Ranch Museum is still a work in progress, but plans call for the eventual additions of a pioneer town Main Street, a petting zoo for children, and a nature trail. A wide variety of old-time agricultural implements, a 1909 settler's "prove-up" shack, and barracks from the nearby World War II–era Hunt Camp Japanese internment facility are already on display. A Live History Day held the second Saturday each June is the best time to stop by for pioneer skills demonstrations and wagon rides. Set up a tour other times of the year by calling (208) 324-5641.

A few miles east of Twin Falls, *Shoshone Falls* ranks among Idaho's most impressive sights. Sometimes called the Niagara of the West, this cataract is actually 212 feet tall, or nearly 40 feet higher than Niagara Falls. Shoshone Falls's main viewpoint is a fine one, but if you'd like a seldom-seen vista, head up the steep trail on the opposite end of the viewpoint parking lot. Up the hill the trail meets a road (now closed to traffic) that becomes a path to several other viewpoints. These spots are undeveloped and unfenced, so use caution, but they'll give you a chance to enjoy the falls in solitude.

Shoshone Falls is best seen in springtime before much of the Snake River's runoff is diverted for the aforementioned agricultural irrigation. But the falls and adjacent Dierkes Lake Park are well worth visitors' attention any time of year. Swimming, fishing, rock climbing, picnicking, and boating are among the available activities, and an easy hike back to Dierkes's "Hidden Lakes" is pleasant (at least if you overlook the behemoth homes rising above the canyon wall). If you ever happen to be here on New Year's Day, be sure to stop by the impoundment above Shoshone Falls to watch crazy water skiers raise funds for local charities in the "Freeze on Skis" event.

South Central Idaho is Oregon Trail country, and one trading post used by the emigrants—the **Rock Creek Stage Station**—can still be seen 5 miles south of Hansen. (Follow the signs off US 30 east of Twin Falls.) Built in 1865 by James Bascom, the log store at the site is the oldest building in South Central Idaho. Interpretive signs tell how the site (also called Stricker Ranch, after a later owner) served the pioneers at the intersection of the Oregon Trail, Ben Holladay's Overland Stage route, and the Kelton Road from Utah. The old Stricker House, also on the grounds, is open Sunday April through October. Shaded picnic facilities are available. Call (208) 423-4000 for more information.

The road south from Hansen continues along Rock Creek into the Twin Falls district of the Sawtooth National Forest, known locally as the **South Hills.** Long considered a private playground by Twin Falls–area residents, the South Hills offer good trails for hiking, horseback riding, cross-country skiing, mountain biking, all-terrain vehicle sports, and snowmobiling. Facilities include several campgrounds and picnic areas, along with the small, family-run **Magic Mountain Ski Area.** The Pike Mountain overlook makes a fitting turnaround for anyone on a scenic drive. Call the Forest Service office at (208) 737-3200 for more information.

Rock Creek Stage Station

Snake River Thrills

When most people think about Snake River floats, they picture raft trips in the shadows of the Grand Tetons in Wyoming. But the Snake River near Twin Falls is becoming the destination of choice for many serious white-water junkies. In years of heavy snowfall, the resulting spring runoff turns the Snake's 14-mile Murtaugh Section (just downstream from Caldron Linn) into a thrill fest for expert kayakers, and several other nearby stretches are nearly as challenging.

These advanced-level river runs shouldn't be taken lightly. Inquire locally on conditions and precautions before you set out. Better yet, get on a guided trip. Area chambers of commerce and sporting goods stores can recommend a good outfitter; Olin and Shelley Gardner of Idaho Guide Service at (208) 734–4998 are among the most experienced in these waters, and they also run canoe trips to the base of Shoshone Falls when water levels allow it. The IGS Web site at www.idahoguide service.com has cool pictures of what you can expect.

During World War II more than 110,000 American citizens of Japanese descent were rounded up from the West Coast and incarcerated farther inland. Many from the Seattle area were transported to the Minidoka War Relocation Center, or *Hunt Camp,* as it came to be known. At one time nearly 10,000 people lived at Hunt, making it Idaho's eighth-largest city. Conditions in the camp were less than ideal. People lived in cramped tar-paper shacks. Guards were posted and prisoners told they would be shot if they moved too close to the barbed-wire fences. Despite the hardship and indignities, about one in ten camp residents wound up serving in the U.S. Armed Forces during World War II.

Little remains of the camp, but it is being protected by the National Park Service as the Minidoka Internment National Monument. Currently, visitors can see the waiting room and guard station, both made of lava. A plaque nearby pays tribute to residents who died in the war, and another shows the layout of the camp. Of particular note are the half-dozen or so ball diamonds—the prisoners found some solace and entertainment in pickup baseball games—and the fields where evacuees grew various crops for the war effort. The site is located a little more than 2 miles north of Highway 25, 7 miles west of Eden. A pair of Idaho highway historical signs—one on Hunt, the other on Prehistoric Man—marks the turn.

The Prehistoric Man sign refers to nearby Wilson Butte Cave, an archaeological site of great importance. Artifacts from *Wilson Butte Cave* near Eden have been carbon dated at 14,500 years old, making them among the oldest findings in the New World. There are no interpretive displays at the cave, but it can be found by driving 2 miles north of the Hunt Camp, then 3⁷⁄₁₀ miles west. Here the road turns to dirt and, in 2 more miles, crosses a canal. A sign another half-mile or so down the road points the way to the cave, still 2 miles away.

Shoshone Falls gets all the publicity, but **Caldron Linn**—or Star Falls, as it's sometimes called—merits its own mighty place in the Snake River Hall of Fame. It was here the 1811 Wilson Price Hunt fur-trapping expedition gave up the river after losing one of its most valuable members, Canadian boatman Antoine Clappine, in the rapids nearby. A year later, according to Cort Conley's *Idaho for the Curious,* Robert Stuart returned to the scene and made this journal entry: "In one place at the Caldron Linn the whole body of the river is confined between two ledges of rock somewhat less than 40 feet apart and here indeed its terrific appearance beggars all description—Hecate's caldron was never half so agitated when vomiting even the most diabolical spells, as is this Linn in a low stage of water."

Caldron Linn can be reached from I-84 by taking Valley Road south of exit 188. After about 3 miles, the road swings east and hits Murtaugh Road a mile east. Follow Murtaugh Road to the canyon and watch for the signs. If you cross the Murtaugh Bridge over the Snake River, you've gone too far. Also keep an eye on kids and pets near Caldron Linn. It's still a nasty, turbulent piece of river real estate.

Lava is the dominant feature of the landscape north of the Snake River Canyon. North and east of Shoshone, the Lincoln County seat, the roadways are rimmed with rugged lava flows that rolled over the land between 2,000 and 15,000 years ago. Some are **lava tubes,** created when a shell formed around a still-flowing river of lava. When the lava moved on, the shell remained. Some of these lava tubes may be explored; the Shoshone office of the Bureau of Land Management at (208) 732-7200 can provide information on locations and necessary equipment.

For another fascinating look at the area's geology, stop by the **Black Magic Canyon** wayside exhibit just south of the Lincoln-Blaine county line at the junction of Highway 75 and West Magic Road. This small but impressive canyon, full of potholes and weirdly sculpted boulders, was carved when pebbles and cobbles from nearby mountain ranges were swept along by melting glacial waters from the last ice age. The best time to explore the canyon is late fall or winter; stay out if there's water in the channel.

Shoshone has seen a bit of a building boom in recent years as people get priced out of Sun Valley 60 miles to the north and even Twin Falls 25 miles to the south. With light traffic and a good supply of audio books, locals have no problem making these distant commutes over the desert. Visitors also have discovered Shoshone's advantages as a base camp, so there's more lodging now, too. The ***Governor's Mansion Bed & Breakfast*** on Highway 75 has five rooms priced $30 to $65. Call (208) 886-2858 for more information or reservations. The ***Manhattan Cafe*** nearby at 133 South Rail Street West is one of Idaho's oldest restaurants, with a basic but extensive menu, daily specials, and plenty of small-town character.

Mini-Cassia Land

Word is getting out about ***Lake Walcott State Park,*** a high-desert oasis situated along the portion of the Snake River stopped short by Minidoka Dam. The park is located within the Minidoka National Wildlife Refuge, where migratory waterfowl including ducks, geese, and tundra swans stop on their fall and spring journeys. Lake Walcott also caters to campers, horseback riders, picnickers, and growing ranks of windsurfers. There's also an eighteen-hole flying disc golf course, so bring your Frisbees. The park is located 10 miles northeast of Rupert on Highway 24. For more information visit the park's Web site at http:// parksandrecreation.idaho.gov/parks/lakewalcott.aspx.

Minidoka Dam itself also is worth a look. Built starting in 1904 the dam became the first federal hydroelectric power project in the Northwest. Along with Milner Dam near Murtaugh, Minidoka Dam made possible the irrigation and settlement of southern Idaho's fertile but dry soil.

Rupert, the Minidoka County seat, has a charming town square that's listed on the National Register of Historic Places. Each year on the day after Thanksgiving, Rupert holds a ***Christmas City USA*** celebration with Santa's arrival, holiday lighting, fireworks, and a chili feed. The ***Minidoka County Historical Society Museum,*** 100 East Baseline Road, is open 1:00 to 5:00 p.m. Monday through Saturday except holidays year-round, with admission by donation. Call (208) 436-0336 if you need more information.

Burley is best known for the ***Idaho Regatta,*** a major powerboating event held annually in late June; call (208) 679-4793 for dates and information. Lesser known and a lot more quiet, but just as fascinating, is the ***Cassia County Historical Museum*** at East Main Street and Highland Avenue, where a large map documents the area's many pioneer trails. Other exhibits tell of Idaho's farming, ranching, mining, and logging history. The museum is open 10:00 a.m. to 5:00 p.m. Tuesday through Saturday, April through September. Call (208) 678-7172 for more information.

Burley's main drag, Overland Avenue, turns into Highway 27, which heads south on a loop drive that takes the traveler back in time to one of the West's best-preserved Victorian towns, mountain scenery, and a world-class rock-climbing area. Seventeen miles south of Burley, the community of

Oakley was settled around 1878 by Mormon pioneers and is famous for its impressive collection of fine historic buildings. In fact all of Oakley has been designated a National Historic District, with particularly notable landmarks including the Marcus Funk residence (on Center Avenue between Poplar and Main), the Oakley Co-op (at Main and Center), and Howells Castle (at Blaine and Poplar). Benjamin Howells, an early settler and judge, also built Howells Opera House, where the Oakley Valley Arts Council continues to present musical performances several times each year. (Call 208-677-ARTS for information.) A tour of Oakley's notable homes is held every year on the third Saturday in June. For more information call (208) 862-3493 or 862-3495.

The peaks rising to Oakley's east are the Albion Mountains, the loftiest in South Central Idaho. Inquire locally or call the Sawtooth National Forest's Burley Ranger District at (208) 678-0430 for directions into the high country. Day hikers and backpackers alike will enjoy a trek to *Independence Lakes,*

"Diamondfield" Jack Davis

Of all the characters in South Central Idaho lore, "Diamondfield" Jack Davis has had an unusually tenacious hold on the region's imagination for his role in the sheepmen vs. cattle owner wars of the 1890s. Hired by cattle magnate John Sparks to keep the rangeland near Oakley free from sheep, Davis earned a reputation as a scrappy fighter—so he was naturally fingered as the prime suspect when two sheepmen were found dead.

The 1897 Davis trial in Albion, then the Cassia County seat, might have been an ordinary one had it not been for the cast of supporting players. Davis's boss, John Sparks, hired James Hawley—the veteran of more than 300 murder cases and a future Idaho governor—to defend his watchman. The prosecution was mounted by William Borah, a young Boise lawyer who went on to become one of Idaho's most famous U.S. senators. The jury swiftly found Davis guilty and sentenced him to hang.

A year later, area ranchers Jim Bower and Jeff Gray confessed to the killings—yet Davis remained on death row, a requested pardon denied.

Other legal maneuverings ensued, with papers filed all the way up to the U.S. Supreme Court. Bower and Gray, tried for the murders, were acquitted on grounds of self-defense. Hawley sought a new trial for Davis, but his motion was denied—and Davis once again was ordered to the gallows. Many stays of execution later, Davis—by then jailed at the Idaho Penitentiary in Boise—was finally pardoned and set free in 1902. His first act on leaving the pen in Boise was stopping for a drink with the city's new mayor, Jim Hawley. Davis moved to Nevada, where he became a successful miner, only to squander his wealth and die in 1949 after being hit by a Las Vegas taxicab.

four tiny blue gems tucked against 10,339-foot Cache Peak. *Lake Cleveland,* another locally popular outdoor playground atop adjacent Mount Harrison, may be accessed by motor vehicle. Camping, picnicking, and fishing are favorite pastimes here. *Pomerelle,* a family-friendly ski area featuring about two dozen runs and the region's only nighttime skiing, also is located on Mount Harrison. Pomerelle is now running its chairlift in summertime, too. See www. pomerelle-mtn.com or call (208) 673-5555 for recorded information, including the ski report.

Southeast of Oakley, Emery Canyon Road provides access to the *City of Rocks National Reserve.* This 14,300-acre area was named by California Trail pioneers passing through in the mid-nineteenth century, some of whom marked their names in axle grease on the ancient granite formations. "During the afternoon, we passed through a stone village composed of huge, isolated rocks of various and singular shapes, some resembling cottages, others steeples and domes," wrote Margaret Frink, who visited in 1850. "It is called City of Rocks, but I think the name Pyramid City [is] more suitable. It is a sublime, strange, and wonderful scene—one of nature's most interesting works." The City of Rocks's hoodoos, arches, caves, and monoliths are the result of erosion, not earthquakes or volcanic activity as some visitors suppose. Most of the rock is part of the Almo Pluton formation, about 25 million years old, while some is part of the 2.5-billion-year-old Green Creek Complex, among the oldest rock in the continental United States. Both kinds can easily be seen at the Twin Sisters formation. The darker "twin" is the older rock, the lighter is from the younger formation.

Today's City of Rocks is in a state of steady development, much of it prompted by the legions of rock climbers who come here to scale the City's challenging spires, some sixty to seventy stories high. In addition to climbers and history buffs, the City beckons stargazers (who value the pitch-black sky), campers, mountain bikers, cross-country skiers, and sightseers. For more information call (208) 824-5519; visit the reserve's Web site at www.nps.gov/ciro/; or stop by the reserve office in nearby Almo, the City's eastern gateway. Nearby *Castle Rocks State Park* offers more rock-climbing terrain and good wildlife watching.

In Almo, look for *Durfee Hot Springs,* which has a 15-by-30 foot natural hot tub, a swimming pool, and a gift shop showcasing works by local artists and crafters. The hot springs, at 2975 South Elba-Almo Road, are open Wednesday through Saturday Memorial Day through Labor Day. Call (208) 824-5701 for more information or to check on off-season hours, which vary due to weather conditions. When you're in the area, be sure to have a meal at the *Almo Creek Outpost,* 3020 South Elba-Almo Road. The steaks are huge (if a bit pricey), the beer is cold, and your dinner may be accompanied by some live old-time music.

For an extended stay in the area, consider the wagon and horseback trips led by Ken Jafek of *War Eagle Outfitters and Guides* in nearby Malta. Jafek's trips travel from Massacre Rocks to City of Rocks along the Raft River Valley, crossing the California Trail in several locations. He also offers hunting, fishing, and camping trips. For information call (208) 645-2455.

From Almo, the Cassia County loop and Highway 77 resume at the crossroads town of Connor. Head north 11 miles to Albion, notable as the former home of the *Albion State Normal School,* one of Idaho's leading teacher-training colleges. The school's beautiful campus later housed a Christian college; today, local residents are trying mightily to preserve the grounds.

The *Marsh Creek Inn,* just south of Albion on Highway 77, is one of Idaho's most pleasant motels. The guest rooms are nothing extraordinary, but it's restful just to stroll the heavily treed grounds, sit on a swing or in the hot tub, and maybe walk the short distance into town. A complimentary continental breakfast featuring fresh, homemade muffins is served in the reception area, housed in a restored log cabin originally built in 1879. Room rates range from $59 to $135. Call (208) 673-6259 or see www.marshcreekinn.com.

Places to Stay in South Central Idaho

GOODING

Cottage Inn
1331 South Main Street
(208) 934-4055
Inexpensive

Gooding Hotel Bed & Breakfast
112 Main Street
(208) 934-4374
(see text)
Inexpensive–Moderate

WENDELL

Hub City Inn
115 South Idaho Street
(208) 536-2326
Inexpensive

HAGERMAN

Billingsley Creek Lodge
1 mile north on US 30
(208) 837-4822
Inexpensive–Moderate

Hagerman Valley Inn
State and Hagerman Streets
(208) 837-6196
Inexpensive

BUHL

Oregon Trail Motel
510 Broadway Avenue
South (US 30)
(208) 534-8814
Inexpensive

TWIN FALLS

Best Western Twin Falls Hotel
1377 Blue Lakes Boulevard
North
(800) 822-8946
fax: (208) 734-7777
Moderate

Comfort Inn
1893 Canyon Springs Road
(800) 228-5150
Moderate

Hampton Inn
1658 Fillmore Street North
(208) 734-2233
Moderate

Monterey Motor Inn
433 Addison Avenue West
(208) 733-5151
Inexpensive

Red Lion Hotel
Canyon Springs
1357 Blue Lakes
Boulevard North
(208) 734-5000
Moderate

Shilo Inn
1586 Blue Lakes
Boulevard North
(800) 222-2244
Moderate

JEROME

Best Western
Sawtooth Inn
2653 South Lincoln Street
(800) 528-1234
Moderate

Days Inn
I-84 exit 173
(208) 324-6400
Inexpensive

SHOSHONE

Governor's Mansion Bed
& Breakfast
315 South Greenwood
(208) 886-2858
(see text)
Inexpensive

HEYBURN

Super 8 Motel
36 South 600 West
(208) 678-7000
Inexpensive

BURLEY

Best Western Burley Inn
800 North Overland
(800) 599-1849
Inexpensive–Moderate

Budget Motel
900 North Overland Avenue
(800) 635-4952
Inexpensive

Fairfield Inn & Suites
230 West Seventh Street
(208) 677-5000
Moderate

ALMO

Old Homestead Bed &
Breakfast
(Closed in winter)
809 East 2975 South
(208) 824-5521
Inexpensive

ALBION

Marsh Creek Inn
on Highway 77
(208) 673-6259
(see text)
Inexpensive–Moderate

Places to Eat in
South Central Idaho

BLISS

Oxbow Cafe (American)
199 East US 30
(208) 352-4250
Inexpensive

HELPFUL WEB SITES FOR
SOUTH CENTRAL IDAHO

Hagerman Fossil Beds National
Monument—www.nps.gov/hafo

Southern Idaho Tourism
www.visitsouthidaho.com

Twin Falls Area Chamber of
Commerce
www.twinfallschamber.com

The *Times-News* (Twin Falls
newspaper)—www.magicvalley.com

City of Rocks National Reserve
www.nps.gov/ciro

Mini-Cassia Chamber of Commerce
www.minicassiachamber.com

GOODING

Rowdy's Pub & Grill (American)
227 Main Street
(208) 934-8003
Inexpensive–Moderate

WENDELL

Cavazos Mexican Food (Mexican)
287 West Avenue H
(208) 536-9921
Inexpensive

Farmhouse Restaurant (American)
I-84 exit 157
(208) 536-6688
Inexpensive–Moderate

HAGERMAN

Larry & Mary's Cafe (American)
141 North State Street
(208) 837-6475
Inexpensive

Snake River Grill (eclectic)
State and Hagerman Streets
(208) 837-6227
(see text)
Inexpensive–Moderate

Sportsman River Resort (American)
18678 US 30
(208) 837-6364
Inexpensive–Moderate

BUHL

Arctic Circle (fast food)
606 Broadway Avenue South
(208) 543-5321
Inexpensive

Garibaldi's (Mexican)
113 Broadway Avenue
(208) 543-6268
Inexpensive–Moderate

TWIN FALLS

Burger Stop (American)
1335 Addison Avenue East
(208) 734-0427
Inexpensive

Gertie's Brick Oven Cookery (Pizza)
602 Second Avenue South
(208) 736-9110
Inexpensive

La Casita (Mexican)
111 South Park Avenue West
(208) 734-7974
Inexpensive

Pandora's (American/brewpub)
516 Hansen Street South
(208) 733-5433
Moderate

Peking Restaurant (Chinese)
824 Blue Lakes Boulevard North
(208) 733-4813
Inexpensive

Rock Creek (steak/ seafood; dinner only)
200 Addison Avenue West
(208) 734-4154
(see text)
Moderate

JEROME

Choate's Family Diner (American)
400 West Main Street
(208) 324-4642
Inexpensive

El Sombrero (Mexican)
143 West Main Street
(208) 324-7238
Inexpensive

SHOSHONE

Manhattan Cafe (American)
133 South Rail Street West
(208) 886-2142
(see text)
Inexpensive

Shoshone Snack Bar (fast food)
Highway 75
(208) 886-2294
Inexpensive

EDEN

Traveler's Oasis Restaurant (American)
I-84 exit 182
(208) 825-4147
Inexpensive

RUPERT

Connor's Cafe (American)
I-84 exit 208
(208) 678-9367
Inexpensive

Playa Azul (Mexican)
531 Fifth Street
(208) 436-6713
Inexpensive

HEYBURN

Stevo's (American)
290 South 600 West
(208) 679-3887
Inexpensive–Moderate

BURLEY

Guadalajara Mexican Restaurant (Mexican)
262 Overland Avenue
(208) 678-8695
Inexpensive

Shon Hing (Chinese)
109 East Main Street
(208) 678-4950
Inexpensive

ALMO

Almo Creek Outpost (American)
3020 South Elba-Almo Road
(208) 824-5577
(see text)
Moderate–Expensive

ALBION

Sage Mountain Grill (American)
255 North Main Street
(208) 673-6696
Inexpensive–Moderate

ALSO WORTH SEEING IN SOUTH CENTRAL IDAHO

Anderson Camp (pool, miniature golf)—Eden

Magic Valley Speedway
south of Twin Falls

Nat–Soo–Pah Hot Springs
Hollister

Shoshone Ice Caves
north of Shoshone

Southeastern Idaho

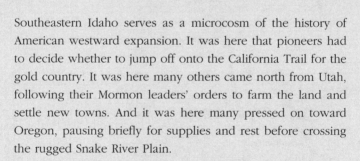

Southeastern Idaho serves as a microcosm of the history of American westward expansion. It was here that pioneers had to decide whether to jump off onto the California Trail for the gold country. It was here many others came north from Utah, following their Mormon leaders' orders to farm the land and settle new towns. And it was here many pressed on toward Oregon, pausing briefly for supplies and rest before crossing the rugged Snake River Plain.

Interstate 86 enters Southeastern Idaho from the west, making a lonely crossing of Power County and part of the Fort Hall Indian Reservation before reaching Pocatello, the region's major city. At Pocatello, Interstate 15 heads north and south; 25 miles south of town, travelers can hop off on U.S. Highway 30 to make a loop around the region via U.S. Highway 89, Highways 34 or 36, and U.S. Highway 91. Drivers may want to extend their explorations of Southeastern Idaho into Utah, since the border between these two states is blurrier than most, as we shall see.

For Southeastern Idaho travel information, call (888) 201-1063, see www.seidaho.org, or write the Pioneer Country Travel Council, P.O. Box 669, Lava Hot Springs 83246.

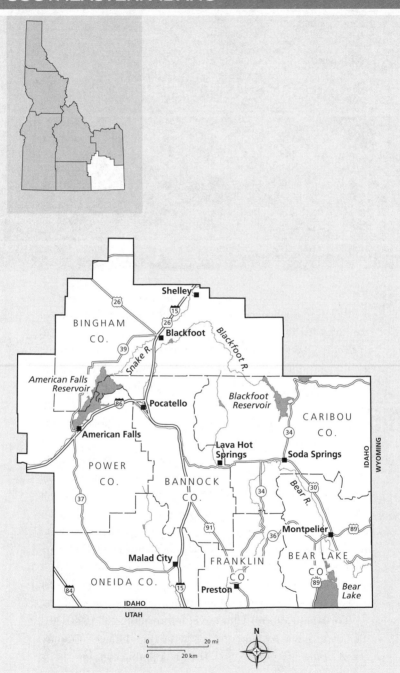

Shelley

BINGHAM
CO.

Blackfoot

Blackfoot R.

Snake R.

American Falls
Reservoir

Blackfoot
Reservoir

Pocatello

CARIBOU
CO.

American Falls

Lava Hot
Springs

Soda Springs

POWER
CO.

BANNOCK
CO.

Bear R.

IDAHO
WYOMING

Montpelier

Malad City

FRANKLIN
CO.

BEAR LAKE
CO.

ONEIDA CO.

Preston

Bear
Lake

IDAHO
UTAH

0   20 mi
0   20 km

N

Trails and Rails

Crossing Power County it's easy to get the feeling you're alone. Most travelers veer off the interstate either east of Burley, where Interstate 84 runs southeast to Utah, or at I-15 at Pocatello. It's not hard to imagine what it might have been like for the pioneer wagon trains crossing the same stretch 150 years ago.

Most of those emigrants traversed southern Idaho without trouble from the Indians. But as traffic along the trail increased, the native peoples grew ever more resentful of the whites invading their land. This may have been the impetus for an August 1862 incident that led to the deaths of ten westward-bound emigrants and an unknown number of Shoshones in two days of fighting amid the lava outcroppings along the Snake River. During the emigrant era, the area became known as the Gate of Death or Devil's Gate because of a narrow, rocky passage through which the wagons rolled (now gone as a result of blasting for the construction of I-86). But stories of the 1862 battles eventually led the locals to dub the area Massacre Rocks.

Massacre Rocks State Park, situated on a narrow strip of land between I-86 and the Snake River, has made the most of its location. Hikers can trace history or see more than 200 species of birds and 300 varieties of desert plants along nearly 7 miles of trails. The park also has notable geologic features, many the result of extensive volcanic activity, others created by the massive Bonneville Flood, the second-largest flood in world geologic history. But things are quieter today. In addition to hiking, fishing, boating, and searching out the local flora and fauna, visitors can spend a peaceful respite in the park's campground, where nightly campfire programs are held each summer. Those making a brief stop in the area can combine a hike with a stop in the visitor

JULIE'S FAVORITES IN SOUTHEASTERN IDAHO

Idaho's World Potato Exposition
Blackfoot

Lava Hot Pools
Lava Hot Springs

Bear Lake
on the Idaho/Utah border

National Oregon/California Trail Center—Montpelier

Napoleon Dynamite **sights**
Preston

Stephens Performing Arts Center
Idaho State campus, Pocatello

center. Exhibits include the diary of Jane A. Gould, who traveled from Iowa to California in 1862 along the Oregon Trail and was in the area at the time of the skirmish with the Shoshones. For more information on Massacre Rocks, call (208) 548-2672 or see the Web site at http://parksandrecreation.idaho.gov/parks/massacrerocks.aspx.

Register Rock, located a few miles west of Massacre Rocks, was a favorite campground along the Oregon Trail, and many visiting emigrants signed their names on a large basalt boulder that is now the centerpiece of a small park. Some signatures date from as early as 1849, and many are still legible. On a smaller rock nearby, J. J. Hansen, a seven-year-old emigrant boy, carved an Indian's head in 1866. Nearly five decades later, after he had become a professional sculptor, Hansen returned and dated the rock again. Register Rock's shady picnic area offers welcome relief from the searing Idaho summer.

For an interesting detour off the interstate between American Falls and Blackfoot, consider taking Highway 39. This 55-mile route (as opposed to 47 miles via the interstate) offers a pleasant two-lane alternative through several small towns and a lot of pretty potato country on the north side of *American Falls Reservoir.* Watch for the signs showing access to fishing on the human-made lake.

South and east of the reservoir, many Native Americans from the Shoshone and Bannock tribes live on the 544,000-acre *Fort Hall Indian Reservation,* which stretches across much of Power, Bannock, and Bingham Counties. Fort Hall is the most populous of Idaho's four reservations, with about 3,200 people living within its boundaries.

The *Shoshone-Bannock Indian Festival* and *All-Indian Rodeos* are held the second week of each August, and the tribes also operate a number of small businesses, including a truck stop and trading post complex at exit 80 off of I-15. Browse at the *Clothes Horse Trading Post,* which features a good selection of Indian beadwork, craft items, and cassette tapes by Native American musicians. Visit the tribal museum, which showcases exhibits on the Shoshone and Bannock people's past. Play a little bingo at the tribe's gaming hall. Or eat at the trading post restaurant, where the specialties include buffalo burgers, buffalo steaks, eggs and buffalo sausage, buffalo stew, and fry bread.

The Oregon Trail really did pass through what is now the Fort Hall Reservation—and there truly was a Fort Hall on what is now reservation land, too. Nathaniel Wyeth established the outpost near the banks of the Snake River in 1834, selling it to the British Hudson's Bay Company three years later. It was a busy place, teeming first with fur trappers and traders and later with emigrants through the mid-1850s. There is nothing left of the original Fort Hall, but there are wagon ruts, emigrant grave sites, and other traces of the fort's history scattered across what is now known as the **Fort Hall Bottoms.** Because the sites are on tribal land, they are not generally open to the public. But if you'd like to have a look, contact Shoshone-Bannock tribal member Red Perry Sr., who leads personal tours through the bottomlands. Perry often can be found at the Fort Hall Museum. If not, call (208) 238-0097 or write Oregon Trail Tours, Route 6 Box 666, Pocatello 83202.

Shelley, up US 91 from Blackfoot, is best known for its annual **Idaho Spud Day** celebration and as the headquarters of **Cox Honey Farms.** The Coxes have been in business since the 1930s, keeping bees all over Southeastern Idaho and even into Wyoming. No tours are available, but you can stop by their little storefront at 456 South State Street in Shelley anytime between 8:00 a.m. and 4:00 p.m. weekdays to pick up gift boxes and a handy brochure listing honey recipes and uses for beeswax (fish bait, mosquito repellent, and lip balm among them). The Coxes also ship gifts throughout the United States. Call (208) 357-3226 or visit www.coxhoneyfarms.com for more information.

North of Blackfoot on I-15, meanwhile, travelers will notice the vast lava beds to the west. **Hell's Half Acre Lava Field,** located midway between Blackfoot and Idaho Falls, is a 180-square-mile flow that has been designated a National Natural Landmark. This is a relatively young lava field, with the last eruptions probably taking place about 2,000 years ago (although the flows near the interstate are probably twice that old). Hikers have two options here: a short educational loop trail (marked by blue-topped poles) that takes about a half-hour to traverse, or a 4.5-mile route that leads to the vent, or source, of the lava flow. The way to the vent is marked by red-topped poles, and the

TOP ANNUAL EVENTS IN SOUTHEASTERN IDAHO

Dodge National Circuit Finals Rodeo
Pocatello (mid-March)

Eastern Idaho State Fair
Blackfoot (late August/early September)

Portneuf Mountain Man Rendezvous
American Falls (late May)

Idaho Spud Day
Shelley (mid-September)

Shoshone-Bannock Festival
Fort Hall (early August)

Festival of Lights
Preston (Thanksgiving through Christmas)

Spuds Aplenty

Blackfoot, located just north of the reservation, narrowly lost an 1880 bid to replace Boise as capital of the Idaho Territory. Instead Blackfoot has become the Potato Capital of Idaho and probably the world. Potatoes have long been synonymous with Idaho, and Blackfoot is the seat and largest town in Bingham County, the state's top spud-producing region. Small wonder, then, that Blackfoot's top attraction is *Idaho's World Potato Exposition,* dedicated to "fun and educational exhibits about the world's most popular vegetable." The world's largest potato chip—of the Pringles variety, 25 inches by 14 inches, the equivalent of eighty regular chips—is on display, as is a photo of Marilyn Monroe modeling an Idaho potato sack. The center also offers "Free Taters for Out-of-Staters," a box of dehydrated hash browns. Picnic grounds are available.

The Potato Expo is located in downtown Blackfoot at 130 Northwest Main Street in the old train depot. The Expo is open from 9:30 a.m. to 5:00 p.m. Monday through Saturday April through October and from 9:30 a.m. to 3:00 p.m. weekdays November through March. Admission is $3.00 for adults, $2.50 for seniors over age fifty-five, and $1.00 for children ages six through twelve. For more information call (208) 785-2517 or see www.potatoexpo.com.

hike takes a full day. Be sure to wear boots with sturdy soles and carry plenty of water.

Pocatello, a city of about 54,000 people, apparently took its name from that of Pocataro, a Shoshone chief, but it owes its prominence—and a lot of its character—to railroading. The Utah and Northern narrow-gauge and Oregon Short Line railways, both part of the Union Pacific system, intersected at Pocatello, and railroad activity spurred settlement and construction. By World War II, more than 4,500 railroad cars passed through Pocatello each day. Rail fans may want to pay a visit to the old *Oregon Short Line Depot* on West Bonneville Street. President William Taft attended the dedication of this building, erected in 1915. The *Yellowstone Hotel,* frequently used by rail passengers, is just across the street from the old depot. The *Pocatello Model Railroad and Historical Society* runs holiday train displays out of Union Pacific Building B-59 southwest of the Union Pacific depot. Stop in any Saturday late November through the last Saturday before Christmas.

Perhaps because of its railroad links, perhaps because it is home to a university, Pocatello has a different feel from Idaho's other large towns: more transient, a bit scruffy, but not without a charm of its own. Like all good-size American towns, Pocatello has its "on-the-beaten-path" commercial strips and its soul—its downtown, or as they call it hereabouts, "Old Town Pocatello."

The first Friday of each month is a good time to visit, with an art walk set from 5:00 to 8:00 p.m., followed by a coffeehouse with live music at the First Congregational Church. (See below.)

The **Continental Bistro** at 140 South Main Street is widely considered one of the best restaurants in town. On a fine summer day, it's possible to peer through the bistro's windows and see the place look abandoned. That's because most patrons favor the restaurant's spacious rear patio, which recalls an Italian formal garden. At lunchtime the bistro offers a good variety of salads, sandwiches, and pasta dishes, most for about $8. Try the Cobb Sandwich: honey-cured turkey, bacon, lettuce, tomato, avocado, and shaved bleu cheese on focaccia bread.

At dinner, the Bistro serves up a varied menu, featuring such dishes as chicken scampi, grilled London broil, and roast vegetable lasagna. Most entrees are in the $13 to $23 range. The restaurant has won a *Wine Spectator* magazine award for many years running and has a list of about 200 selections. The Continental Bistro also has a pub featuring sixteen microbrews on tap and live music each Wednesday night in the summer. (Wednesday evening is also "inexpensive beer night," with all micros priced at $1.50 apiece starting at 4:00 p.m.) The Continental Bistro is open for dining from 11:00 a.m. to 10:00 p.m. Monday through Saturday, with the patio generally open May through October. The pub is open until 1:00 a.m. nightly except Sunday. For more information or reservations, call (208) 233-4433.

Pocatello has some beautiful architecture in its central core. Stroll along **Garfield Avenue** 2 blocks west of Main Street to see some fine examples. The church at 309 North Garfield, shared by the local Congregationalists and Unitarian Universalists, dates back to 1904. The **Standrod House** at 648 North Garfield was built in 1901, its light gray and red sandstone quarried in nearby McCammon and hauled to the site by horse-drawn wagons. The city of Pocatello acquired and renovated the Standrod House in the 1970s and for a time it regained its status as community center. Now, however, it is off-limits to the public.

Across the Union Pacific tracks from the downtown core, railroad history also permeates **Kinport Junction,** a recently renovated seventy-year-old brick-and-timber warehouse along the tracks at 815 South First Avenue. The Pocatello Co-Op natural foods market is here, along with several restaurants, helping Kinport rival the Continental Bistro as a prime destination for Southeastern Idaho foodies. See www.kinportjunction.com for the latest on this development.

Even if you've taken the Sho-Ban tour of the original Fort Hall site, the **Fort Hall Replica** in Pocatello's Ross Park is worth a visit. Exhibits at the replica

Fort Hall Replica

include a blacksmith's shop and extensive displays on Indian lifestyles. A videotape on Fort Hall's history may be viewed on request. The Fort Hall replica is open daily from 10:00 a.m. to 6:00 p.m. from Memorial Day through Labor Day; from 10:00 a.m. to 2:00 p.m. from after Labor Day through the end of September; and from 10:00 a.m. to 2:00 p.m. Tuesday through Saturday during April and May. Admission is $2.50 for adults, $2.00 for seniors, $1.50 for youths ages twelve to seventeen, and $1.00 for children ages three to eleven. Ross Park also includes a pool, rose garden, picnic areas, a playground, and a small zoo. For more information call (208) 234-1795.

The ***Bannock County Historical Museum,*** also located in Ross Park, is a good place to learn more about Pocatello's railroading past; other exhibits include war memorabilia, Indian artifacts, a restored stagecoach, and rooms that offer glimpses into how early Pocatello lived and worked. The museum is open from 10:00 a.m. to 6:00 p.m. daily Memorial Day weekend through Labor Day and 10:00 a.m. to 2:00 p.m. Tuesday through Saturday the rest of the year. Admission is $1 for adults and 50 cents for children ages six to twelve. The phone number is (208) 233-0434.

Pocatello is also home to Idaho State University, which enrolls about 12,750 students. Notable attractions on the campus include the ***Idaho Museum of Natural History*** at Fifth Avenue and Dillon Street and the hilltop 123,000-square-foot ***L. E. and Thelma E. Stephens Performing Arts Center,*** which looks something like a cross between a Mormon temple and the Taj Mahal. For more information on activities and events at ISU, see www.isu.edu.

Hot Baths and Pioneer Paths

The entire state of Idaho is justly famous for its hot springs. But perhaps no other town has been so blessed with wondrous thermal activity as **Lava Hot Springs,** situated along US 30 and the Portneuf River 35 miles southeast of Pocatello.

Tucked in a mile-high mountain valley near the north edge of the Wasatch Range, Lava Hot Springs once served as a winter campground for the Bannock and Shoshone Indian tribes, who thought the local springs held healing powers. Geologists believe the springs have been a consistent 110°F for at least fifty million years. The springs are rich with minerals—calcium carbonate, sodium chloride, and magnesium carbonate being most prevalent—but have no sulfur and, therefore, none of the nose-wrinkling odor typical of many hot springs.

The town has two main attractions, both operated by the Lava Hot Springs Foundation, a State of Idaho agency. A huge free-form Olympic pool complex on the west side of town has one-third of an acre of water surface, 50-meter racing lanes, a 10-meter diving tower, two hydro slide tubes, and a surrounding carpet of green grass for sunbathing; another 25-yard pool nearby meets Amateur Athletic Union standards. The 25-yarder was recently enclosed and is now open year-round. The larger pool is open mid-May through August from noon to 9:00 p.m. weekdays and from 11:00 a.m. to 9:00 p.m. Saturday, Sunday, and holidays. The Lava Hot Pools on the east side of town are perfect for mellow soaking. These four hot pools—open every day of the year except Thanksgiving and Christmas—are set amid the sunken gardens of an extinct volcano and range in temperature from 102° to 112°F. Hours at the hot pools are 8:00 a.m. to 11:00 p.m. April through September and 9:00 a.m. to 10:00 p.m. October through March, except on Friday and Saturday evenings, when they remain open until 11:00 p.m. A $9.00 fee buys all-day admission to both the pools and the hot baths; single admission to either runs $5.00 for adults and youth ages twelve and up and $4.50 for seniors and children ages four through eleven. A $30 family pass, available Monday through Thursday except holidays, admits everyone in an immediate family to all the pools. Suits, towels, and lockers may be rented, and group rates are available. Call (800) 423-8597 or visit www.lavahotsprings.com for more information.

The pools, hot baths, and Portneuf River tubing have made Lava Hot Springs justly popular, so quite a few other tourist-oriented businesses have sprung up to serve visitors. Motel rates are very reasonable for a resort area; many rooms (some including private hot mineral baths) go for less than $75 a night. One of the most interesting spots in town is the **Lava Hot Springs**

Inn, a European-style bed-and-breakfast complete with an on-site massage therapist and five outdoor natural mineral-water pools. (One is 80 feet long.) Rooms here start at about $70 and go to $200 for two family-size suites that can sleep eight to ten people. The larger one has a kitchen. The inn supposedly has its own ghost, too. For more information call (208) 776-5830; write Lava Hot Springs Inn, 95 East Portneuf Avenue, Lava Hot Springs 83246; or see www.lavahotspringsinn.com.

Lava Hot Springs has a full calendar of summer special events, including a mountain man rendezvous and *Pioneer Days* celebration in mid-July. But autumn may be the best time of all to visit; room rates dip even lower at some establishments, and the surrounding hills are ablaze with some of Idaho's most colorful fall foliage. If you're a fan of Thai food, be sure to have a meal at the *Riverwalk Cafe,* 695 East Main Street. This small, family-run restaurant serves authentic, inexpensive fare every day but Monday. Call (208) 776-5872. For more information on Lava Hot Springs, call (888) 201-1063 or see www .lavahotsprings.org.

Back on US 30 heading east from Lava Hot Springs, consider one of three short side trips to Black Canyon, Maple Grove Hot Springs, or the ghost town of Chesterfield. *Black Canyon* is one of Idaho's hidden geological gems. The gorge gets its start just downstream of the town of Grace, which is located about 5 miles south of US 30 via Highway 34. Turn west on Center Street in town (Turner Road) and pause at the bridge to see the chasm opening up. As the Bear River rolls across the farmland surrounding Grace, it quickly widens and deepens into a canyon rivaling those on the Snake River. Sadly, however, there's no public access to the rim along the deepest parts, and a modest fishing access spot near the Utah Power plant southwest of Grace just doesn't do the canyon justice. But take a peek where you can—some farmers along the Black Canyon Lane southwest of Grace via Turner and Hegstrom Roads might let you look if you ask permission. East of Grace there are interesting interpretive signs detailing how the Last Chance Canal Company struggled to provide irrigation to this region.

Situated south of Grace, *Maple Grove Hot Springs* is a bit farther off the beaten path than other southeastern Idaho thermal retreats, but it's worth the drive. This secluded resort offers daily soaking in several beautiful pools, eight campsites, and a 1955 vintage 31-foot Detroiter trailer that can sleep at least four. The setting is really picturesque, too, on the Oneida Narrows Reservoir of the Bear River, with excellent wildlife watching, fishing, and boating. To get to Maple Grove from Grace, continue south on Highway 34. After 15 miles, watch for 13800 North

Human-made Lava

With all the lava in Idaho, you wouldn't think people would pay much heed to another pile of the stuff. Ah, but when it's a human-made lava flow bubbling over the landscape before your eyes—well, that's enough to generate interest. And that's just what happens north of Soda Springs at the Monsanto Chemical Company.

Monsanto, which produces elemental phosphorous—a substance used in laundry detergents, soft drinks, toothpaste, and other products—dumps the resulting slag from its electric furnaces. The slag, 1,400°F hot, fills trucks bearing special cast-steel pots. The trucks then pour the molten rock onto the slag pile five times each hour, twenty-four hours a day. You can almost imagine the local kids asking each other, "Whaddya wanna do tonight, watch MTV, cruise US 30, or go to the slag heap?"

Road, and turn left. Make an immediate right on Maple Grove Road and continue south about 3 miles to the hot springs. For more information (including directions from other points in southeastern Idaho), see www.maplegrovehotsprings.com, call (208) 851-1137, or write to Maple Grove Hot Springs, 11386 North Oneida Narrows Road, Thatcher 83283.

Most extinct Western towns owed their existence to mining, but **Chesterfield** had its roots in agriculture. Mormon pioneers settled the town in 1880 along the old Oregon Trail. The town reached its peak in the 1920s with a population of about 500 people. After that, however, Chesterfield slowly began to shrink. After World War II, few local boys came home, and the town lost its post office a couple of years later.

No one lives year-round in Chesterfield today, but the town's memory remains remarkably well preserved. About two dozen buildings still stand, with plans to rebuild a few others. The most notable remaining structure is the old Chesterfield LDS Ward meetinghouse, which the Daughters of Utah Pioneers have preserved as a museum. Daffodils and a manicured lawn greet visitors, while exhibits inside the handsome brick building include photos of many early settlers, an old pump organ, and a tribute to the prolific Western novelist Frank Robertson, a local boy who grew up to write 128 books (including eight each in 1935 and 1936).

The museum may be toured May through October by checking with the caretaker couple who live nearby at 3111 Moses Lane. (Look for signs giving directions.) Many descendants of early Chesterfield residents come back each Memorial Day for a luncheon and reunion. Nearby Chesterfield Reservoir is a good fishing spot, too. Chesterfield is located 10 miles north of the town of Bancroft and 15 miles north of US 30.

Continuing east on US 30, the traveler reaches Soda Springs, Caribou County's seat and largest town. The area was another major point along the Oregon Trail, with many emigrants stopping to camp and sample the water from the area's abundant natural springs. Most are gone now, but evidence remains of two of the most famous. One pioneer spring is preserved under a small pavilion in **Hooper Springs Park,** located 2 miles north of the center of town. DRINK DEEPLY OF NATURE'S BEST BEVERAGE, a plaque advises. Hooper Springs is named for W. H. Hooper, who was a leading Salt Lake City banker, Utah congressman, and president of the Zion's Cooperative Mercantile Institution, at one time Intermountain region's major home-grown department store chain. He had a summer home in Soda Springs and helped the town's soda water reach international markets.

Another spring regularly gave off a sound like that of a steamboat. It's now drowned beneath Alexander Reservoir, but **Steamboat Spring** has not disappeared altogether; on a clear day it can still be viewed puffing and percolating beneath the water's surface. The best way to see evidence of the spring is to

Geyser Park

play a round on the ***Oregon Trail Golf Course.*** Look south to the reservoir from either the No. 1 green or the No. 8 tee. From those vantage points you also can see what are probably the only Oregon Trail wagon ruts on a golf course, a phenomenon that was once featured in *National Geographic.* Traces of the wagons' wheels cut across the No. 9 fairway and skirt the No. 1 green before traveling across the No. 8 fairway. Still another famous local spring tasted almost exactly like beer—and produced similar effects once drunk—but it, unfortunately, has vanished completely.

Several other Soda Springs attractions are of particular note. The town has the world's only captive geyser, the centerpiece of the aptly named ***Geyser Park.*** The gusher was discovered in 1937 as the town attempted to find a hot-water source for its swimming pool. The drill hit the geyser, which was later capped and controlled by a timer. These days it erupts every hour on the hour (unless strong west winds are blowing, which would send the 150-foot-high spray cascading over nearby businesses). The surrounding park offers a pleasant place to rest while waiting for the next "show."

North of town, the Nature Conservancy and the Bureau of Land Management have established a preserve at ***Formation Springs.*** Here visitors see crystal-clear pools amid a wetlands area at the base of the Aspen Mountains. The springs that feed the pools and nearby creek system deposit high concentrations of calcium carbonate, giving the site its unusual geology. Formation Cave, about 20 feet tall and 1,000 feet long, is among the impressive features, and abundant wildlife may be seen.

Bear Lake Country

Two designated scenic routes traverse the state's extreme southeastern corner, intersecting in Soda Springs. The ***Pioneer Historic Byway*** follows Highway 34 northeast to Wyoming, skirting the shores of Blackfoot Reservoir and Grays Lake, and the south to Preston and Franklin, two of Idaho's oldest towns. The ***Bear Lake–Caribou Scenic Byway*** follows US 30 and 89 through Montpelier and south to Bear Lake, a 20-mile-long recreational paradise straddling the Idaho-Utah border. We'll look at the region following a clockwise direction southeast from Soda Springs and back north toward Pocatello.

Settled in 1864 by Mormon families, Montpelier was named for the capital of Brigham Young's home state, Vermont. Outlaw Butch Cassidy visited here in 1896, joining with two other men in robbing the local bank of $7,165. The bank they supposedly robbed is gone now, but the building in which it stood remains on Washington Street downtown.

Montpelier also is home to the ***National Oregon/California Trail Center,*** built at the junction of US 30 and 89 at the site known in the 1850s as Clover Creek, a popular emigrant rest stop. Through living history, artwork, and exhibits, the center explains how early travelers made it over the "Big Hill," a nearby ridge that many pioneers considered among the roughest obstacles on the way west; how they lived in the wagon trains; and how they encountered such characters as Thomas "Peg Leg" Smith, a nineteenth-century mountain man who had to amputate his own leg. Smith opened a trading post at what is now Dingle, Idaho, and reportedly made $100 a day catering to the emigrants' needs. The center is open daily in the summer from 9:00 a.m. to 5:00 p.m. and by reservation the rest of the year. Admission is $8 for ages thirteen and up, $6 for seniors sixty and up, and $5 for youngsters ages five through twelve. (Children four and under get in free.) For more information call (866) 847-3800 or see www.oregontrail center.org.

Although southeast Idaho is geographically and politically part of the Gem State, spiritually the region is closely aligned with Utah and Mormonism. Nowhere is this more true than in the towns and counties bordering the Beehive State. In fact the 1863 settlers who arrived in what was to become Paris, Idaho, thought they were in Utah until an 1872 boundary survey set the record straight.

The imposing and beautiful ***Paris Stake Tabernacle*** was a labor of love for the local Mormon settlers, who spent half a decade building the Romanesque-style church, completed in 1889. A *stake* is the term used by the Church of Jesus Christ of Latter-day Saints to describe a geographical area; the Paris, Idaho, stake was the first organized outside the Utah territory, and the tabernacle was built to serve the Mormon communities and congregations that sprung up within a 50-mile radius of the town.

The tabernacle—designed by Joseph Young, a son of Brigham—was built from red sandstone hauled by horse- and ox-drawn wagons from a canyon 18 miles away. In the winter the rock was pulled by sled over frozen Bear Lake. A former shipbuilder crafted the ceiling, using pine harvested in nearby forests. Tours are offered daily through the summer; arrive mid-day and you may be treated to music from the tabernacle's Austin pipe organ.

A monument on the tabernacle grounds honors Charles Coulson Rich, the man sent by Brigham Young to settle the Bear Lake Valley. It was Rich who, on one of his many missions for the church, went to Europe to find the skilled craftsmen recruited by the Mormons to help build their new churches and towns in the American West. Rich had six wives and fifty children and ultimately became an apostle in his church. Despite his contributions, Paris was named not for Rich but for Frederick Perris, who platted the town site. One of the first settler cabins, built in 1863 by Thomas Sleight and Charles Atkins, is still standing and may be seen in a park near the tabernacle.

Several intriguing side canyons south of Paris beckon independent-minded motorists from well-traveled US 89. *Bloomington Canyon,* west of the tiny town of the same name, leads to a pristine little lake and meadows filled with wildflowers. *Minnetonka Cave,* located west of St. Charles, is the largest developed limestone cave in Idaho and among the state's more spectacular underground wonderlands. Ninety-minute tours weave through a half-mile of fantastic formations and fossils of preserved tropical plant and marine life in nine separate chambers, the largest of which is about 300 feet around and 90 feet high.

In the late 1930s the federal government began development of Minnetonka Cave via the Works Progress Administration, constructing a trail from St. Charles Canyon and installing interior paths, steps, and railings. But the cave was open only for a couple of years before World War II began, halting efforts at improvement. After the war the Paris Lions Club operated the cave for a time. It is now managed by the U.S. Forest Service as part of the Caribou-Targhee National Forest. Tours of Minnetonka Cave are given every half-hour from 10:00 a.m. to 5:30 p.m. each day from around Memorial Day through Labor Day. The cost is $5 for adults, $4 for children ages six through

Idaho's "Loch Ness"

Photographers find Bear Lake at its most beautiful at sunrise, when the water frequently glints pink, red, and gold as it catches the waking orb's rays. But locals say sunset visitors are more likely to spy the **Bear Lake Monster,** a serpentlike creature said to live underwater along the lake's east shore. Rumors of the beast have circulated for centuries, first by Native Americans and mountain men, later by Joseph Rich (a son of Mormon pioneer Charles Coulson Rich), who reported his findings in an 1868 article for the *Desert News* of Salt Lake City. Sightings were especially prevalent around 1900, when people reported strange creatures of up to 90 feet long that could move as fast as running horses.

According to a local tourism brochure, for a long time no one could find a bottom to Bear Lake. People thought perhaps Bear Lake was connected to Scotland by underground tunnels and that the Bear Lake monster was actually the famous Loch Ness monster. Today Bear Lake–area folks speculate the "creature" could be anything from ice formations or a cloud on the water to a large school of fish or elk swimming across the lake. "No one is willing to say if it is real or not," the pamphlet adds. "That is up to you to decide. But be on the lookout for the monster, and please report any sightings."

fifteen, or $20 for a family. Children ages five and under get in free. Visitors should be prepared for lots of steps and cool temperatures; good walking shoes and a jacket are recommended. Several campgrounds are available up St. Charles Canyon. For more information on the cave or surrounding forest, call (208) 847-0375.

St. Charles serves as gateway to *Bear Lake,* one of the bluest bodies of water in North America. Explanations for its turquoise tint vary, but it's usually credited to a high concentration of soluble carbonates.

Bear Lake also is unique because it boasts several species of fish found nowhere else. In addition to the rainbow and cutthroat trout so plentiful throughout the Rockies, Bear Lake is home to the Bonneville cisco, a sardine-like whitefish that spawns each January and is popular year-round for bait. Check with the Idaho Department of Fish and Game at (800) 635-7820 for regulations on angling for cisco or other fish; information and licenses also are available at sporting goods dealers throughout the state. Bear Lake State Park is on the Internet at http://parksandrecreation.idaho.gov/parks/bearlake .aspx.

In addition to fish, Bear Lake Country is thick with animals and birds. The *Bear Lake National Wildlife Refuge* at the lake's north end draws Canada geese; sandhill and whooping cranes; redhead, canvasback, and mallard ducks; and the nation's largest nesting population of white-face ibis. Deer, moose, and smaller mammals are also known to wander through the refuge's 19,000 acres. Check with the refuge office in Montpelier or call (208) 847-1757 for information on waterfowl hunting, boating, and hiking opportunities.

The Utah end of Bear Lake is far more commercially developed than Idaho's shores. Bear Lake Boulevard in and near Garden City, Utah, is lined with resorts and restaurants, but there are very few visitor services north of the border. That's one reason *Bear Lake Bed & Breakfast* stands out—that and the fact the inn sits high on a hill overlooking the lake. The inn is a good base for summer lake activities, but it's also popular with winter sports enthusiasts, with a 380-mile network of snowmobile trails starting just outside the door. Five rooms (three with private baths) rent for $75 to $115 in summer and $70 to $90 in winter. Ask about massages and murder-mystery dinners. For more information call (208) 945-2688; write Bear Lake Bed & Breakfast, 500 Loveland Lane, Fish Haven 83287; or see www.bearlakebedandbreakfast.com.

Southwest of Bear Lake, US 89 makes a scenic 45-mile swing through the Wasatch National Forest and Logan Canyon before meeting US 91 at Logan. From there it's a short drive back north into Idaho, where our explorations

Gosh! Preston is Flippin' Sweet!

If you've seen the 2004 indie film hit **Napoleon Dynamite,** you're probably wondering whether Preston is really like the slightly time-warped town seen in the movie. The answer is: Heck, yes! If you come to Preston, you really will see such landmarks as the King's store where Summer Wheatley works, the Pop'N Pins bowling alley where Kip and Uncle Rico plot their business empire, and the Deseret Industries Thrift Store where Napoleon buys the awesome leisure suit he wears to the big dance. You can even stay overnight at the Plaza Motel, where the cast and crew bunked while making the movie.

Preston is having fun with its film-inspired fame. An annual Napoleon Dynamite Festival draws several thousand people to town each June for look-alike contests, tours, tetherball tournaments, and live performances by the real-life Happy Hands Club.

A pilgrimage to Preston is a must for *Dynamite* devotees, but even casual fans will enjoy taking the self-drive tour of movie locations including Pedro's house, Preston High School, and Napoleon Dynamite Lane. Stop in the Preston Chamber of Commerce office at 49 North State Street for a map. The chamber also has plenty of boondoggle key chains, T-shirts, and other sweet souvenirs for sale. For more information call (208) 852-2703 or see www.prestonidaho.org.

continue at Franklin. (For more information on the Beehive State, check out *Utah Off the Beaten Path.*)

Franklin, founded in 1860, beats out Paris for the title of Idaho's oldest settled town by three years. But like the pioneers at Paris, Franklin's early townsfolk thought they were part of Utah until the 1872 survey confirmed the town's location in what was to become the state of Idaho. Franklin's museum is called the **Relic Hall,** and it houses many artifacts and photos of pioneer life. A park complete with picnic grounds and a fireplace now surrounds the hall. Two of Franklin's most interesting sights are located just outside of town on the Old Yellowstone Highway. (Turn west at the Daughters of the Utah Pioneers marker north of town.) The ruins on the north side of the road are those of what is likely the **oldest flour mill** in the state of Idaho. And just across the road, the **Yellowstone Rock** shows the old route to the nation's first national park. After Yellowstone received its national park designation, large boulders with arrows pointing the way were placed along what was then the main road to the park to help travelers find their way. This may be the last such marker still in existence.

The scenic **Cub River Canyon** east of US 91 between Franklin and Preston is home to the **Cub River Guest Ranch** and the **Deer Cliff Inn.** Family-run since 1940, this retreat offers rustic cabins and a restaurant featuring seasonal streamside patio dining. Menu items mostly range between $10 and $20 and include steaks, chicken, shrimp, trout, halibut, and lobster. The restaurant is open for dinner May through October, daily in summer, and Thursday through Saturday in spring and fall. Call (208) 852-0643 for more information on the restaurant or (208) 852-2124 for details on accommodations. Drive on up the canyon for beautiful Wasatch Mountain scenery, especially in fall when the maples turn a dazzling red.

Brigham Young, the Mormon leader, urged his followers to heed the golden rule when dealing with Native Americans. "Treat them in all respects as you would like to be treated," he said in an 1852 speech. Indeed the Mormons who settled Idaho early on made pacts with the local Indian chiefs to share crops and live together peacefully. Still there were tensions, and they boiled over in January 1863 in the **Battle of Bear River** 2.5 miles north of Preston. More Indians died in this little-known incident than in any other; there were more casualties—as many as 400 men, women, and children killed—than at Wounded Knee, Sand Creek, or Little Big Horn. The battle was triggered by the death of a miner on Bear River during an Indian attack; Colonel Patrick Connor of the Third California Infantry, stationed at Fort Douglas near Salt Lake City, used the incident as an excuse to make war. William Hull, a local pioneer who witnessed the battle, gave this account of its aftermath: "Never will I forget the scene, dead bodies were everywhere. I counted eight deep in one place and in several places they were three to five deep. In all we counted nearly 400; two-thirds of this number being women and children." A monument along the east side of US 91 north of Preston makes note of the battle, and the actual battle site was nearby along aptly named Battle Creek. Not far north of the Battle of Bear River site, another wayside commemorates **Red Rock Pass.** It was through here that prehistoric Bonneville Lake breached its shores about 14,500 years ago, unleashing one of history's greatest floods.

Malad City, the seat of Oneida County, is more on the beaten path (I-15) than off, but it has a few spots to recommend a stop. The **Iron Door Playhouse** offers a full theatrical menu of about six productions each year including Broadway fare, youth-oriented shows, dinner theater, cowboy poetry, and melodramas. The playhouse is located at 59 North Main Street in what was once one of the nation's first JCPenney stores, since remodeled into a modern theater. Call (208) 766-4705 for reservations or information on upcoming events.

And what about that "Iron Door" name? *Malad* is French for "sick," and—like the Malad Gorge and Malad River in South Central Idaho—Malad City and its nearby (and much longer) Malad River reportedly earned their names when a party of trappers became sick after drinking from the stream. But those early trappers probably didn't feel nearly as sick as did Glispie Waldron, who, in 1890, may have blown his chance at finding a buried treasure.

It seems that during the 1860s and 1870s, Malad City was a major stop for freight wagons taking supplies from Utah north to the mines of Idaho and Montana, as well as those returning with gold. This traffic also made Malad a favorite target of robbers and other ne'er-do-wells, one group of which reportedly hid the loot from a stagecoach holdup somewhere in the Samaria Mountains located southwest of town, planning to retrieve it later. Waldron was traveling in the area in 1890 when he reportedly spied an iron door covering a cave. He tied his coat to a nearby tree to mark the spot, intending to return. But he didn't make it back for a couple of years, and by then, his coat was gone. To this day treasure seekers are still searching for the fabled iron door and the riches that may lie behind it. If you're interested in trying your own luck, stop by the Oneida County **Pioneer Museum** at 27 Bannock Street in Malad City for tips on where to look.

If you haven't had your fill of Southeastern Idaho water recreation by now, check out **Downata Hot Springs Resort,** located near the town of Downey. Aside from a pool and waterslides, this year-round resort offers everything from RV and tent camping and indoor lodging to water aerobics classes. Downey is on US 91, 6 miles south of its junction with I-15. Call (208) 897-5736 for more information or see www.downatahotsprings.com.

HELPFUL WEB SITES FOR SOUTHEASTERN IDAHO

City of Pocatello
www.pocatello.us

Greater Pocatello Chamber of Commerce—www.pocatelloidaho.com

Idaho State Journal **(Pocatello newspaper)**—www.journalnet.com

Shoshone-Bannock Tribes
www.shoshonebannocktribes.com

Places to Stay in Southeastern Idaho

AMERICAN FALLS

American Motel
2814 Pocatello Avenue
(208) 226-7271
Inexpensive

Hillview Motel
2799 Lakeview Road
(208) 226-5151
Inexpensive

BLACKFOOT

Best Western Blackfoot Inn
750 Jensen Grove Drive
(208) 785-4144
fax: (208) 785-4304
Inexpensive–Moderate

Riverside Inn
I-15 exit 93
(208) 785-5000
Inexpensive–Moderate

POCATELLO/CHUBBUCK

AmeriTel Inn
1440 Bench Road
(Pocatello)
(800) 600-6001
fax: (208) 234-0000
Moderate–Expensive

Black Swan Inn
746 East Center (Pocatello)
(208) 233-3051
Moderate–Expensive

Comfort Inn
1333 Bench Road
(208) 237-8155
Moderate

Holiday Inn
1399 Bench Road
(Pocatello)
(800) 200-8944
fax: (208) 238-0225
Moderate

Motel 6
291 West Burnside Avenue
(Chubbuck)
(800) 466-8356
Inexpensive

Red Lion Inn
Pocatello
1555 Pocatello Creek Road
(Pocatello)
(208) 233-2200
fax: (208) 234-4524
Moderate

LAVA HOT SPRINGS

Lava Hot Springs Inn
94 East Portneuf
(208) 776-5830
(see text)
Moderate–Expensive

Riverside Inn & Hot Springs
255 East Portneuf
(208) 776-5504
Moderate

SODA SPRINGS

Caribou Lodge
110 US 30
(208) 547-3377
fax: (208) 547-2663
Inexpensive

ALSO WORTH SEEING IN SOUTHEASTERN IDAHO

American Falls Reservoir
north of American Falls

Bingham County Historical Museum—Blackfoot

Idaho Museum of Natural History
Pocatello

Pebble Creek Ski Area
Pocatello

Rails and Trails Museum
Montpelier

Grays Lake National Wildlife Refuge—
north of Soda Springs

J-R Inn
179 US 30
(208) 547-3366
Inexpensive

Trail Motel
213 East 200 South
(208) 547-0240
Inexpensive

MONTPELIER

Best Western Clover Creek Inn
243 North Fourth Street
(800) 528-1234
fax: (208) 847-3519
Inexpensive–Moderate

Three Sisters Motel
112 South Sixth Street
(208) 847-2324
Inexpensive

FISH HAVEN

Bear Lake Bed & Breakfast
Milepost 2 US 89
(208) 945-2688
(see text)
Moderate

PRESTON

Plaza Motel
427 South US 91
(208) 852-2020
Inexpensive

Places to Eat in Southeastern Idaho

AMERICAN FALLS

China City (Chinese)
220 Harrison
(208) 226-7038
Inexpensive

Melody Lanes Cafe (American)
152 Harrison
(208) 226-2815
Inexpensive

BLACKFOOT

El Mirador (Mexican)
620 West Bridge Street
(208) 785-1595
Inexpensive

Homestead Family Restaurant (American)
1355 Parkway Drive
(208) 785-0700
Inexpensive–Moderate

POCATELLO

Buddy's (pizza/ISU favorite)
626 East Lewis
(208) 233-1172
Inexpensive–Moderate

Continental Bistro (fine dining)
140 South Main
(208) 233-4433
(see text)
Moderate–Expensive

Food for Thought (salads/sandwiches)
504 East Center
(208) 233-7267
Inexpensive

Grecian Key (Greek)
314 North Main Street
(208) 235-3922
Inexpensive

Mama Inez (Mexican)
390 Yellowstone Avenue
(208) 234-7674
Inexpensive–Moderate

Red Hot Roasters (coffeehouse)
737 East Clark Street
(208) 233-0902
Inexpensive

Remo's (Italian)
160 West Cedar
(208) 233-1710
Moderate

LAVA HOT SPRINGS

Riverside Restaurant (fine dining)
255 East Portneuf
(208) 776-5504
Moderate

Riverwalk Cafe (Thai)
695 East Main Street
(208) 776-5872
(see text)
Inexpensive

SODA SPRINGS

Betty's Cafe (American)
US 30 west of town
(208) 547-4802
Inexpensive

Cedar View Supper Club (American)
2525 US 30
(208) 547-3301
Inexpensive–Moderate

MONTPELIER

Butch Cassidy's Restaurant & Saloon (American)
230 North Fourth
(208) 847-3501
Inexpensive–Moderate

PRESTON

Big J Burgers (fast food)
196 North State Street
(208) 852-2800
Inexpensive

Deer Cliff Inn (American)
up Cub River Canyon
(208) 852-0643
(see text)
Inexpensive–Moderate

Mis Amores (Mexican)
101 North State Street
(208) 852-7133
Inexpensive-Moderate

MALAD CITY

**Me 'n' Lou's Diner
(American)**
75 South 300 East
(208) 766-2919
Inexpensive–Moderate

Eastern Idaho

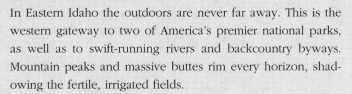

In Eastern Idaho the outdoors are never far away. This is the western gateway to two of America's premier national parks, as well as to swift-running rivers and backcountry byways. Mountain peaks and massive buttes rim every horizon, shadowing the fertile, irrigated fields.

Eastern Idaho is defined by three routes: Interstate 15, busy around Idaho Falls, then rather lonely on its trek north to Montana; U.S. Highway 20, which carries traffic to West Yellowstone, one of Yellowstone National Park's major entrances; and U.S. Highway 26, a popular route to Jackson Hole and Grand Teton National Park. As might be expected, summertime traffic is thick on US 20 and 26. Fortunately, several possible alternatives give travelers the chance to break away from the pack or make a loop tour of the region. The most popular of these, the Teton Scenic Byway and adjacent Mesa Falls Scenic Byway, are still well traveled—yet on these routes, you'll complete your trip feeling you've at least seen something other than the bumper of the vehicle in front of you.

For additional Eastern Idaho travel information, call (800) 634-3246 or (208) 356-5700; write Yellowstone/Teton Territory, 420 West Fourth South, Rexburg 83440; or see www.yellow stoneteton.org.

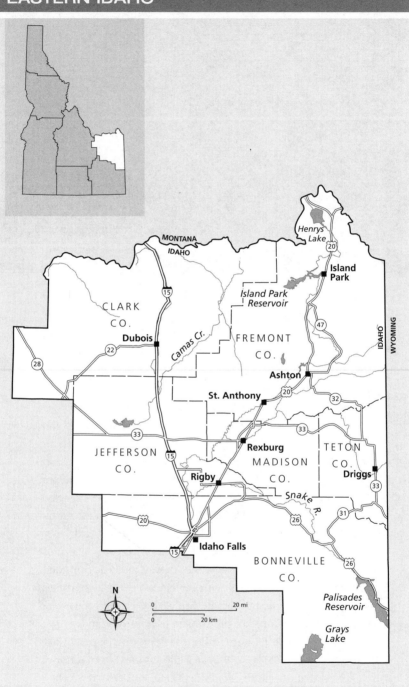

MONTANA
IDAHO

Henrys
Lake

Island
Park

Island Park
Reservoir

CLARK
CO.

Dubois

Camas Cr.

FREMONT
CO.

Ashton

IDAHO

WYOMING

St. Anthony

JEFFERSON
CO.

Rigby

Rexburg

MADISON
CO.

TETON
CO.

Driggs

Snake R.

Idaho Falls

BONNEVILLE
CO.

Palisades
Reservoir

Grays
Lake

N

0   20 mi
0   20 km

The Upper Snake River

Even within the city limits of Idaho Falls, nature makes her presence known. Unlike Twin Falls, where a set of Snake River cascades gave the town its name, Idaho Falls got its name before any falls really existed. The city of about 53,000 people started life as Eagle Rock, taking that name from a ferry built in 1863 by Bill Hickman and Harry Rickards. (The ferry was positioned near a small rock island on which bald eagles frequently nested in a juniper tree.) In its early days Eagle Rock served as a major fording point for miners heading to the riches of central and western Idaho; the community also was known as Taylor's Crossing or Taylor's Bridge for the early span built by James "Matt" Taylor. Later, Eagle Rock served as the center of railroad activity in the new Idaho Territory, but all that changed in 1887 when the Union Pacific moved its headquarters south to Pocatello and Eagle Rock's population plummeted. By 1891 a team of Chicago developers—Charles N. Lee, W. G. Emerson, D. W. Higbee, J. B. Holmes, and Bernard McCaffery—had descended on Eagle Rock. Seeing the rapids on the Snake River, they encouraged the locals to change the town's name to Idaho Falls. But it was not until 1911 that human-made falls were completed, giving the city legitimate claim to its name.

Since then Idaho Falls has made good use of its riverside location. The 2.5-mile *Idaho Falls Greenbelt* runs between the falls area and downtown, offering office and shop workers a pleasant place to spend the lunch hour. On weekends local residents flock to the greenbelt to enjoy a picnic, often sharing their food with the numerous ducks and geese who call the area home. Joggers, cyclists, strollers, and in-line skaters also enjoy the greenbelt's picturesque view. Another good outdoor destination, especially with children, is the *Tautphaus Park Zoo*. This once-decrepit facility has improved vastly

JULIE'S FAVORITES IN EASTERN IDAHO

Willard Arts Center Idaho Falls	**Idaho Centennial Carousel** Rexburg
Tautphaus Park Zoo Idaho Falls	**Mesa Falls Scenic Byway** near Ashton
Jefferson County TV & Pioneer Museum—Rigby	**Harriman State Park** near Island Park

over the past decade. Exhibits include an Australian outback area, a bi-level otter home, penguins, zebras, a children's petting zoo, a great pond filled with Idaho waterfowl, and an "Asian Adventure" exhibit with red pandas and sloth bears. Call (208) 528-5552 or see www.idahofallszoo.org for updates. Zoo admission is $5.00 for age thirteen and up, $2.50 for children ages four through twelve, and $3.50 for seniors age sixty-two and up. Children age three and under get in free. Summer hours (Memorial Day through Labor Day) are 9:00 a.m. to 8:00 p.m. Monday and 9:00 a.m. to 5:00 p.m. Tuesday through Sunday. In May and September the zoo is open daily from 9:00 a.m. to 4:00 p.m. In April and October it's open weekends only from 9:00 a.m. to 4:00 p.m. The closing times noted here are when the last admission is sold; the zoo gates remain open an hour after that. The zoo is closed November through March. Tautphaus Park is between Rollandet Avenue and South Boulevard east of Yellowstone Avenue in south Idaho Falls.

The big attraction downtown is the **Museum of Idaho,** which incorporated and expanded upon the former Bonneville County Historical Museum. Occupying both the former Carnegie Library and 20,000 feet of new space, the museum is now the largest in Idaho. Exhibits include a full-size, fleshed-out Columbian mammoth; a walk-through replica of the town of Eagle Rock as it may have appeared in 1891; a children's discovery area; and displays showing Eastern Idaho's role in the atomic age. The museum, located at 200 North Eastern Avenue, is open from 9:00 a.m. to 8:00 p.m. Monday and Tuesday and 9:00 a.m. to 5:00 p.m. Wednesday through Saturday. Admission is $6 for adults and $4 for youth age eighteen and under. Family passes cost $19 ($15 on Monday night). For more information call (208) 522-1400 or see www .museumofidaho.org.

The Idaho Falls Arts Council has its headquarters in the **Colonial Theater and Willard Arts Center.** Broadway shows and touring musicians come here frequently. The center also has a regular menu of arts classes for children and adults, and the Carr Gallery at the center has twelve shows a year featuring artists from around the state. For information on upcoming events, call (208) 522-0471; write the Idaho Falls Arts Council, 498 A Street, Idaho Falls 83402; or see www.idahofallsarts.org.

Across the street from the arts center at 439 A Street, **Vino Rosso** is a popular wine bar offering more than twenty ever-changing wines by the glass, eight craft beers on tap, and appetizer plates. You'll also find wireless Internet access and live entertainment a few nights each week. Vino Rosso is open Tuesday through Saturday at 11:00 a.m., closing at 8:00 p.m., except Friday and Saturday, when it's open until 9:00 p.m. Call (208) 525-8466 for more information.

TOP ANNUAL EVENTS IN EASTERN IDAHO

Mountain Arts Celebration/Hot Air Balloon Festival (early July)

Idaho Falls Chukars baseball (June–September)

Fourth of July Events Idaho Falls

Idaho International Dance and Music Festival, Rexburg (late July–early August) (see text)

Grand Targhee Bluegrass Music Grand Targhee (mid-August)

If a full meal is what you have in mind, there are plenty of good restaurants in downtown Idaho Falls. The **Snake Bite** at 401 Park Avenue is a longtime favorite. Try the Blue Snake burger with bleu cheese and mild chili peppers, or the house salad with cranberry vinaigrette dressing. **Grandpa's Southern Barbecue** at 1855 West Broadway Street—about 2 miles west of downtown—has devoted fans from all over southern Idaho who say it serves the best barbecue in the state. Save room for a slice of sweet potato pie.

Idaho Falls has an abundance of interesting architecture. The city's landmark structure is the **Idaho Falls Temple** of the Church of Jesus Christ of Latter-day Saints, located along the Snake River at 1000 Memorial Drive, its spire visible for miles. The temple's visitor center is open daily from 9:00 a.m. to 9:00 p.m. Free tours are available, and exhibits highlight Mormon history, art, and culture.

Elsewhere in the city, the Idaho Falls Historic Preservation Committee has prepared several informative pamphlets detailing walking tours. For example, the **Ridge Avenue Historic District** has sixty-seven notable buildings, with styles ranging from Queen Anne to craftsman to colonial revival. One of the most auspicious structures on the tour is the **First Presbyterian Church** at 325 Elm Street, a neoclassical building complete with Roman dome and Ionic portico. You can pick up brochures at area visitor centers and museums.

US 26, the road from Idaho Falls to Grand Teton National Park, isn't exactly off the beaten path. Sometimes in our hurry to get somewhere else, however, we miss seeing something interesting right along our way. Such is the case with the big, unusual looking building at 4523 US 26, a few miles north of Idaho Falls. For years I drove by wondering: Was it a school? A barn? Actually, it was both: a school built in 1899 and a barn erected shortly thereafter. Both structures now sit on the same site and serve as home to the **Country Store Boutique,** a fascinating antiques and gift emporium run by Eric and Melanie Seneff.

The Country Store Boutique boasts 15,000 square feet of the old, new, and unusual. Unlike many shops featuring antiques and collectibles, the Country Store Boutique doesn't feel musty and overstuffed. There's room to move around amid the solid old wood furniture, the antique glassware, and the Indian pottery and jewelry. The boutique also carries quilts, rugs, baskets, arrowheads, sheet music, folk art, and more. It's a great place to shop for a gift or for your home. The store is open from 10:00 a.m. to 6:00 p.m. Monday through Saturday. Call (208) 522-8450 for more information.

Do you watch television? If so, you may want to make a pilgrimage to Rigby, hometown of **Philo T. Farnsworth,** who invented the cathode-ray tube and made TV possible. No couch potato, Farnsworth was a natural whiz at all things mechanical.

Born in Utah in 1906, he moved to a farm near Rigby when he was a boy. Fascinated by electricity, he played violin in a dance orchestra to earn money for books on the topic. Farnsworth was fourteen years old when he got the idea for TV while plowing a field, and one day he sketched out his ideas on a blackboard at Rigby High School. By 1927 Farnsworth—then living in California—was able to prove his idea worked by transmitting a single horizontal line from a camera in one room to a receiving screen in another. He was just twenty-one.

In 1930 electronics giant RCA offered to buy Farnsworth's invention for a cool $200,000 and give him a job, but the inventor—preferring to preserve his independence—turned them down flat. That refusal apparently triggered the patent war between Farnsworth and RCA, which claimed one of its own

Neat Seats

If you get tired walking around Idaho Falls, a bench will probably be close at hand—and not just any bench, either. In 2005, the city arts council, the Idaho Falls Historic Downtown Foundation, and the City of Idaho Falls teamed up to install **Art You Can Sit On,** twenty regionally inspired public benches around the city center, with plans for more around town.

Fourteen different artists created the benches from concrete, wood, bronze, copper, marble, and river rock. Designs range from the whimsical (see the "Skateboard" bench by Carol Popenga at Park and A Streets) to the sublime ("Rest Surprise" by Lisa Bade at the Idaho Falls Public Library at 457 West Broadway Street). Eastern Idaho's natural beauty and wildlife are well represented, too, in such benches as "Trout" by Davidjohn Stosich at Shoup and A Streets and "Geese" by Marilyn H. Hansen on the 400 block of A Street. Stop by the arts council office for a walking tour brochure featuring the "sculptural seats."

employees, Vladimir Zworykin, had actually invented television. Zworykin had been tinkering with TV, but it wasn't until he visited Farnsworth's lab and saw the Idaho native's invention that he was able to duplicate Philo's principles and work. RCA eventually filed suit against Farnsworth, but the inventor prevailed, especially after his former high-school science teacher produced a 1922 sketch of Philo's television theory.

Farnsworth never finished high school, yet by the time he died in 1971 he had earned 300 patents and an honorary doctorate from Brigham Young University. His other notable inventions included the baby incubator, and at the time of his death, he was working on the theory of nuclear fission. Zworykin still sometimes gets credit for Farnsworth's television invention, but the truth is coming out—and someday Farnsworth's name may be as famous as those of fellow inventors Thomas Edison and Alexander Graham Bell.

The *Jefferson County TV and Pioneer Museum* has extensive displays about Farnsworth's life and work, including several handwritten journals, his Dictaphone, a Farnsworth television, much of his science book collection, and copies of just about anything ever written about the inventor. Other exhibits detail the early history of Jefferson County and its communities, including a Hall of Fame honoring local boys author Vardis Fisher and NFL great Larry Wilson. You also can see a jar of peaches canned in 1886! Museum hours are from 1:00 to 5:00 p.m. Tuesday through Saturday or by appointment. Suggested donation is $2 for adults and $1 for children. The museum is at 118 West First South in Rigby; just look for the high tower. The phone number is (208) 745-8423.

Feeling the need for relaxation? East of Idaho Falls near Ririe, *Heise Hot Springs* features a swimming pool with waterslide and a soothing 105°F mineral hot bath. But this popular resort doesn't stop there; visitors also can camp amid tall cottonwood trees, tee off on a nine-hole par twenty-nine golf course, grab a bite at the pizza parlor, or spread a picnic on the lawn. Heise Hot Springs is open year-round except for about three weeks in late October and November. For more information or current hours, call (208) 538-7312.

Mountain River Ranch, also near Ririe, offers wintertime sleigh rides nearly every night in December and weekends through February 14; meal options with these include Cornish game hen ($29) or prime rib ($39). Ask about reduced prices for children. In summer the ranch has a fee-fishing pond (no license needed), an RV park, and five rustic rooms for rent. For more information call (208) 538-7337; write to Mountain River Ranch, 98 North 5050 East, Ririe 83443; or see www.mountainriverranch.com.

The *Cress Creek Nature Trail* is yet another worthy stop east of Ririe off the Heise Road. This well-marked path gives visitors a chance to learn about

I Scream, You Scream . . .

The heavily Mormon country of Eastern Idaho and Utah reportedly has some of the highest ice-cream consumption rates in the United States. Some theorize this is because members of the Church of Jesus Christ of Latter-day Saints deny themselves other hedonistic pleasures like alcohol and caffeine. But it may also simply be because there's a lot of excellent ice cream made by places like **Reed's Dairy,** located on the western outskirts of Idaho Falls at 2660 West Broadway (just west of Broadway and Bellin, on the north side). Reed's makes about forty flavors, including such favorites as Moo Tracks (vanilla with peanut butter and chocolate chips) and Chunky Monkey (banana with nuts and chocolate chips). You'll usually have your pick of eighteen at any one time. Cones, shakes, sundaes, frozen yogurt, and sandwiches are available; there is informal seating inside and out; and self-guided tours are offered, too. Reed's Dairy is open Monday through Saturday from 8:00 a.m. to 10:00 p.m. in the summer and until 9:00 p.m. the rest of the year. For more information call (208) 522-0123.

The **Rainey Creek Country Store** is another can't-miss spot on the region's ice-cream circuit. This convenience store at the junction of US 26 and Highway 31 is famous for serving square ice-cream cones. Actually, it's the ice cream that is square—not the cones—but you get the idea. The staff scooped up 18,761 cones on the Fourth of July weekend in 2007, setting a new store record that may be broken by the time you read this. Rainey Creek offers twenty-four flavors, including huckleberries-and-cream, the favorite. Summertime store hours are 7:00 a.m. to 9:00 p.m. Monday through Saturday and 8:00 a.m. to 8:00 p.m. Sunday. The rest of the year hours are 7:00 a.m. to 8:00 p.m. Monday through Saturday and 9:00 a.m. to 7:00 p.m. Sunday. Phone (208) 483-2151.

There are only two legitimate excuses for passing up Rainey Creek: You are a diabetic or otherwise unable to eat ice cream, or you plan to head over Pine Creek Pass for a huckleberry shake in Victor.

Reed's Dairy

the flora, fauna, and geology of Eastern Idaho, all while enjoying some tremendous views. At one point the panorama stretches from the Caribou Mountain Range south of the Snake River all the way to the Beaverhead Range on the Montana border. The Blackfoot Mountains, Big Southern Butte and East Twin Butte, the Lost River Mountain Range, and the Menan Buttes can all be seen as well.

US 26 continues to follow the Upper Snake River toward its origin in Wyoming. The Swan Valley–Palisades area is one of Eastern Idaho's least populated and most scenic stretches. Several U.S. Forest Service campgrounds along Palisades Reservoir provide excellent bases for enjoying the region's good fishing and boating.

The **Lodge at Palisades Creek** is considered one of the top fly-fishing lodges in the West. This rustic-yet-elegant resort sits within casting distance of the South Fork of the Snake River and Palisades Creek, and the fly-fishing is so good that dinner is served until 10:00 p.m. to accommodate guests who wish to stay in the river well into the evening. Accommodations options include nine log cabins and a two-bedroom chalet, all overlooking the river. The lodge is spendy, as we say here in Idaho—$250 to $550 per person per day, plus guide service. For more information call (208) 483-2222 or write The Lodge at Palisades Creek, P.O. Box 70, Irwin 83428. The lodge's Web site is at www.tlapc.com, and its e-mail address is palisades@tlapc.com.

At Swan Valley, the traveler has a choice: Continue on US 26 to Alpine, Wyoming (the southern gateway to Jackson Hole), or take Highway 31 over Pine Creek Pass, elevation 6,764 feet. The latter provides access to Idaho's Teton Valley, the area we will explore next.

Teton Valley

Wyoming's Teton Range ranks among the world's most magnificent chains of mountains. The classic view of the Tetons is from the east, but Idaho's Teton Valley offers a less-crowded, equally scenic approach to the famed peaks. Highways 31, 33, and 32 (in that order, from south to north) have been designated Idaho's **Teton Scenic Byway.** Along the way the drive winds through several small towns—Victor, Driggs, and Tetonia—oriented to outdoor recreation.

If you drive in via Highway 31 over Pine Creek Pass, the first town you'll see is Victor. Hang a right here and you'll be bound for Teton Pass. Turn left, and you're 9 miles from Driggs. But before you leave Victor, consider stopping for a huckleberry milkshake at the **Victor Emporium,** 45 North Main Street. This old-fashioned soda fountain also sells sandwiches, along with fishing gear and Idaho souvenirs.

Driggs is the jumping-off spot for **Grand Targhee Ski & Summer Resort,** just over the border in Alta, Wyoming, but accessible only via the Tetons' Idaho side. Targhee is well known for getting a pile of snow, typically more than 500 inches each winter, including plenty of powder. The resort has added a detachable quad lift serving Peaked Mountain and bringing its lift-accessed terrain to 2,000 acres. There are plenty of programs for skiers and snowboarders of all levels, including a special "Magic Carpet" serving the beginners' area. But Targhee is also a target of extreme skiers, with several instructional workshops typically planned each winter.

Grand Targhee is worth a visit in warmer weather, too. Take the chairlift to the top of Fred's Mountain for a great Teton vista. There's also good mountain biking, horseback riding, tennis, hiking, swimming, and a climbing wall, plus activities and child care for kids of all ages. Resort staff even will arrange a fly-fishing, river-rafting, or soaring expedition nearby. Grand Targhee is also the site for several summer music festivals including the long-running Targhee Bluegrass Festival in mid-August. (Call for current dates.) For more information on Grand Targhee, call (800) TARGHEE; write to Grand Targhee Resort, 3300 East Ski Hill Road, Alta, WY 83422; or see www.grandtarghee.com.

Whether you want to carbo load for a mountain bike trek or enjoy one of the most unusual dining experiences in the West, you will not go hungry in the Teton Valley.

The ultimate Teton Valley dining experience may be at the **Lost Horizon Dinner Club** at 755 East Alta Road in Alta, Wyoming. Technically, like Grand Targhee, Lost Horizon shouldn't even be included in an Idaho guidebook. But since the only road there runs through Idaho, the Gem State can make at least partial claim to these treasures. Chuck and Shigeko Irwin serve a ten-course Chinese-Japanese meal once each evening on Friday and Saturday. In between the courses of the three-hour meal, guests can wander through the Irwins' 6,000-foot home, taking in the Teton views. Cost is $40 per person, and diners are asked to reserve a spot by calling (307) 353-8226 about two weeks ahead of time. Complimentary RV parking is offered after dinner. The Irwins have a life— they like to travel extensively and spend a good bit of time out of town—so don't be too disappointed if Lost Horizon is temporarily closed when you'd like to visit. Just consider it another reason to return to the Teton Valley.

The Teton Valley also has several unusual spots to bed down for one night or longer. The **Pines Motel–Guest Haus,** at 105 South Main in Driggs, is an unusual combination of mom-and-pop motel and bed-and-breakfast inn. Originally a two-story log cabin built about 1900, the building has been enlarged and is now home to John and Nancy Nielson and their family. Many travelers who stay at the Pines seem to wind up part of the Nielsons' extended clan,

Drive-In Delights

If you grew up in the '50s, '60s, or '70s, chances are you spent your share of summer nights parked in front of a massive outdoor movie screen, either fighting with your siblings or smooching with your sweetie. Drive-in movie theaters are dying out across much of North America, but there remain a fair number in the Gem State.

Appropriately enough for Idaho, the one just south of Driggs is called the **Spud Drive-In.** The Spud's giant potato is a landmark throughout the region, and its hamburgers are pretty famous, too. For twenty-four-hour movie information, call (208) 354-2727. Elsewhere in Idaho, you'll still find drive-in theaters at Idaho Falls, Twin Falls, Caldwell, Grangeville, Parma, Pocatello, Rexburg, and Soda Springs.

The Spud Drive-In also is one venue for the annual Spudfest Drive-in Family Film & Music Festival, held in mid-August. According to its organizers, the event celebrates the best independent filmmakers making family films. Recent festival hits include *Mobsters and Mormons,* which explored what might happen if *The Sopranos* moved to Salt Lake City; *The Snurks,* from the creators of *A Bug's Life;* and *5 Sides of a Coin,* about the birth of hip-hop culture.

Spudfest's executive producer is Teton Valley resident Dawn Wells, who played Mary Anne on the 1960s TV show *Gilligan's Island.* For more information see www.spudfest.org.

returning for holiday dinners and corresponding with the family. Outdoors, a stone fireplace, gas grill, lawn chairs, and play area offer summertime fun and relaxation. Local people and tourists alike turn out for Driggs's annual antiques show, held in the Nielsons' backyard almost every Fourth of July.

The Pines Motel–Guest Haus has seven rooms, including one suite with adjoining rooms, ranging in price from $55 to $80 double occupancy. Children twelve and under are welcome at no extra charge; pets are permitted for an additional $10 nightly. When requested, the Nielsons serve a big country-style breakfast on antique dishes in one of the original log-cabin rooms. The meal is $15 extra per person for guests (half-price for children twelve and under). For more information or reservations, call (800) 354-2778; write the Pines Motel–Guest Haus, P.O. Box 117, Driggs 83422; or send e-mail to the pines@tetontel.com.

Moose Creek Ranch is famous for its wild mustangs, which are adopted, trained, and ultimately added to the remuda. This is a working dude ranch, where guests are encouraged to learn as much as they can about horse care during their stay. But it's not all chores: Moose Creek visitors also enjoy lots of riding, plus hiking, swimming, and white-water rafting. Visitors stay in comfortable cabins or a five-bedroom ranch home and enjoy great Western grub. Special kids' programs are available, too. The cost of a weeklong stay is about $1,300 for adults, with lower rates for children. Shorter-term stays are available, too. Call (208) 787-2871 or (208) 313-4840 for more information, or e-mail info@moosecreekranch.com.

On the road to Grand Targhee, **_Teton Tepee Lodge_** caters to skiers and boarders. It's a cross between a hostel and a guest lodge, with small but pleasant rooms ($100 double occupancy) radiating from a cavernous common area and a bunkhouse-style dorm downstairs. Dorm bunks cost $40 a night for teens and adults, $30 for children under fourteen. For more information call (307) 353-8176; write Teton Tepee Lodge, 470 West Alta Road, Alta, WY 83422; or see www.tetonteepee.com/.

Yellowstone Country

Just west of Tetonia the Teton Scenic Byway continues north on Highway 32, terminating in Ashton, where the Mesa Falls Scenic Byway begins. Highway 33 continues west to Rexburg, the largest city in the Teton Valley. En route plan a stop at the **_Teton Dam Site,_** just a mile and a half north of Highway 33 near Newdale. A big pyramid of earth is all that is left of the Teton Dam, which collapsed June 5, 1976, killing eleven people and causing nearly $1 billion in damage. (The nearby Idaho state highway historical marker erroneously puts the death toll at fourteen.) The dam—widely opposed by environmentalists— had just been completed and its reservoir was still being filled when the breach occurred, unleashing eighty billion gallons of water toward Wilford, Sugar City, Rexburg, and Idaho Falls. Fortunately most Teton Valley residents heard

Global Hoedown

Little Rexburg, Idaho, is more globally minded than most towns of 27,000. Mormon-owned Brigham Young University–Idaho has several hundred international students and many American students who have served church missions all over the planet. But for one week during midsummer each year, Rexburg really starts to resemble a mini–United Nations. That's when about 300 folks from scores of foreign lands arrive to perform in the **_Idaho International Dance and Music Festival,_** a sort of Olympics for the arts. Past years' events have attracted dancers from Slovakia, India, Sweden, Malaysia, China, Russia, and dozens of other nations. In addition to daily dancing, visitors also can expect lots of Western—as in cowboy—entertainment, including a rodeo and barbecue. For more information or a schedule for the next festival, call (208) 356-5700 or see www.rexcc.com.

about the coming torrent and were able to evacuate before the waters swept through their towns.

The **Teton Flood Museum,** at 51 North Center Street in Rexburg, tells the tale in exhibits, photos, and a fascinating video called *One Saturday Morning.* (Ask at the front desk to view the tape.) Other displays at the museum showcase handmade quilts and a collection of more than 300 salt-and-pepper shakers. The Teton Flood Museum is open from 9:00 a.m. to 4:00 p.m. Monday through Saturday from June through August, and 10:00 a.m. to 3:00 p.m. Monday through Friday the rest of the year. Admission is $1 for adults and 50 cents for children. For more information phone (208) 359-3063.

While in Rexburg, don't miss the **Idaho Centennial Carousel,** located in Porter Park. The merry-go-round was built in 1926 by the Spillman Engineering Company of North Tonawanda, New York, and brought to Rexburg in 1952. By the late 1970s, the old carousel had been severely damaged by vandalism and the Teton Dam floodwaters. Now, however, the carousel is completely restored and truly one of a kind. Sherrell Anderson, a master carver, replaced more than fifty broken legs and ten tails for the carousel's horses, then created twelve new horses that match the originals in style but are festooned with symbols of Idaho.

The lead horse, "Centennial," is decorated with the state tree (whitepine), the state bird (mountain bluebird), the state flower (syringa), the state gemstone (star garnet), and the state seal. On the opposite side, the "Chief Joseph" horse is a gray Appaloosa (Idaho's state horse) fitted with ornamentation including a bear-claw necklace and a shield bearing the portrait of the great Nez Perce leader. The carousel's center also is decorated with pictures and symbols from all over the Gem State, including scenes of Hells Canyon, Balanced Rock, and Harriman State Park, as well as a moose, grizzly bear, and white-tailed deer. The Idaho Centennial Carousel is open for rides from noon to 7:00 p.m.

Idaho Centennial Carousel

Monday through Saturday during the summer months (except on days with bad weather). It can be reserved for group use; for more information call (208) 359-3020.

The *Menan Buttes,* rising southwest of Rexburg, are another National Natural Landmark and offer a fun spot for even the littlest hikers (although steep and challenging treks are available for those who want more adventure). The two 10,000-year-old buttes are composed of glassy basalt lava, found in only a few places in the world. The buttes are 800 and 500 feet high, with craters that measure a half-mile wide and about 300 feet deep. The buttes are north of the small town of Menan, or they may be reached by taking Highway 33 west of Rexburg.

St. Anthony, northeast of Rexburg on US 20, is famous for the sand dunes north of town. Like the dunes at Bruneau in Southwestern Idaho, the *St. Anthony Sand Dunes* are among the highest in the United States, but the St. Anthony complex is much larger than that at Bruneau—about 150 square miles total. The St. Anthony dunes are particularly popular with all-terrain vehicle enthusiasts. Small, rolling hills are suitable for beginners, and hills up to 500 feet in height offer challenges for more experienced riders. But because the dunes are under consideration for wilderness designation—and because sagebrush and other vegetation at the site provide critical habitat for deer, elk, and sage grouse—visitors must ride on the open sand only. For more information call the Bureau of Land Management (which oversees the dunes) at (208) 524-7500.

Ashton, another 14 miles east of St. Anthony on US 20, is the gateway to the *Mesa Falls Scenic Byway* (Highway 47), a beautiful 25-mile route that runs right by the viewpoints for Lower and Upper Mesa Falls and offers good views of the Teton Range, too. This is one scenic drive that takes barely longer than the more direct highway route, so by all means indulge.

At Lower Mesa Falls, an overlook appropriately dubbed Grandview provides a panorama featuring the Henry's Fork of the Snake River and the 65-foot falls, which are seen at some distance. Camping and picnicking are available nearby. Upper Mesa Falls, on the other hand, are viewed up close and personal. By descending a series of walkways, it's possible to stand right at the brink of the 114-foot Upper Falls, bask in its thunderous roar, and possibly see a rainbow. Benches offer the traveler an opportunity to sit and reflect on the falls and the tall pines all around. Big Falls Inn at Upper Mesa Falls, constructed around the turn of the century and used by travelers en route to Yellowstone National Park, now serves as a visitor information center. From Upper Mesa Falls the byway continues 12 miles to US 20, returning to the main route near Island Park.

Yellowstone's Back Door

A side trip from the Mesa Falls Scenic Byway takes travelers into the little-known *Bechler District of Yellowstone National Park*—an isolated area marked by broad meadows and abundant waterfalls. Remarkably, this rich region was almost lost to a reservoir in the early twentieth century, when Idaho farmers prevailed on Congressman Addison Smith to seek the Bechler area's removal from Yellowstone National Park so a dam could be built for irrigation water. In hearings, Smith insisted to his peers that the region was nothing more than a swamp. But fortunately naturalist William Gregg got word of the scheme and launched a crusade to save the Bechler district. The dam idea was finally crushed by public outcry.

To detour about 40 miles round-trip to "the Bechler," which sits astride the Idaho-Wyoming border, watch 4 miles outside Marysville (itself just east of Ashton) for the Cave Falls Road (1400 North) and follow it for 19 miles. A Forest Service campground sits just past the Wyoming border. Nearby, a picnic area affords a view of Cave Falls, which drop along the entire width of Falls River. An easy 1-mile trail leads through the pine forest to Bechler Falls. Longer trails in the region can take you to magnificent meadowlands and dramatic waterfalls, including Union Falls and Albright Falls; check at the Bechler ranger station (located at the end of a short spur road off the Cave Falls Road) for details and permits, which are required for overnight treks.

Island Park is among Idaho's top recreation areas. Aside from being a town of some 200 people, Island Park is a geological feature—a caldera, or volcanic basin, about 15 miles in diameter. The caldera was created when a volcano originally situated in the area erupted continuously for thousands of years before finally collapsing. This is also the land of the Henry's Fork, considered one of America's premier trout streams. The river was named for Andrew Henry, who passed through the area in 1810 as part of a fur-trapping expedition and established a trading post. These days numerous outfitters offer guide services and equipment for anglers, snowmobilers, and other recreationists.

Big Springs, located northeast of Island Park, is the source of much of the Henry's Fork flow and the home of some truly impressive rainbow trout. A National Natural Landmark, the springs are one of a kind, issuing at the rate of 92,000 gallons per minute from the same rhyolitic lava flows that created the caldera. The Targhee National Forest has a campground at the site. No fishing is allowed at Big Springs, but the trout will happily accept handouts of bread tossed by visitors. The John Sack Cabin, listed on the National Register of Historic Places, sits nearby and is open to visitors July 4 through Labor Day.

Mack's Inn Resort, on the banks of the Henry's Fork between Island Park and West Yellowstone, Montana, is another spot Idaho families have enjoyed for generations. The resort sports a variety of accommodations ranging from cabins of several sizes to condos, along with an RV park. Recreational amenities include float trips, paddleboats, miniature golf, basketball, volleyball, horseshoe pits, and more. Call (208) 558-7272 for more information; write Mack's Inn Resort, P.O. Box 10, Mack's Inn 83433; or see www.macksinn.com.

Island Park can be a noisy place in winter, what with all the snowmobilers racing across the white fields of snow. But solace isn't hard to find for those seeking a more serene wintertime experience. **Harriman State Park** has some of the state's best cross-country skiing, and the park is closed to snow machines. That's largely because the park is also a wildlife refuge, home to bald eagles, trumpeter swans, sandhill cranes, elk, deer, moose, and coyotes. Skiers and snowshoers are likely to catch glimpses of these and other animals during any winter trip through the park.

Harriman is peaceful in summertime, too. Trails ranging in length from 1 mile to 5.5 miles meander along the Henry's Fork, Silver Lake, and Golden Lake, or up to the top of a ridge where the Teton Range may be viewed. Again these paths are open only to nonmotorized use by hikers, mountain bicyclists, and horseback riders. Visitors may bring their own horse or rent one in the park.

Harriman State Park is also home to the **Railroad Ranch,** a collection of buildings erected in the early twentieth century by investors from the Oregon Short Line Railroad. Over time the ranch became a favorite retreat of prominent American industrialists and their families. It was E. H. Harriman, founder of the Union Pacific Railroad, who envisioned the ranch as a refuge for wildlife. Ironically, he never really got to enjoy the ranch, but his son and daughter-in-law, E. Roland and Gladys Harriman, spent six weeks of most summers at the ranch, and a cabin remains furnished much as they used it.

Over a half-century about forty buildings were constructed at the Railroad Ranch. Twenty-seven of these original structures still stand, and many are included in tours given during the summer months. No camping is available in the park, but you can rent the four-bedroom ranch manager's log house for $190 for four adults; extra adults are $12 a person per night. Fully furnished with a screened-in sun porch, knotty-pine walls, and a stone fireplace, it sleeps up to eight people and makes a great base for either a fly-fishing trip or winter outing. Like all accommodations at the park, it's accessible only by cross-country skis or snowshoes in winter. Another nicely furnished historic cabin, the three-bedroom Cattle Foreman's House, can sleep up to four adults for $140 plus an additional two people for $12 each. This cabin has two queen beds, bunk beds, a wood-burning stove, and a full kitchen. Harriman also has a bunkhouse that sleeps from fifteen to forty people at a per-person, per-night cost of $12, with a minimum fee of $180 per night. Finally, Harriman has two yurts accommodating up to six people for $45 per night. For reservations or more information about Harriman State Park, call (208) 558-7368; write Harriman State Park, 3489 Green Canyon Road, Island Park 83429; or see the Web site at www.idahoparks.org/parks/harriman.aspx.

From Island Park, it's possible to take back roads to the last area of Eastern Idaho on our itinerary, the opal mines of Clark County. A2, a county road, runs from just north of Island Park west to Kilgore and on to Spencer, which sits on I-15. Spencer is reportedly the only place in North America where opals are abundant enough to mine commercially. Several businesses in the Spencer-Dubois area sell finished gemstones and opal jewelry. The *Spencer Opal Mine* is open to the public for digging on summer holiday weekends (Memorial Day, Father's Day, the Fourth of July, and Labor Day) and occasional other summer weekends; call for dates. The cost is $40 per digger per day for up to five pounds of opal-bearing rock; extra pounds cost $8 apiece. When the mine isn't open, the headquarters (open daily from 8:00 a.m. to 8:00 p.m. mid-May through mid-September) has a "mini-mine" where visitors can pay $10 per adult or $5 per child for one pound of rock.

The opals rest in layers at the mine, and visitors dig in windrows of opal-bearing rock ranging in size from gravel to small boulders. The mine recommends the following tools be taken to the site: rock hammer, three- or four-pound crack hammer, points and chisels, eight- or ten-pound sledge hammer, bucket, spray bottle, gloves, sturdy shoes or boots, and safety glasses (which are required). Bring drinking water and a lunch, too; water to wash the mined rock is available on-site.

For more information call (208) 374-5476; write Spencer Opal Mines, 27 Opal Avenue, Spencer 83446; or see www.spenceropalmines.com. In the off-season, the mine owners can be reached at (928) 859-3752.

Places to Stay in Eastern Idaho

IDAHO FALLS

Hampton Inn
2500 Channing Way
(208) 529-9800
fax: (208) 529-9455
Moderate

Hilton Garden Inn
700 Lindsay Boulevard
(208) 522-9500
fax: (208) 522-9501
Moderate

Littletree Inn
888 North Holmes
(800) 521-5993
fax: (208) 523-7104
Inexpensive

Motel West
1540 West Broadway
(800) 582-1063
fax: (208) 524-1144
Inexpensive–Moderate

Red Lion Hotel on the Falls
475 River Parkway
(800) RED-LION
fax: (208) 529-9610
Moderate

Shilo Inn Suites Hotel
780 Lindsay Boulevard
(800) 222-2244
fax: (208) 522-7420
Moderate

Towne Lodge
255 E Street
phone/fax: (208) 523-2960
Inexpensive

RIGBY

Blue Heron Inn
4175 East Menan–Lorenzo
Highway
(866) 745-9922
Moderate–Expensive

South Fork Inn Motel
425 Farnsworth Way
(208) 745-8700
Inexpensive

SWAN VALLEY

South Fork Lodge
US 26
(877) 347-4735
fax: (208) 483-7007
Expensive

IRWIN

**The Lodge at Palisades
Creek**
(208) 483-2222
(see text)
Expensive

VICTOR

Moose Creek Ranch
215 East Moose Creek
Road
(800) 676-0075
fax: (208) 787-2284
(see text)
Moderate–Expensive

DRIGGS

Best Western Teton West
476 North Main Street
(208) 354-2363
fax: (208) 354-2962
Inexpensive–Moderate

Grand Targhee Resort
(Alta, Wyoming)
(800) TARGHEE
(see text)
Moderate–Expensive

Pines Motel–Guest Haus
105 South Main
(800) 354-2778
(see text)
Inexpensive–Moderate

Teton Tepee Lodge
(Alta, Wyoming)
(800) 353-8176
Moderate–Expensive

REXBURG

**Best Western
Cottontree Inn**
450 West Fourth South
(800) 662-6886
fax: (208) 356-7461
Moderate

CJ's Motel
357 West 400 South
(208) 356-5477
fax: (208) 359-1794
Inexpensive

Days Inn
271 South Second West
(800) 329-7466
fax: (208) 356-9242
Inexpensive

ST. ANTHONY

GuestHouse International
Henry's Fork Inn
115 South Bridge
(208) 624-3711
Inexpensive–Moderate

ASHTON

**Jessen's RV Park/
Bed & Breakfast**
1146 South US 20
(800) 747-3356
Inexpensive

Log Cabin Motel
1001 Main
(208) 652-3956
Inexpensive

ISLAND PARK

Mack's Inn Resort
US 20
(208) 558-7272
fax: (208) 558-9305
Inexpensive–Moderate

HELPFUL WEB SITES FOR EASTERN IDAHO

Idaho Falls Chamber of Commerce
www.idahofallschamber.com

Island Park area information
www.westyellowstonenet.com

Yellowstone National Park
www.nps.gov/yell/

Yellowstone Teton Territory
www.yellowstoneteton.org

Pond's Lodge
(208) 558-7221
Inexpensive-Moderate

Sawtelle Mountain Resort
4133 Lodge Pole
(208) 558-9366
Moderate

DUBOIS

Cross Roads Motel
391 South Reynolds
(208) 374-5258
Inexpensive

Places to Eat in Eastern Idaho

IDAHO FALLS

Brownstone Restaurant & Brewhouse (brewpub)
455 River Parkway
(208) 535-0310
Inexpensive–Moderate

The Cellar (fine dining)
3520 East.17th Street
(208) 525-9300
Expensive

Grandpa's Southern Barbecue (soul food)
1855 West Broadway Street
(208) 522-1890
(see text)
Inexpensive

A Little Bit of Mexico (Mexican)
465 East Anderson Street
(208) 528-8185
Inexpensive

O'Brady's (American)
1438 West Broadway
(208) 523-2132
Inexpensive–Moderate

The Sandpiper (steaks/seafood)
750 Lindsay Bouelvard
(208) 524-3344
Moderate

The Snake Bite (eclectic)
401 Park Avenue
(208) 525-2522
(see text)
Inexpensive–Moderate

Vino Rosso (wine bar)
439 A Street
(208) 525-8466
(see text)
Moderate

SWAN VALLEY

South Fork Lodge (fine dining)
Highway 26
(208) 483-2229
Moderate–Expensive

VICTOR

Knotty Pine (American)
58 South Main
(208) 787-2866
Moderate

Victor Emporium (soda fountain/lunch counter)
45 North Main Street
(208) 787-2221
(see text)
Inexpensive

DRIGGS

Lost Horizon Dinner Club (Japanese/Chinese)
755 East Alta Road (Alta, Wyoming)
(307) 353-8226
(see text)
Expensive

The Royal Wolf (American)
65 Depot Street
(208) 354-8365
Moderate

ALSO WORTH SEEING IN EASTERN IDAHO

Idaho Falls Aquatic Center

Idaho's Vietnam Veterans Memorial
Idaho Falls

Kelly Canyon Ski Area
east of Heise

Hess Heritage Museum
near Ashton

Flat Ranch Preserve (Nature Conservancy)
Island Park

Warbirds Café (American)
Driggs Reed Memorial
Airport
(208) 354-2550
Inexpensive-Moderate

REXBURG

Frontier Pies (American)
460 West 4th South
(208) 356-3600
Inexpensive

Me n' Stan's (American)
167 West Main Street
(208) 356-7330
Inexpensive

Pineapple Grill
(Island Fare)
383 South 2nd West
(208) 356-4398
Moderate

ST. ANTHONY

The Relay Station
(American)
593 North 2600 East
(208) 624-4640
Moderate

ASHTON

Frostop Drive-In
(fast food)
26 North US 20
(208) 652-7762
Inexpensive

Trails Inn Restaurant
(American)
213 Main
(208) 652-9918
Inexpensive–Moderate

ISLAND PARK

Hyde Lodge Restaurant
(fine dining)
3400 North US 20
(208) 558-7068
Moderate

Lodgepole Grill
(American)
3907 Phillips Loop Road
(208) 558-9379
Inexpensive–Moderate

ROBERTS

BJ's Bayou (Cajun)
Downtown Roberts
(208) 228-2331
Inexpensive–Moderate

Central Idaho

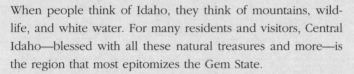

When people think of Idaho, they think of mountains, wildlife, and white water. For many residents and visitors, Central Idaho—blessed with all these natural treasures and more—is the region that most epitomizes the Gem State.

Few highways traverse Central Idaho; those that do are separated and isolated by mountain ranges. We'll explore this region in a counterclockwise fashion, starting on Highway 28 north from the ghost town of Gilmore to Salmon and environs. From Salmon, we'll head south on U.S. Highway 93, offer a few suggestions for sights in the Lost River Valley, then pick up Highway 75 for its trip to the Sawtooth National Recreation Area and Sun Valley. We'll finish by crossing the high desert on U.S. Highway 20.

For more Central Idaho travel information, call (800) 634-3347 or write the Central Idaho Rockies Association, P.O. Box 2420, Sun Valley 83353.

Lemhi River Valley

Highway 28 is also known as the **Sacajawea Historic Byway**—so named because the Lemhi River Valley, which Highway 28 parallels from the town of Leadore north to

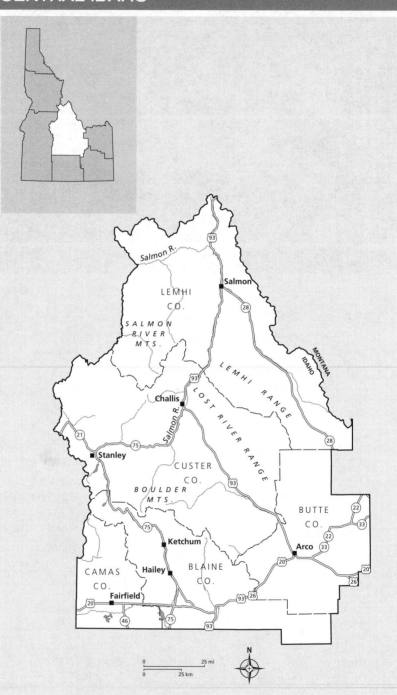

Salmon, was the birthplace of one of America's greatest heroines, Sacajawea. (Although national scholars prefer the spelling "Sacagawea," "Sacajawea" is more popular in Idaho.) This Shoshone Indian woman was an invaluable asset to the Lewis and Clark Expedition two centuries ago, as we shall see.

Central Idaho was the site of a major mining boom in the late nineteenth and early twentieth centuries, and the ghost town of **Gilmore** stands in mute testimony to those days. To get there watch for the historical marker telling of Gilmore near milepost 73, then take the road west immediately across the highway. Gilmore sat about a mile and a half west over a gravel, washboarded road, and its two dozen or so remaining buildings come into view almost immediately. ENJOY BUT DO NOT DESTROY, weathered signs warn the visitor. Look for the remnants of an old railroad bed. This was the Gilmore and Pittsburgh Railway—a branch railroad from Montana—which helped Gilmore's mines produce more than $11.5 million in silver and lead before a power plant explosion ended operations in 1929.

A most rewarding side trip is possible from Highway 28 to **Lemhi Pass,** where Meriwether Lewis became the first white American to cross the Continental Divide in August 1805. Traveling ahead of the rest of the Lewis and Clark Expedition, Captain Lewis was searching for the Shoshone Indians in hopes they could provide horses to help the Corps of Discovery travel overland. On August 12, Lewis's party moved west into the mountains from what is now Montana's Clark Canyon Reservoir, following what Lewis called a "large and plain Indian road . . . I therefore did not despair of shortly finding a passage over the mountains and of tasting the waters of the great Columbia this evening." Soon after, Lewis and his men reached a stream that he dubbed "the most distant fountain of the mighty Missouri in search of which we have spent so many toilsome days and restless nights." After pausing for a drink

JULIE'S FAVORITES IN CENTRAL IDAHO

Lemhi Pass
east of Tendoy

Greyhouse Inn Bed and Breakfast
Salmon

Galena Lodge
north of Ketchum

Silver Creek
west of Picabo

Craters of the Moon National Monument—west of Arco

from the stream, Lewis and his men continued to the top of the ridge, where Lewis later wrote he saw "immense ranges of high mountains still to the west of us with their tops partially covered with snow." It was a point of reckoning for the expedition. Lewis had crossed the divide, but the sight of those mountains meant there would be no easy passage to the Columbia.

The day after reaching Lemhi Pass, Lewis and his party came upon several Shoshones, who led the whites to their chief, Cameahwait. Lewis convinced the chief to accompany him back over the pass, where Clark and the rest were waiting with their baggage. It was to be a most extraordinary meeting, for it turned out that Cameahwait was the long-lost brother of Sacajawea, the Shoshone woman who—together with her husband Charbonneau and their infant son—had accompanied the Corps of Discovery after their winter stay in the Mandan Villages of North Dakota. Because of this family coincidence, the expedition was able to get the horses it needed.

To visit Lemhi Pass turn east at the small settlement of Tendoy. The steep and winding 26-mile loop drive to the pass isn't recommended for large RVs or vehicles towing trailers, but most pickup trucks and passenger vehicles in good shape will make it with no problem. (The Montana approach to the pass is much less steep; apparently a busload of Lewis and Clark buffs made it to the top that way.) Face west at the pass to see the ridge upon ridge of mountains Lewis described. At 7,373 feet, Lemhi Pass is the highest point on the Lewis and Clark Trail and one of the most pristine, too. It's a great place to watch a sunset. The primitive Agency Creek Campground sits 7.5 miles from the summit on the Agency Creek Road. Agency Creek, run by the Bureau of Land Management, has a vault toilet and picnic tables. Before returning to the highway, note the grave of Chief Tendoy, an Indian leader who commanded respect and influence. The burial site is sacred to Indians, and visitation by the general public is not considered appropriate. The small store at Tendoy sells gas and food; it's another 20 miles north to Salmon, where all services are available.

River of No Return

Even though it has just one stoplight, the Lemhi County seat of Salmon is one of Idaho's busiest recreation gateways. This is the outfitting spot for many trips on the Main Salmon, Idaho's "River of No Return." Many raft excursions run several days, but if time is limited, **_Kookaburra Guided Whitewater Trips_** offers a full-day trip for about $95 for adults, $80 to $85 for kids and teens, including a tasty lunch. Call (888) 654-4386 or see Kookaburra's Web site at www.raft4fun.com.

Salmon salutes Idaho's most famous native daughter at the ***Sacajawea Interpretive, Cultural, and Education Center.*** The site includes a small visitor center, an outdoor trail with interpretive panels, and several pieces of impressive public art, including a larger-than-life statue of the young Shoshone woman holding her baby, Jean Baptiste Charbonneau, nicknamed "Pomp" by William Clark. (The statue, by Agnes Vincen "Rusty" Talbot, also can be seen in front of the Idaho Historical Museum in Boise, where its production was funded in part by $8,000 in donations from Idaho schoolchildren.) Sacajawea Heritage Days, held annually in mid-August, feature frontier and Native American living history demonstrations. The Sacajawea Center is just south of Salmon on Highway 28. The grounds are open all year during daylight hours. The interpretive center is open daily late May through late September, and weekends only in May and October. For more information call (208) 756-1188 or see www.sacajaweacenter.org.

The ***North Fork Cafe,*** at the little town of the same name on US 93, is a popular stop for hungry Idaho river runners, anglers, and hunters. Breakfast offerings include eggs topped with homemade chili, plate-size pancakes, and corned beef hash and eggs. At lunchtime, guests chow down on a variety of sandwiches. Steaks, fish, chicken, and hickory-smoked barbecued ribs are among the dinner offerings, and don't forget the huckleberry pie—it's among the best in the state, when it's in season. The North Fork Cafe is open from 6:30 a.m. to 9:00 p.m. in the summer and 7:00 a.m. to 8:00 p.m. daily in winter. The phone number is (208) 865-2412 or (888) 432-0240.

Even if you're not planning a river trip on the Main Salmon from North Fork, you may want to drive the river road a ways anyhow. The road is paved for about 16 miles, then it's a good packed gravel byway.

There's a small settlement at Shoup, which until 1991 had the last hand-cranked telephone system in the United States. Another 2 miles west, the Class III+ to IV ***Pine Creek Rapids*** are the highlight of most short river trips on

TOP ANNUAL EVENTS IN CENTRAL IDAHO

Sun Valley Ice Show
(mid-June through September)

Sawtooth Mountain Mamas Arts and Crafts Fair, Stanley (mid-July)

Sun Valley Symphony
(late July–early August)

Sacajawea Heritage Days
Salmon (mid-August)

Wagon Days
Ketchum (Labor Day weekend)

Swing 'n' Dixie Jazz Jamboree
Sun Valley (mid-October)

this stretch of river. William Clark, making a reconnaissance trip in the area in August 1805, may have seen these rapids from a nearby bluff. The wild river, coupled with the canyon's sheer rock cliffs, convinced Clark he and Lewis would need to find a safer route west.

West of Pine Creek Rapids, a wayside has been built at the **Shoup Rock Shelter,** a site dating from perhaps 8,000 years ago. Pictographs can be seen here. The North Fork Road ends at River Mile 46, where the Corn Creek boat ramp marks the start of the Salmon's federally designated Wild and Scenic stretch. Permits are required to float the 79-mile section from here to Long Tom Bar. Near the put in, Salmon River Lodge offers everything from drop-in meals to guided hunting, floating, fishing, and pack trips. Rates start at $85 per person per night; campsites are available too. For lodging reservations or more information, call (800) 635-4717 or see www.salmonriverlodge.com.

It's worth driving north from North Fork on US 93 toward the Montana border. This area is attracting lots of lone-wolf entrepreneurs for whom Salmon apparently is just too dang big a town.

At Gibbonsville, just before the highway starts its climb to Lost Trail Pass, pull in for a meal at **Ramey's Broken Arrow.** Situated in a building that dates to 1897, the Broken Arrow serves delicious and authentic pork carnitas, enchiladas, tacos, and more, with most entrees priced from $9 to $12. The Broken Arrow also has rustic cabins ($45) and RV spaces ($20) for rent. The restaurant is open for dinner Thursday through Sunday from Mother's Day weekend through the first weekend in November. Special annual events include a cowboy poetry festival in June and a bluegrass camp out the weekend after Labor Day. Call (208) 865-2241 or see www.thebrokenarrow.com for more information.

South of Salmon on US 93, two notable Western-style resorts have lately come under the same management. Near the road, **Twin Peaks Ranch** ranks among the oldest dude ranches in the United States. Guests who have never been on horseback can learn to ride in the rodeo arena before setting off on gentle trails, while more experienced riders have the option of traveling high into the Idaho Rockies. Several stocked ponds provide a challenge to anglers, and guided trips are offered to seldom-fished private streams. Twin Peaks also offers scenic and white-water floats on the Salmon River, as well as guided hunts for elk and deer. Twin Peaks caters to one-week stays, priced at $1,718 to $2,055 in summer, with reduced rates for children and for off-season stays. Some shorter stays are possible, depending on availability. For more information call (800) 659-4899; write Twin Peaks Ranch, P.O. Box 774, Salmon 83467; or see www.twinpeaksranch.com. Twin Peaks also runs nearby **Williams Lake Lodge,** an alpine fishing retreat at a lake full of fat rainbow trout. All

Williams Lake Lodge

Twin Peaks stays include a trip to Williams Lake, and especially avid anglers can spend their whole week there.

Back on US 93, the *Greyhouse Inn Bed and Breakfast* is 12 miles south of Salmon. This beautiful Victorian building was once a hospital in Salmon and was trucked to its current location in the early 1970s. Proprietors Sharon and David Osgood offer four guest rooms in the main house, two with private baths. Or ask about more private accommodations in the Carriage House or Lewis and Clark cabins. The Osgoods provide a full breakfast to get guests primed for a day of hiking, hunting, floating, or fishing. Have them give you directions to Goldbug Hot Springs (sometimes called Elk Bend Hot Springs), on Warm Springs Creek about 11 miles away. It's one of the finest hot springs in Idaho. Rates at the Greyhouse are $79 to $150 a night in summer, $65 to $125 in winter. For current information call (800) 348-8097; write the Greyhouse Inn, 1115 US 93 South, Salmon 83467; or see www.greyhouseinn.com.

For lodgings of a different sort, check out the *Dugout Ranch,* homestead of Richard "Dugout Dick" Zimmerman. Dugout Dick—born in 1916—has been on this piece of land 19 miles south of Salmon since 1948, and he says he helped put in the road and the bridge over the Salmon River. But it wasn't until 1969 that he started digging caves and multiroom tunnels out of the hillside.

He now has about a dozen, and yes, they are available for rent at a cost of $25 a month or $5 a night. Rooms are outfitted with a woodstove and a bed, although visitors should bring their own sleeping bags.

Dugout Dick's accommodations are certainly spartan and not to everyone's taste, but a handful of people—including a couple from Idaho Falls and a teacher from Missoula—find the caves so cozy they consistently spend their weekends at the Dugout Ranch. One of Idaho's true characters, Dugout Dick has been featured on CNN and National Public Radio, in *National Geographic* magazine, and in several books. He'll be glad to tell you a few tales, too. If you stop by the ranch and find it deserted, don't worry—Dick is probably just out on his grocery run to Salmon. Have a look around, and he'll be back before you know it.

It's 60 miles from Salmon to Challis on US 93, with the road following the Salmon River the whole way. In Challis, the locals like to eat at ***Antonio's Pizza and Pasta*** at Fifth and Main uptown. Every Friday Antonio's offers an all-you-can-eat soup, salad, and breadsticks bar from 11:00 a.m. to 3:00 p.m. for about $7. The wide-ranging menu also includes calzones, sandwiches, burgers, and about a dozen dinner entrees. You won't leave hungry. Antonio's is open from 11:00 a.m. to 10:00 p.m. Monday through Thursday, 11:00 a.m. to 11:00 p.m. Friday and Saturday, and noon to 10:00 p.m. Sunday, with somewhat reduced hours in winter. The phone number is (208) 879-2210.

At Challis, travelers need to choose between taking US 93 south to Arco or hopping off on Highway 75, which continues along the Salmon River. Either way, the scenery is glorious.

US 93 streaks south through the Lost River Valley. Fourteen miles southeast of Challis at about milepost 150, the road bisects ***Grand View Canyon,*** a short but impressive gorge forged about 350 million years ago. Another 20 miles south, plan a stop at the ***Mount Borah*** interpretive area to marvel at Idaho's highest mountain and learn about the 1983 earthquake that struck this area (see sidebar).

South of Mount Borah, watch for the Trail Creek Road sign and turn right for a "shortcut" to Sun Valley. Trail Creek Road (Forest Road 208) is open in the summer months and accessible to passenger vehicles, although the westernmost section descending into Wood River Valley is steep and rocky. It's a good idea to inquire locally or check with the Forest Service in Ketchum (208-622- 5371) to assess road conditions.

Halfway to Sun Valley along Trail Creek Road, Forest Road 135 heads south from the byway toward ***Wild Horse Creek Ranch,*** another classic Idaho guest ranch well suited for family reunions and group retreats. Year-round, the ranch offers a luxurious base camp for mountain activities ranging

The Borah Earthquake

On the morning of October 28, 1983, an earthquake measuring 7.3 on the Richter scale rocked Idaho's Lost River region. This temblor was the strongest in the continental United States in a quarter-century, and it proved more powerful than the two high-profile California earthquakes in 1989 and 1994, which combined killed 123 people. But because Central Idaho is so sparsely populated, the damage was correspondingly less, though not insignificant: Two children were killed in Challis, and area residents lost property valued in the millions.

Geologically, the quake made its mark, too. A side road from US 93 leads to a viewing area where it's easy to see the scarp left in the quake's wake, 21 miles long and 10 to 14 feet high. This rock ledge at the base of the Lost River Range stands in raw testimony to the temblor.

Mount Borah gained 2 feet in elevation during the 1983 quake, which means it now stands at 12,662 feet. The mountain, earlier christened Beauty Peak, was renamed in 1933 for William Borah, the "Lion of Idaho," who served in the U.S. Senate from 1907 to 1940. Experienced mountaineers say Borah Peak can be climbed up and back in a day, but trekkers need to be well prepared mentally and physically for the strenuous, if not technical, ascent. Check with the Forest Service office on Custer Street in Mackay for more information—and to let them know of your plans. For more information call (208) 588-2224.

from fishing and hiking to cross-country skiing and snowmobiling. Ten guest rooms rent for between $100 and $125 a night, double occupancy; there is a minimum of ten people. Kids can camp out in tepees if they like. Wild Horse Creek also can set you up with everything from a two-hour trail ride to an extended big-game hunt. For more information call (208) 588-2575 or write Wild Horse Creek Ranch, 4387 Wild Horse Creek Road, Mackay 83251. Past the Wild Horse Creek turnoff, Forest Road 135 follows the East Fork of the Big Lost River to Copper Basin, spectacularly situated between the Pioneer Mountains and the White Knob Mountains.

Back on US 93, it's 26 miles from Mackay to Arco. But we'll now return our attention to Highway 75. Just as US 93 did north of Challis, Highway 75 hugs the Salmon River tightly here, making for slow but stupendously scenic driving. It's easy to spend an entire day lingering here and there along the 55-mile drive from Challis to Stanley. Interesting stopping spots along the way include **Torrey's Resort and RV Park,** which offers good food and cozy cabins at a popular float trip takeout west of Clayton, and the **Sunbeam area** with its history and hot springs.

To many Idahoans unable to take lengthy and often expensive river trips down the Main or Middle forks of the Salmon River, a day float down this stretch of the Salmon is a minivacation and a whole lot of fun. Quite a few excursions leave from Sunbeam Village, including those offered by **White Otter Outdoor Adventures.** Whether you want lots of white-water rapids or a calm scenic float, the Salmon delivers. Fun-seekers have their choice of oar boats, where the guide does all the work; paddle rafts, in which floaters help propel the boat downriver; and one-person inflatable kayaks that can be maneuvered by just about anyone fourteen or older. Cost for a half-day float with snack (including taxes) is $67 per teen or adult and $56 for kids; full-day trips including a deluxe meal run $86 for adults and teens, $76 for the small fry. Children must be at least four years old—eight in high-water season—to go floating. Call (208) 726-4331 or see www.whiteotter.com for reservations or more information. (Note: In attempts to protect salmon-spawning areas, Sawtooth National Recreation Area officials occasionally close this part of the river to boating in late summer. So check with outfitters or the SNRA at 208-727-5013.)

Several accessible hot springs are located along Highway 75 west of Sunbeam. East to west there's the very visible **Sunbeam Hot Springs,** complete with bathhouse; **Basin Creek Hot Spring,** located near a campground of the same name; **Campground Hot Spring,** actually located in the Basin Creek Campground (walk into the bushes at Site 4); **Mormon Bend Hot Spring,** good for late-summer soaking (since a river crossing is necessary); and **Elkborn Hot Spring.** Although these springs are all located near the highway, soakers are apt to feel a million miles away as they lean back and gaze at the blue sky above.

The Stanley Basin

If the Tetons are the West's most magnificent mountain range, Idaho's Sawtooths run a close second. Stanley, situated at the Highway 75–Highway 21 intersection, is the hub of Sawtooth country—in fact, it's the only place in the United States where three National Forest Scenic Byways converge. In summer there's camping, fishing, and boating on the Salmon River and at Redfish Lake, and there are hikes high into the mountains and adjacent wilderness areas. But for many people winter is prime time in the Stanley Basin because that's when snowmobiling season starts. The area has more than 200 miles of groomed trails and outfitters poised to help visitors with everything from snow machine rental to lodging and meals.

For example, **Sawtooth Rentals** charges $100 to $160 per day for a snowmobile; expert guides, snowsuits, boots, helmets, and gloves are available for rent, too. The company also has its own motel, with rooms starting at about $65 in winter, $85 in summer. For more information call (208) 774-3409.

Stanley is the departure point for most trips on the **Middle Fork of the Salmon River,** which many people regard among the world's premier white-water trips. The classic Middle Fork trip covers 105 miles of river over six days, with prices between $1,750 to $2,000 per person. Many outfitters run the Main Salmon; for help in choosing and booking a trip on the Middle Fork or other Idaho rivers, contact the Idaho Outfitters and Guides Association at (208) 342-1919, or see its Web site at www.ioga.org. Many Middle Fork outfitters also have listings on www.idahosmiddlefork.com.

The **Idaho Rocky Mountain Ranch** south of Stanley ranks among the Gem State's most renowned guest ranches. Built in 1930 and listed on the National Register of Historic Places, and surrounded by more wilderness than anywhere in the continental United States, the ranch offers an abundance of activities (although it sometimes seems visitors are happiest just relaxing on the huge front porch of the central lodge, with its view of the Sawtooth Mountains). On-site diversions include a hot springs swimming pool, horseback riding, fishing in the Salmon River or the stocked catch-and-release pond, exploring the 900-acre property on foot or bike, horseshoes, and wildlife viewing. Rafting, rock climbing, and visits to nearby ghost towns are available as well.

Idaho Rocky Mountain Ranch has seventeen cabin accommodations and four lodge rooms, all with private baths. A continental breakfast buffet plus full hot breakfast menu greet guests each morning, and dinners are served nightly. Five nights a week, diners enjoy multicourse meals designed and prepared by a culinary institute–trained chef and on-site baker. Entree choices might include seared Lava Lake lamb, pancetta-wrapped ahi tuna, and house-made tricolor ravioli. There also are weekly barbecues and Dutch oven cookouts. Rates (including breakfast, dinner, and use of the ranch facilities) range from $275 to $445 double occupancy, depending on accommodations chosen and length of stay. Children's and single occupancy rates are available. For more information or reservations, call (208) 774-3544; write Idaho Rocky Mountain Ranch, HC 64, Box 9934, Stanley 83278; or see www.idahorocky.com.

Stop at the **Galena Summit** overlook for another great view of the Sawtooth Mountains and the headwaters of the Salmon River. It's hard to believe this tiny trickle of a stream becomes the raging River of No Return, the longest river flowing within one state in the continental United States. Some of Idaho's best telemark skiing can be found on the Stanley Basin (or Humble Pie) side of Galena. Gentler terrain is available in the vicinity of Galena Lodge, situated at the base of the mountain on the Sun Valley side. The lodge features hearty food along with ski rentals, lessons, and overnight ski-hut accommodations. From Galena Summit it's about a half-hour drive to the Sun Valley–Ketchum area.

Wood River Valley

The Wood River Valley is more famously known as Sun Valley–Ketchum, site of America's first destination ski resort. In 1935 Union Pacific chief Averell Harriman dispatched Count Felix Schaffgotsch to find the perfect setting for a European-style ski haunt. After scouring the West, the count finally found what he was looking for near the scruffy Idaho mining town of Ketchum. Ironically, when the Sun Valley resort opened in 1936, there was barely enough snow to cover the slopes. But today, Sun Valley has state-of-the-art snowmaking capabilities, and it's widely considered one of the best ski areas in North America (though the experience doesn't come cheap; single-day high-season lift tickets are nearing $80).

Skiing is the big draw here, of course, but there are other reasons to visit, too. Eating is another favorite pastime in the Wood River Valley; without a doubt, the area is home to some of the state's best and most creative restaurants. The dining scene seems in a state of constant evolution, but a few perennial favorites include the creative **Ketchum Grill,** the casual **Pioneer Saloon,** and **Whiskey Jacques',** which features raucous live entertainment in addition to its menu of pizza, sandwiches, and salads. For an unusual winter dining experience, take a sleigh ride from the Sun Valley Inn to **Trail Creek Cabin.** The horse-drawn sleigh rides run three times nightly, Tuesday through Saturday mid-December through March. Call (208) 622-2135 for more information.

In the summertime Sun Valley offers a wide selection of special events. The **Sun Valley Summer Symphony,** the largest free admission symphony in the United States, features concerts in a pavilion on the Sun Valley Resort lawn and various other venues from late July to mid-August. Call (208) 622-5607 for performance dates and programs. But probably no local summer attraction is as unique as the **Sun Valley Ice Show.** The biggest stars in figure skating— Katarina Witt, Nancy Kerrigan, Brian Boitano, and Sasha Cohen, to name a few—appear each summer. General admission tickets start at $29; dinner buffet tickets also are available. Contact the Sun Valley Sports Center at (208) 622-2135 for more information.

Of course, Sun Valley is an excellent base from which to explore the neighboring Pioneer, Boulder, Smoky, Sawtooth, and White Cloud Mountains. **Venture Outdoors,** a Wood River Valley–based outfitter, offers a variety of guided adventures ranging from its five-hour "Take a Llama to Lunch" trek (priced at $95 per person) to multiday llama packing and mountain biking trips. Venture Outdoors also leads sea kayaking expeditions to locales as close as Magic Reservoir and as far as the Oregon Coast. For more information see www.venout.com; call (800) 528-LAMA; or write Venture Outdoors, P.O. Box 2251, Hailey 83333.

Ernest Hemingway spent part of his last years in Ketchum, and fans of his writing will find several local spots worth a stop. First there's the **Hemingway Memorial** located along Trail Creek east of town; take Sun Valley Road east from the stoplight in downtown Ketchum, and watch for the sign on your right. A short path leads to a memorial as spare as Papa's prose, topped by a rugged bust of the author and embellished by this passage Hemingway wrote in 1939 while in Idaho:

> *Best of all he loved the fall*
> *the leaves yellow on the cottonwoods*
> *leaves floating on the trout streams*
> *and above the hills*
> *the high blue windless skies*
> *. . . now he will be part of them forever.*

Hemingway first came to Idaho in 1939 and visited many times over the next two decades. In 1959 he and his wife, Mary, finally bought a home in Ketchum, but by 1961, apparently depressed over his failing health, he was dead, the victim of a self-inflicted shotgun blast. He is buried in the Ketchum Cemetery, located just north of the downtown area. Look for two pine trees growing closely together near the rear of the graveyard; there you'll find the plots of Ernest Miller Hemingway and his last wife, Mary. Like Jim Morrison's grave in Paris, Hemingway's burial site sometimes attracts people who want to spend some time with the writer's spirit. On one visit this author had been preceded by a pilgrim who had left behind a pack of Dutch Masters little cigars—three left out of the box as if in homage—and an empty bottle of Maker's Mark whiskey.

For more local history, check out the **Ketchum–Sun Valley Heritage and Ski Museum.** Located in the former Civilian Conservation Corps–built Forest Service complex at 180 First Street East in Ketchum, the museum has a great collection of early ski gear and pioneer memorabilia. Hours are 11:00 a.m. to 3:30 p.m. Monday through Friday and 1:00 to 4:00 p.m. Saturday, with admission by donation. Call (208) 726-8118 for more information.

Sun Valley and Ketchum are full of interesting places to stay. If you'd like to sleep where Hemingway and countless other celebrities have slept, check into the venerable **Sun Valley Lodge,** which may have the most comfortable beds in Idaho. Rooms start at about $209 in peak season and $149 in the shoulder seasons; call (800) 786-8259 for reservations. The **Lift Tower Lodge** has some of Sun Valley–Ketchum's least expensive rooms, still priced about

Preserving the Past

Heroes, rogues, scoundrels, and saints . . . they're all well represented at the **Blaine County Historical Museum,** located at Main and Galena Streets in Hailey. This is the repository for the Joe Fuld Political Button Collection, among the largest of its type in the world. Fuld was an early Hailey businessman who started collecting political memorabilia in the late nineteenth century and wound up with more than 5,000 items of campaign souvenirs, not just buttons but handkerchiefs, pencils, posters, an ashtray used by Teddy Roosevelt, even the inaugural ball program from 1881.

The museum also has a corner devoted to **Ezra Pound,** the iconoclastic writer born in Hailey in 1885. Pound's parents left Idaho when Ezra was only fifteen months old, but the poet seemed ever after to consider himself an Idahoan. Perhaps he felt the state's outpost image was one well suited to his own renegade reputation. Pound went on to pen thousands of poems (including the epic Cantos series), but he outraged many when he embraced fascism and started making anti-American broadcasts from Europe during World War II. Pound later renounced totalitarianism, and he is now best remembered as a champion of other writers, including T. S. Eliot and Ernest Hemingway.

The Blaine County Historical Museum is open Memorial Day weekend through October. Hours are from 11:00 a.m. to 5:00 p.m. Monday through Saturday and 1:00 to 5:00 p.m. Sunday. Admission is by donation. For more information call (208) 788-1801. Off-season tours for five people or more are available. Call (208) 788-2348 or (208) 788-3497 to make arrangements.

$80 to $95 despite recent upgrades. The motel's namesake, salvaged from the 1939-vintage exhibition chairlift on Sun Valley's Bald Mountain, is a local landmark. Call (800) 462-8646 to book a room.

The area also has several notable B&Bs, including the European-style **Knob Hill Inn.** A Relais & Chateaux–affiliated inn, the Knob Hill has twenty-six guest suites and rooms, each with a balcony and mountain views. The location is good, just a short stroll from downtown Ketchum. Rates run $250 for a king room, $325 for a fireplace room, $400 for a suite, and $500 for a penthouse suite; all include breakfast. For more information see www.knobhillinn .com; write 960 North Main Street, Ketchum 83340; or call (800) 526-8010.

Hailey and Bellevue, the two "lower valley" towns, are much less known than Ketchum and Sun Valley. That's not saying they lack in glitz, however: Actors Bruce Willis and Demi Moore may no longer be a couple, but both still have homes in the area. Both also served on the board of **Company of Fools,** a theatrical troupe that presents most of its performances in Hailey at the Liberty Theatre. Willis has even appeared onstage in the company's productions of Sam Shepard's *Fool for Love* and *True West.* Company of Fools was the first Idaho theater to attain "constituent" status from Theatre Communications Group, which puts it in the same league with such top playhouses as the Guthrie in Minneapolis, Lincoln Center Theater in New York, and the Seattle Rep. (Others are the Boise Contemporary Theater and the Idaho Shakespeare Festival.) For tickets or information on upcoming shows, call (208) 788-6520 or see the Web site at www.companyoffools.org.

Camas Lilies and Lava Beds

South of Bellevue more vehicles topped with ski racks travel the intersection of Highway 75 and US 20 than any other in Idaho. Most are heading north to Sun Valley, of course, but a growing number are destined for **Soldier Mountain** near Fairfield. Lift tickets at Soldier Mountain cost less than half what they do at Sun Valley, so it's a good family bargain. The skiing's not bad, either, with three dozen runs and 1,400 feet of vertical drop. Soldier also offers snowcat skiing. For more information on current hours and prices, call (208) 764-2526 or see www.soldiermountain.com.

Named for a fire lookout on the westernmost peak of the Soldier Mountain Range, the **Iron Mountain Inn** at 325 West US 20 in Fairfield specializes in charbroiled steaks and prime rib. The latter is served Friday and Saturday night for $13.95 for eight ounces and $16.95 for twelve ounces. The Iron Mountain Inn is open from 11:00 a.m. to 10:00 p.m. Wednesday through Sunday. There's an RV park on the premises, too. The phone number is (208) 764-2577.

This part of Central Idaho is known as the Camas Prairie for the beautiful blue flowers that were such an important food source for the Indians. (Yes, part of North Central Idaho near the Nez Perce reservation is known as the Camas Prairie, too.) The week before Memorial Day is generally the best time to see the flowers in midbloom; they're at their best the spring after a wet winter.

North of Fairfield the **Soldier Mountain Ranch and Resort** offers golf, fishing, tennis, and swimming in the summer; cross-country skiing and snowmobiling come winter; and gorgeous sunrises and sunsets year-round. Couples seeking a romantic weekend should ask about the honeymoon suite in the main lodge, featuring a fireplace, sunken tub with mirrors all around it, and a European-style tiled bathroom boasting an oversize shower with two showerheads, all for $100 a night. The resort also has a variety of other accommodations priced from $70 (terrace and poolside rooms in the main lodge) to $200 (the 1892 Homestead/Tree House, which has rustic charm and modern features and can sleep up to a dozen people). The resort is a good site for family reunions and retreats. Call (208) 764-2506 for more information or reservations.

East of the Highway 75/US 20 junction, drivers soon spy *Silver Creek,* a fly-fishing dream stream. This was Hemingway's favorite fishing hole, and avid anglers say it's one of the best anywhere in the world, period. The Nature Conservancy protects part of Silver Creek with a wonderful preserve that also features a short nature trail. Silver Creek runs close to the little ranching town of Picabo, which some lexicologists say is Indian for "silver water." If the town's name—pronounced like the children's game—sounds familiar, it's probably because Picabo's namesake is Picabo Street, the now-retired champion Olympic and World Cup skier who grew up plying the slopes at Sun Valley. Picabo actually grew up in another tiny Wood River Valley town, Triumph, and somehow that town's name seems apt for her, too.

U.S. Highways 20 and 26 come together at Carey. From here, it's 25 miles east to *Craters of the Moon National Monument.* From Native Americans to early white explorers to the Apollo astronauts, people long have been fascinated with the strange landscapes of this region. Indians probably never lived on the harsh lava lands, but artifacts found in the area show they visited, probably to hunt and gather tachylite—a kind of basaltic volcanic glass—for arrow points. In the early twentieth century, Boisean Robert Limbert extensively explored the lava flows; it was his work and an article he penned in *National Geographic* that led to Craters of the Moon being named a national monument in 1924. In 1969 a group of Apollo astronauts preparing to go to the moon first visited Craters to get a feel for what the lunar landscape might be like.

The same experiences are available today. Though Craters has a popular 7-mile loop drive offering opportunities for several short hikes, it also has a surprisingly accessible designated wilderness area that receives much less use than the rest of the monument. The best time to visit is in the spring, when delicate wildflowers cover the black rock, or in fall after the often-extreme heat of the desert summer abates. In winter the loop road is closed to vehicular traffic but may be enjoyed by cross-country skiers or on snowshoes.

There are two predominant types of lava at Craters: the jagged aa (pronounced "ah-ah," Hawaiian for "hard on the feet") and the smoother pahoehoe (also Hawaiian, meaning "ropey" and pronounced "pa-hoy-hoy"). Both may be seen on the North Crater Flow loop trail, a good introduction to the monument's geology. Also consider an overnight stay in Craters's campground; the sites set amid the lava make an absolutely perfect setting for telling ghost stories (although you'll have to do so without a campfire; no wood fires are permitted, because the only available trees are the ancient and slow-growing limber pines). Craters of the Moon National Monument is 18 miles west of Arco. Admission is $8 per vehicle (free with a federal "America the Beautiful" pass). For more information call (208) 527-3257 or see www.nps.gov/crmo.

The Arco area has lately staked a claim as one of the West's best *hang gliding* sites. Most of the action takes place off nearby King Mountain due east of the tiny settlement of Moore, 8 miles north of Arco on US 93. For more information on hang gliding and paragliding opportunities, pick up the King Mountain brochure, available at the Arco visitor center, 132 West Grand Avenue.

The lava lands surrounding Arco and Craters of the Moon are but a small part of the huge Great Rift section of Idaho, which covers nearly 170,000 acres across the eastern Snake River Plain. For a view of the whole expanse, try a hike or drive up *Big Southern Butte,* the 300,000-year-old monolith towering 2,500 feet above the surrounding landscape. To get to the butte, follow the signs west from Atomic City. The dirt road up Big Southern Butte is steep, with a 2,000-foot elevation gain and some 15+ percent grades. It's a challenging hike but one that can be accomplished in a long day's excursion or relatively easy overnight trip. The winds can be fierce atop the butte, but hardy, early-waking campers may be rewarded with a view of the Teton Range against the rising sun.

Places to Stay in Central Idaho

NORTH FORK

North Fork Motel
US 93
(208) 865-2412
Inexpensive

One Hundred Acre Wood Bed & Breakfast
north of town on US 93
(208) 865-2165
Inexpensive–Moderate

River's Fork Inn
Highway 93
(208) 865-2301
Inexpensive

SHOUP

Salmon River Bed & Breakfast
3175 Salmon River Road
(208) 394-2226
Inexpensive–Moderate

Salmon River Lodge
30 miles west at Corn Creek
(800) 635-4717
(see text)
Inexpensive–Moderate

SALMON

Greyhouse Inn Bed & Breakfast
12 miles south on US 93
(800) 348-8097
(see text)
Moderate

HELPFUL WEB SITES FOR CENTRAL IDAHO

Idaho Mountain Express
(Sun Valley–area newspaper)
www.sunvalleycentral.com

Sun Valley/Ketchum Chamber of Commerce—www.visitsunvalley.com

Stanley-Sawtooth Chamber of Commerce
www.stanleycc.org

Craters of the Moon National Monument—www.nps.gov/crmo

Twin Peaks Ranch
south on US 93
(800) 659-4899
fax: (208) 894-2429
(see text)
Expensive

Wagons West Motel
503 US 93 North
(208) 756-4281
fax: (208) 756-8194
Inexpensive

CHALLIS
Northgate Inn
US 93
(208) 879-2490
Inexpensive

River House Resort Bed
and Breakfast
US 93 15 miles north of
Challis
(208) 876-4123
Moderate

MACKAY
Bear Bottom Inn
412 West Spruce Street
(208) 588-2483
Inexpensive

Wild Horse Creek Ranch
4387 Wild Horse Creek
Road
(20 miles west off of
Trail Creek Road)
phone/fax: (208) 588-2575
(see text)
Moderate

STANLEY
Idaho Rocky
Mountain Ranch
south on Highway 75
(208) 774-3544
fax: (208) 774-3477
(see text)
Expensive

Mountain Village Resort
Highways 21 and 75
(800) 843-5475
fax: (208) 774-3761
Moderate

SUN VALLEY/KETCHUM
Best Western
Kentwood Lodge
180 South Main Street
(Ketchum)
(800) 805-1001
fax: (208) 726-2417
Moderate–Expensive

Clarion Inn of Sun Valley
600 North Main Street
(Ketchum)
(800) 262-4833
fax: (208) 726-3761
Moderate–Expensive

Knob Hill Inn
Highway 75 (Ketchum)
(800) 526-8010
fax: (208) 726-2712
(see text)
Expensive

Lift Tower Lodge
703 South Main Street
(Ketchum)
(800) 462-8646
(see text)
Moderate

Sun Valley Resort
(800) 786-8259
fax: (208) 622-3700
Expensive

HAILEY
Hitchrack Motel
619 South Main
(208) 788-1696
Inexpensive–Moderate

Wood River Inn
601 North Main
(208) 578-0600
Moderate

BELLEVUE
High Country Motel
765 Main Street South
(208) 788-2050
Moderate

FAIRFIELD
The Prairie Inn
US 20
(208) 764-2247
fax: (208) 764-2244
Moderate

Soldier Mountain Ranch
9 miles northwest
(208) 764-2506
fax: (208) 764-2927
www.soldiermountainranch
.com/directions.html
(see text)
Moderate–Expensive

ARCO
Arco Inn
540 Grand Avenue West
(208) 527-3100
Inexpensive

D-K Motel
316 South Front Street
(800) 231-0134
Inexpensive

Lost River Motel
405 Highway Drive
(208) 527-3600
Inexpensive

Places to Eat in Central Idaho

GIBBONSVILLE

Ramey's Broken Arrow
(Mexican)
US 93
(208) 865-2241
(see text)
Moderate

NORTH FORK

North Fork Cafe
(American)
US 93
(208) 865-2412
(see text)
Inexpensive

One Hundred Acre Wood
(fine dining)
US 93
(208) 865-2165
Moderate–Expensive

SALMON

Bertram's Brewery
(American/microbrewery)
101 South Andrews Street
(208) 756-3391
Inexpensive–Moderate

Buddy's Family Dining
(American)
609 US 93 North
(208) 756-3630
Inexpensive

CHALLIS

Antonio's (pizza/pasta)
(208) 879-2210
(see text)
Inexpensive

MACKAY

Amy Lou's Steakhouse
(American)
US 93
(208) 588-9903
Moderate

Bear Bottom Inn (eclectic)
412 West Spruce Street
(208) 588-2483
Inexpensive–Moderate

STANLEY

Mountain Village
(American)
(208) 774-3317
Inexpensive–Moderate

SUN VALLEY/KETCHUM

Chandler's (fine dining)
240 South Main Street
(208) 726-1776
Moderate–Expensive

Cristina's Restaurant
(brunch and bakery)
520 Second Street East
(Ketchum)
(208) 726-4499
Moderate

KB's Ketchum Burritos
(Mexican)
Sixth and Washington
(208) 726-2232
Inexpensive

Ketchum Grill
(contemporary American)
520 East Avenue
(208) 726-4660
Moderate

Pioneer Saloon
(American)
320 North Main Street
(Ketchum)
(208) 726-3139
Moderate–Expensive

Roosevelt Tavern
(eclectic)
280 North Main Street
(208) 726-0051
Inexpensive–Moderate

Sun Valley Lodge Dining Room (continental)
(208) 622-2150
Expensive

HAILEY

CK's Real Food
(Northwest cuisine)
320 South Main Street
(208) 788-1223
Moderate

ALSO WORTH SEEING IN CENTRAL IDAHO

Challis Hot Springs

Land of the Yankee Fork State Park
near Challis

Sawtooth National Fish Hatchery
near Stanley

EBR-1 nuclear reactor site
near Arco

DaVinci's (Italian)
17 West Bullion Street
(208) 788-7699
Moderate

**Red Elephant Saloon
(American)**
107 South Main Street
(208) 788-6047
Inexpensive–Moderate

**Sun Valley Brewing
Company (eclectic)**
202 North Main Street
(208) 788-5777
Inexpensive–Moderate

Zou 75 (French Asian)
416 North Main Street
(208) 788-3310
Moderate

FAIRFIELD

**Iron Mountain Inn
(American)**
US 20
(208) 764-2577
(see text)
Moderate

ARCO

**Deli Sandwich Shop
(shakes and sandwiches)**
119 North Idaho Street
(208) 527-3757
Inexpensive

**Pickle's Place
(American)**
440 South Front Street
(208) 527-9944
Inexpensive

Index

About the Author

An Idaho resident since 1989, Julie Fanselow is among the state's most widely published writers. In addition to this book, she is the author of *Traveling the Lewis and Clark Trail* and *Traveling the Oregon Trail* (Globe Pequot), and she has contributed to many national and regional magazines. Julie is a member of the American Society of Journalists and Authors. She lives with her family in Boise. For more information see www.juliefanselow.com.